THE
EVERYTHING®
AIR FRYER
COOKBOOK

Dear Reader,

My name is Michelle (holding up candle), and I'm a kitchen appliance junkie. Seriously, I have a rice cooker, Instant Pot®, dehydrator, slow cooker, sous vide machine, and now an air fryer. Although my rice cooker and slow cooker have been delegated to the back of the closet because the Instant Pot® can do their jobs, my air fryer is absolutely unique. I haven't found another appliance that can pull off the crispy, crunchy magic that my new favorite appliance can achieve. But, *shhhh*, don't tell the others. They think I love them all equally!

So, of course, my first trials were with French fries and chicken wings. There is only one word to describe the results, and that's *fantastic*! I have baked both of these for years in my oven, and although tasty, these items not only cook quicker in the air fryer, but the exteriors are crisped all the way around. Because they are cooked in the metal mesh basket and the hot air circulates, the heat simultaneously cooks underneath as well as on top. I would absolutely suggest starting with some of these easier recipes just to get the hang of your appliance and to boost your confidence.

Your next step is to move on to recipes that will require accessories when cooking with your air fryer. Most brands have specific side accessories that you can purchase, but as long as a dish fits in your cooking basket and is oven safe, you can use small cooking pots, pans, and ceramic dishes that you may already have in your cabinets. With the right dish or accessory, small lasagnas, cakes, casseroles, and frittatas can be at your fingertips in under an hour!

If you've held fried foods at an arm's length since you can't even remember, then the air fryer is for you. You still get that crunch and breading from fried foods without the added grease, fat, calories, and yucky feeling after eating that type of junk food.

Happy eating,

Michelle Fagone

Welcome to the EVERYTHING® Series!

These handy, accessible books give you all you need to tackle a difficult project, gain a new hobby, comprehend a fascinating topic, prepare for an exam, or even brush up on something you learned back in school but have since forgotten.

You can choose to read an Everything® book from cover to cover or just pick out the information you want from our four useful boxes: e-questions, e-facts, e-alerts, and e-ssentials.

We give you everything you need to know on the subject, but throw in a lot of fun stuff along the way too.

We now have more than 400 Everything® books in print, spanning such wide-ranging categories as weddings, pregnancy, cooking, music instruction, foreign language, crafts, pets, New Age, and so much more. When you're done reading them all, you can finally say you know Everything®!

QUESTION

Answers to common questions

FACT

Important snippets of information

ALERT

Urgent warnings

ESSENTIAL

Quick handy tips

PUBLISHER Karen Cooper

MANAGING EDITOR Lisa Laing

COPY CHIEF Casey Ebert

ASSOCIATE PRODUCTION EDITOR Jo-Anne Duhamel

ACQUISITIONS EDITOR Zander Hatch

DEVELOPMENT EDITOR Brett Palana-Shanahan

EVERYTHING® SERIES COVER DESIGNER Erin Alexander

Visit the entire Everything® series at www.everything.com

THE EVERYTHING®
AIR FRYER COOKBOOK

300 easy and delicious recipes
for your favorite foods!

Michelle Fagone of CavegirlCuisine.com

Adams Media
New York   London   Toronto   Sydney   New Delhi

To my two weird and fantastic girls, who are growing up way too fast:
I wish you a life of good food and great love.

To my crazy and supportive husband:
Thanks for making me laugh for over twenty years.
Your dry, witty humor is the perfect yin to my slapstick and low-brow yang.

To my insane parents:
Thanks for always loving me, taking my side, and keeping me right-ish.

Adams Media
An Imprint of Simon & Schuster, Inc.
100 Technology Center Drive
Stoughton, MA 02072

An Everything® Series Book.
Everything® and everything.com® are registered trademarks of Simon & Schuster, Inc.

First Adams Media trade paperback edition November 2018

ADAMS MEDIA and colophon are trademarks of Simon & Schuster.

For information about special discounts for bulk purchases, please contact Simon & Schuster Special Sales at 1-866-506-1949 or business@simonandschuster.com.

The Simon & Schuster Speakers Bureau can bring authors to your live event. For more information or to book an event contact the Simon & Schuster Speakers Bureau at 1-866-248-3049 or visit our website at www.simonspeakers.com.

Interior design by Colleen Cunningham
Photographs by James Stefiuk

Manufactured in the United States of America

5 2021

Library of Congress Cataloging-in-Publication Data
Fagone, Michelle.
The everything® air fryer cookbook / Michelle Fagone of CavegirlCuisine.com.
Avon, Massachusetts: Adams Media, 2018.
Series: Everything.
LCCN 2018031909 | ISBN 9781507209127 (pb) | ISBN 9781507209134 (ebook)
Subjects: LCSH: Hot air frying. | LCGFT: Cookbooks.
Classification: LCC TX689 .F34 2018 | DDC 641.7--dc23
LC record available at https://lccn.loc.gov/2018031909

ISBN 978-1-5072-0912-7
ISBN 978-1-5072-0913-4 (ebook)

Contents

Acknowledgments

A big thank you to the folks at Adams Media for your devoted support and assistance over the past several years. Your confidence and professionalism are infectious, and I am completely grateful for our "cookbook friendship"! A special "holla" to Jackie, Bethany, and Zander!

((Hugs)) to my *Cavegirl Cuisine* friends. In the past six years you have provided such a supportive virtual environment for us to learn and cook together. You have always been a constant source of smiles and inspiration, for which I am so incredibly appreciative.

Introduction

WE ALL KNOW THAT deep-fried foods are bad for us on so many levels, but there is something about that crunch that is so satisfying. The food is tasty, the meals are convenient, but really, inside and out, eating this way is not a lifestyle that our bodies can maintain.

Make the decision to choose fresher foods and to cook them in a healthier manner—with an air fryer! It's true that the air fryer won't produce an identical twin of a breaded, deep-fried food, but it comes really close. And instead of grease, you'll be tasting the actual ingredients while still achieving the satisfying mouthfeel of crunchy foods.

The Everything® Air Fryer Cookbook will not only provide you with three hundred easy-to-follow, simple-to-prepare recipes, but it will also give you the tools you need to start preparing air-fried foods. And don't think that all foods are battered and "fried" in this cookbook. You will essentially learn to air-bake muffins and cakes, such as Chocolate-Espresso Muffins and Confetti Cake; to air-roast chicken and vegetables, such as Salsa Chicken and Nutty Roasted Acorn Squash; and even to air-grill beef and seafood, such as Cowboy Flank Steak and Seared Sea Scallops.

By cooking in an air fryer you will be using a significantly lower amount of oil in the preparation of your food, but the heat will still give your food that crispiness on all sides. In addition, because air fryers have a quicker cooking time, more nutrients will stay intact. Since you can taste more of your actual food, you can start experimenting with herbs and seasonings to impart great flavor instead of relying solely on grease. Sure, there are some recipes in this book that call for bottled ingredients, but most such recipes have sidebars on how to make those ingredients from scratch, eliminating fillers and preservatives that are often needed to give those products a stable shelf life. And don't forget to flip through Chapter 15 to find many quick and delicious homemade dips and sauces.

So, are you ready to dive in and learn to cook with this convenient appliance? Read on and start cooking delicious, healthier meals.

CHAPTER 1

Air Fryer Essentials

The air fryer is an easy, healthier alternative to conventional fryers and will quickly become your go-to appliance in your kitchen. The air fryer is so much more versatile than you might think—it's not just useful for those French fries and onion rings! In fact, there's an air-fried meal for almost every taste, diet, or mood from breakfast to desserts and everything in between. But before you get to cooking, you'll need to know about your new appliance. This chapter will cover not only what an air fryer is and the benefits of using one, but also what to look for when purchasing an air fryer and tips on how to use and clean it.

What Is an Air Fryer?

Air fryers work by baking foods with a constant stream of hot air circulating around the food, cooking it evenly and quickly, crisping up edges as it does its job. An air fryer cooks foods quicker than a conventional oven; it doesn't heat up your living space, and it is easy to clean. Although similar to a convection oven, an air fryer is smaller in size and convenient to place on the countertop. And while both these appliances use hot air and cook food from all angles, the air fryer utilizes Rapid Air Technology, circulating the heat with speed.

ALERT

There are many reasons to give up traditionally cooked fried foods, which are prepared by submerging foods in heated oil. Fried foods are high in bad fats and calories. Also, when oil is heated beyond its smoke point—the temperature at which an oil begins to smoke, as with deep-frying—certain oils break down and produce toxic fumes and free radicals. In addition, deep-frying foods is just messy, with its splatter in your kitchen or even on you!

Using an air fryer is not only a better alternative for your health but for your safety as well. Unlike a traditional deep fryer, which can be a fire hazard and should be used with extreme caution, most air fryers have an auto-shut-off feature. Air fryers also offer quick and safe cooking so you don't anguish over oil spills or cooking on an open flame.

The Benefits of Air Frying

In addition to the health benefits of air frying, you'll find there are a few other benefits as well:

- **It won't heat up your whole house/apartment.** When cooking casseroles or thicker cuts of meat, your traditional oven can warm up, providing a heat source that is not always welcomed, especially on those long, hot summer days. Apartment or efficiency dwellers with limited living space will appreciate the contained heat of the air fryer, which will keep their air conditioner from working overtime.

- **It's faster than your oven.** Although it's not as fast as a deep fat fryer, the air fryer has quicker cooking times than an oven due to the circulating heat. This is particularly nice for your busy family when your tribe is hungry. Instead of trying to calm your "hangry" (hungry + angry) crowd, reduce your cook time and get those bellies filled with quick and tasty recipes.

- **It can help with picky eaters.** Picky vegetable eaters or parents of picky vegetable eaters can find benefit in the transformative ways of the air fryer. A little breading and a fresh dip can turn zucchini into tasty fries. And a little cornflake breading on some cod can be the gateway recipe from fish sticks to a simple salmon fillet. So be creative and get everyone involved.

- **It's portable.** A benefit of cooking in the air fryer is that it is contained. So for those hit-the-road, no-boundaries renegades, the air fryer is perfect in your Airstream when traveling from the biggest ball of twine to the awe-inspiring redwoods. No need to worry about splashing hot soup or cracklin' bacon burning your skin. Use this handy appliance to heat up or prepare a quick and delicious meal while on the road.

- **It works wonders on frozen foods.** Students and folks looking for a quick snack can also benefit from the air fryer by cooking frozen foods. Yes, the microwave is faster, but it doesn't create that crunchy exterior. The air fryer is great on frozen foods such as French fries, fish sticks, or egg rolls. As a general rule, cut the cooking time in half of what is recommended on the package. If more cooking time is needed, slowly increase the time by a minute or two so as to not overcook the final product.

When Purchasing an Air Fryer

Fortunately and unfortunately there are several brands, sizes, and shapes of air fryers. This book was based on a four-person air fryer with a 1-pound, 2.75 quart capacity and 1,425 watts, which is the typical middle-of-the-road size. There are larger models and there are smaller ones as well. Depending on your chosen model, the size of your food batches will vary, but cooking times should not be affected. Conveniently, until you find your groove with your appliance, you can just pull out your basket during the cooking process and check the results to view if the food needs extra cooking.

There are a variety of settings offered by the different models. Some of the newest types offer digital settings that allow the user to be in control of the temperature and time. Other models have analog dials as well as preset temperatures for a variety of fresh and frozen foods.

FACT

A meat thermometer is one of those fairly inexpensive kitchen gadgets that are well worth the price. You neither want to overcook nor undercook your meats. With the varying shapes and sizes of air fryers, being able to test the internal temperature of your steak, chicken, fish, pork, and other meats will help guarantee that your food will be cooked to perfection.

Because the air fryer basket is going to be used with most of your air-fried foods, finding a model with a basket that has a quick-release button is crucial and will make your life easier. This button helps release the mesh basket containing food from the bottom basket for easy shaking or flipping of the food, which is necessary when using this appliance.

Air Fryer Accessories

Most air fryers come with the basic fryer basket; however, there are many other recipes that can be made with the purchase of a few accessories, including a cake barrel, pizza pan, and even a skewer rack. But before you purchase any of these, check two things. One, make sure they work with your size and brand of air fryer. Most of the accessory packages fit models ranging from a 2.75-quart to a 5.8-quart air fryer. Two, check your cupboards, as you may already have some small, oven-safe dishes that will work in your new appliance.

Here are some of the common air fryer accessories:

- **The Cake Barrel:** The cake barrel accessory comes in both a round and a square version. This nonstick cake pan is used for desserts, casseroles, and egg dishes. And as a bonus both barrels have a handle, making retrieval from the appliance a cinch.

- **The Grill Pan:** The grill pan is a nonstick accessory that replaces the basket on the air fryer and is used for grilling fish, meat, and vegetables. The basket is removable from the handle, and the grill pan slides right in its place. Because there are no side walls, the pan allows for a bit more room. Also, with the perforated base, the airflow is able to cook underneath while still providing those beautiful grill lines.
- **The Rack:** This metal holder is a round metal rack that allows for a second layer of food in the air fryer. One nonconventional use is for cooking lightweight food like bacon, which tends to fly around with the airflow. You can turn your rack upside down on top of your bacon to hold it in place while cooking.
- **The Pizza Pan:** The pizza pan is a nonstick shallow pan that allows you to make mini pizzas as well as provides a flat surface for a variety of other recipes, such as biscuits, corn bread, Dutch pancakes, and even the delectable Giant Oatmeal Raisin Cookie for One found in the dessert chapter of this book!
- **The Silicone Liners:** Silicone cupcake liners or baking cups are oven safe and great for mini meatloaves, cupcakes, on-the-go frittatas, little quick breads, and muffins. They are reusable and dishwasher safe, making cleanup a snap!
- **The Skewer Rack:** The skewer rack contains four metal skewers, which can be used for meat and vegetable shish kebabs. With the food elevated slightly above the fry basket, the cooking time is shortened by allowing more room for the airflow to do its job. Just as you would do before outdoor grilling, if you only have wooden skewers, be sure to soak them in water for about 30 minutes prior to cooking, to avoid burning.

Accessory Removal

Cooking with a pot in an appliance is a great idea until it's time to remove the inserted cooking dish. Because of the tight space, it is almost impossible to use thick oven mitts to reach down and grip the pot evenly without tipping one side of the cooking vessel and spilling the cooked food. There are a few ways around this:

1. Wooden or silicone-tipped tongs are a good purchase for air frying. Because most air fryer baskets and accessories have a nonstick surface,

a good pair of nonmetal tongs are recommended for helping to flip those larger food items, such as egg rolls, that don't benefit from just a quick shake of the basket, as is the case with most fries and chips.

2. Heat-resistant mini mitts or pinch mitts are small, food-grade silicone oven mitts and are especially helpful when lifting pots, racks, and barrels out of an air fryer after the cooking process. They are more heat resistant and less cumbersome than traditional oven mitts, which can prove to be bulky in the tight fryer basket.

ESSENTIAL

Creating an aluminum-foil sling is a quick, inexpensive, homemade fix to the problem of lifting a heated dish out of an air fryer. Take a 10" × 10" square of aluminum foil and fold it until you have a 2" × 10" sling. Place this sling underneath the bowl or pan before cooking so that you can easily lift up the heated dish.

Oil and Your Air Fryer

One of the main and obvious benefits when first deciding to purchase an air fryer is the fact that you no longer want to consume deep-fried foods, whether for health purposes or weight issues. But oil and butter are still used in some air frying, just not to the extent that deep-frying calls for. Some recipes in this book will advise to "lightly grease" a pan. Because this seems to be such a personal choice in this day and age, use your preferred method and oil type.

FACT

If you want to cut back on the oil even more, instead of giving your basket a light spray or brush of oil, simply cut a piece of parchment paper to the size of the bottom of your basket. It will help keep the batter or other ingredient on your items without adding additional calories.

And although your grill basket is most likely of the nonstick variety, a light spritz or brush of oil directly on the basket is necessary with some foods, as indicated in the recipes. Try to avoid using commercial nonstick sprays, as they may contain chemicals that can cause your basket to get sticky or start to flake. True oils and butter, without additives, yield better results.

To avoid heavy drizzling of oil on your food, purchase one of the many types of misters, sprayers, and spritzers in which you can use your oil of choice to lightly spray onto foods to encourage browning and crisping. Many prefer this to commercial spray oil, which may contain chemicals and preservatives that may have a denigrating effect on the nonstick components and accessories of your air fryer.

A basting or silicone pastry brush uses more oil than a sprayer does but is helpful on certain dishes that require a brush of melted butter on the dough or breaded food, such as phyllo tarts or biscuits.

FACT

For a cheap fix, grab the bigger unused paintbrush out of your kids' multipack of paintbrushes. Or if you have one of those cheap sponge brushes used in painting (unused, of course!), that works too. And if you've exhausted those options and are still at an impasse, fold a paper towel in half. Tightly roll the paper towel into a small tube. Using scissors, cut up about 2" several times on one end to create a small mop. There you go—brush away!

Air Frying Tips

Although the air fryer is an easy appliance to use, there is always a learning curve associated with any new cooking method. The first rule is that you shouldn't overcrowd your fryer basket. Most foods will have to be cooked in batches to yield the best crunch. You will also have to take this into consideration when purchasing your air fryer. How big is your family? How large are the batches that you'll be preparing? The larger the air fryer capacity, the larger the batches, and the quicker the results.

Once the batches are in the air fryer, it is essential to flip or shake the food at least once or more during the cooking process. This will ensure that the circulating air will touch all sides of the food. After the first flip, some foods, especially those that need to be browned, may need a brush or spritz of oil or butter. That's right: although you are giving up the deep-frying oil, a fraction is required for maximum crispiness.

ALERT

The recipes in this book usually suggest a preheat time of 3 minutes. Some models require 5 minutes. Check your user manual to determine the best time for yours. Although some brands claim you don't need to preheat, skipping this step can alter cooking times. Preheating allows the unit to heat up to the required temperature, which allows the cooking time to be accurate.

Smoke and Your Air Fryer

Some fattier cuts of meat, like bacon or marbled steaks, will render fat when cooking. This can create white smoke and can be eliminated by adding 1 to 2 tablespoons of water in the fryer drawer prior to cooking. If it happens in the middle of your cooking time and you didn't anticipate smoke, simply open the drawer and add needed water. If there is black smoke present, unplug the machine and determine the culprit, as food could have attached itself to the heating element, causing the smoke. Remove the rogue food immediately, clean, and continue cooking.

Sweat the Small Stuff!

Air frying isn't just about the frying, or even the baking, roasting, and grilling. It's about the small stuff too. Before garnishing an Asian stir-fry with cashews, give them a quick toss in sesame oil and air-fry them for a surprising flavorful crunch. Before enjoying a fresh tomato soup, make some quick Grilled Cheese Croutons to create big smiles. Toast pine nuts for another dimension of flavor before pulsing them into a fresh pesto. The air fryer is one of those appliances that will not only feel right at home on your countertop but will not collect dust waiting to be used. And one more quick tip:

hard-boiled eggs can be made in 15 minutes without breaks from bumping around in boiling water. Yes, that's right. Check out the recipe in Chapter 2. That extra protein added to a Cobb salad, on-the-go bite, or even a few luscious deviled eggs will lift your mood without dirtying up dishes!

Cleaning and Seasoning Your Air Fryer

After using your air fryer, unplug the appliance and allow it to completely cool. Adding cooler water to a hot fryer basket can cause warping. Although the removable parts are dishwasher safe, some people suggest washing the parts by hand with warm, soapy water to lengthen the life of those nonstick, coated parts. Wipe down and remove excess fat or oil from the warming drawer and nonremovable parts, inside and out, with hot water and a dishcloth or kitchen sponge.

Also, once dry, the basket can be *seasoned*. Oftentimes you only hear about this term with cast-iron pans, but the air fryer basket can also benefit from seasoning. Place your air fryer basket in the appliance and heat for 5 minutes at 400°F. Remove the basket and, when cool enough to touch, simply spread a thin layer of coconut oil on your basket using a paper towel. Heat the basket in the appliance for an additional 2 minutes. This will help extend the life of the nonstick coating on the basket.

Breakfast

Pork Sausage Patties

It's not only easy to make your own sausage, but you can also control what goes into the food. This sausage can be made in larger batches and can be easily frozen for future morning meals!

HANDS-ON TIME: 10 minutes
COOK TIME: 20 minutes

INGREDIENTS | YIELDS 8 SAUSAGE PATTIES

12 ounces lean ground pork
1 teaspoon fresh thyme leaves
1 tablespoon brown sugar
Pinch ground nutmeg
¼ teaspoon salt
¼ teaspoon freshly ground black pepper
1 tablespoon water

1. Preheat air fryer at 350°F for 3 minutes.

2. In a large bowl, combine pork, thyme, sugar, nutmeg, salt, and pepper. Form into eight patties.

3. Pour water into bottom of air fryer. Place four patties in fryer basket and cook 5 minutes. Flip patties. Cook an additional 5 minutes. Repeat with remaining patties.

4. Transfer to a plate and serve warm.

PER SERVING Calories: 58 | Fat: 1.6 g | Protein: 8.9 g | Sodium: 97 mg | Fiber: 0.0 g | Carbohydrates: 1.2 g | Sugar: 1.1 g

Spicy Scotch Eggs

A Scotch egg is a gastropub classic made by forming sausage or meat around a cooked egg, coating it in bread crumbs, and then deep-frying it. With the air fryer, you skip the bath in hot oil and go straight for the goodness without all of the guilt.

HANDS-ON TIME: 5 minutes
COOK TIME: 12 minutes

INGREDIENTS | YIELDS 4 EGGS

½ pound ground chorizo, loose or removed from casings
4 soft-boiled eggs, peeled
1 large egg
1 cup plain bread crumbs

1. Preheat air fryer at 375°F for 3 minutes.

2. Gently form chorizo around peeled eggs.

3. In a small bowl, whisk large egg. In another small bowl, add bread crumbs.

4. Dip chorizo-covered eggs in whisked egg and then dredge in bread crumbs.

5. Place eggs in air fryer basket. Cook 6 minutes. Turn. Cook an additional 6 minutes. Serve warm.

PER SERVING Calories: 322 | Fat: 22.2 g | Protein: 19.7 g | Sodium: 775 mg | Fiber: 0.3 g | Carbohydrates: 6.2 g | Sugar: 0.7 g

Maple-Sage Breakfast Links

The maple syrup lends a sweetness against the savory spices and the pinelike flavor of the sage. And these links are void of any preservatives and fillers that store-bought counterparts may be filled with.

HANDS-ON TIME: 10 minutes
COOK TIME: 9 minutes

INGREDIENTS | YIELDS 8 SAUSAGE LINKS

12 ounces ground mild pork sausage, loose or removed from casings

1 teaspoon rubbed sage

2 tablespoons pure maple syrup

Pinch cayenne pepper

¼ teaspoon salt

¼ teaspoon freshly ground black pepper

1 tablespoon water

1. Preheat air fryer at 350°F for 3 minutes.

2. Combine pork, sage, maple syrup, cayenne pepper, salt, and black pepper. Form into eight links.

3. Pour water into bottom of air fryer. Place links in air fryer basket. Cook 9 minutes.

4. Transfer to a plate and serve warm.

PER SERVING Calories: 130 | Fat: 8.8 g | Protein: 6.5 g | Sodium: 483 mg | Fiber: 0.1 g | Carbohydrates: 4.9 g | Sugar: 3.3 g

Air-Fried Maple Bacon

What's better than bacon? Maple bacon! This sweet and salty treat will wake you up with a smile. It's also delicious on breakfast sandwiches, crumbled up into your favorite salads, and even dipped in a little chocolate for some bacon candy. Sinful, truly sinful!

HANDS-ON TIME: 5 minutes
COOK TIME: 12 minutes

INGREDIENTS | SERVES 4

2 tablespoons water

4 slices bacon, halved

2 teaspoons maple syrup, divided

My Bacon Is Flipping Around!

The flow of air in the air fryer sometimes blows the lightweight bacon around. Depending on the air fryer model, either check and shake your bacon often or use the rack that came with your fryer and flip it upside down on top of the bacon to hold it down while cooking.

1. Preheat air fryer at 400°F for 3 minutes.

2. Pour water into bottom of air fryer. Place 4 bacon halves in air fryer basket. Cook 3 minutes. Flip bacon. Brush 1 teaspoon maple syrup on bacon. Cook an additional 3 minutes. Transfer to a paper towel–lined plate.

3. Repeat with remaining bacon and serve warm.

PER SERVING Calories: 51 | Fat: 3.0 g | Protein: 3.6 g | Sodium: 162 mg | Fiber: 0.0 g | Carbohydrates: 2.2 g | Sugar: 2.0 g

Homemade Tater Tots

Tater Tots have been a favorite breakfast treat, side dish, and even casserole topper for many years. But did you know how easy they are to make? For a switch-up, substitute sweet potatoes and trade the savory spices for a little cinnamon and nutmeg to create an awesome side to most any ham dish!

HANDS-ON TIME: 15 minutes
COOK TIME: 38 minutes

INGREDIENTS | SERVES 4

2 medium Russet potatoes, peeled and quartered

1¼ teaspoons salt, divided

1 tablespoon all-purpose flour

1 tablespoon minced sweet onion

¼ teaspoon garlic powder

¼ teaspoon smoked paprika

¼ teaspoon freshly ground black pepper

1. In a large pot over high heat add potatoes and enough water to cover them. Add 1 teaspoon salt. Cook 5–6 minutes until potatoes are fork-tender. Drain.

2. When potatoes are cool enough to handle, grate. Using a cheesecloth or paper towels, squeeze excess water out of grated potatoes.

3. Transfer squeezed potatoes to a large bowl. Add flour, onion, garlic powder, paprika, ¼ teaspoon salt, and pepper. Using a 2-tablespoon scooper, form tight balls with mixture. Using your hands, shape balls into tot forms.

4. Preheat air fryer at 350°F for 3 minutes.

5. Working in batches, add half of tots to lightly greased air fryer basket. Cook 8 minutes. Gently toss. Cook an additional 8 minutes or until browned. Transfer each batch to a paper towel–lined plate and serve warm.

PER SERVING Calories: 73 | Fat: 0.1 g | Protein: 1.6 g | Sodium: 326 mg | Fiber: 1.7 g | Carbohydrates: 17.1 g | Sugar: 0.8 g

Hard-"Boiled" Eggs

This is the easiest way to make hard-"boiled" eggs. There is no need for boiling and steaming and water and a saucepan… Just place them in the air fryer and, voilà, perfection! Also, the shells will stay intact due to the absence of boiling water making them bump around.

HANDS-ON TIME: 5 minutes
COOK TIME: 15 minutes

INGREDIENTS | YIELDS 4 HARD-"BOILED" EGGS

4 large eggs
1 cup ice
1 cup water

1. Preheat air fryer at 250°F for 3 minutes.

2. Place eggs in silicone muffin cups to avoid eggs from bumping around and cracking during the cooking process. Add eggs in cups to air fryer basket. Cook 15 minutes.

3. Add ice and water to a medium bowl. Transfer eggs to this water bath immediately to stop the cooking process. After 5 minutes, peel and eat.

PER SERVING Calories: 77 | Fat: 4.4 g | Protein: 6.3 g | Sodium: 62 mg | Fiber: 0.0 g | Carbohydrates: 0.6 g | Sugar: 0.6 g

Soft-"Boiled" Eggs

For a full, healthy breakfast experience, serve the soft-"boiled" eggs with a plate of fresh fruit and steamed asparagus. Steamed asparagus? Oh, yes, the spears are divine dipped in the gooey deliciousness of that heavenly yolk.

HANDS-ON TIME: 5 minutes
COOK TIME: 8 minutes

INGREDIENTS | YIELDS 4 SOFT-"BOILED" EGGS

4 large eggs
1 cup ice
1 cup water

1. Preheat air fryer at 250°F for 3 minutes.

2. Place eggs in silicone muffin cups to avoid eggs from bumping around and cracking during the cooking process. Add eggs in cups to air fryer basket. Cook 8 minutes.

3. Add ice and water to a medium bowl. Transfer eggs to this water bath immediately to stop the cooking process. After 5 minutes, peel and eat.

PER SERVING Calories: 71 | Fat: 4.3 g | Protein: 6.3 g | Sodium: 148 mg | Fiber: 0.0 g | Carbohydrates: 0.4 g | Sugar: 0.2 g

Individual Egg and Cheese Soufflés

Serve these immediately so you can enjoy the "fluff." Also, don't be afraid to change up the ingredients in the bottom of your ramekin. Try chopped mushrooms, cooked sausage, diced avocado, or whatever else your taste buds request!

HANDS-ON TIME: 5 minutes
COOK TIME: 10 minutes

INGREDIENTS | SERVES 3

6 teaspoons grated sharp Cheddar cheese
¼ cup chopped deli ham
¼ cup diced tomato
2 tablespoons chopped scallion
3 large eggs
2 tablespoons whole milk
¼ teaspoon salt
¼ teaspoon freshly ground black pepper
⅛ teaspoon smoked paprika

1. Preheat air fryer at 275°F for 3 minutes.

2. Lightly grease three 7-ounce standard ramekins. Divide cheese, ham, tomato, and scallions equally among the ramekins.

3. In a small bowl, whisk eggs, milk, salt, pepper, and paprika. Pour into ramekins.

4. Add ramekins to air fryer basket. Cook 10 minutes.

5. Serve immediately while still fluffy.

PER SERVING Calories: 120 | Fat: 7.9 g | Protein: 9.9 g | Sodium: 495 mg | Fiber: 0.5 g | Carbohydrates: 2.4 g | Sugar: 1.4 g

Easy Egg Cups

These protein-packed egg cups are great for those busy weekday mornings. Filled with protein, this breakfast will ensure that you will be satisfied longer and your energy level will be elevated. Add your favorite fillings by trying different meats, cheeses, and vegetables for a change of pace.

HANDS-ON TIME: 5 minutes
COOK TIME: 9 minutes

INGREDIENTS | SERVES 4

3 large eggs
Pinch salt
Pinch freshly ground black pepper
2 pieces cooked bacon, crumbled
4 teaspoons shredded Cheddar cheese
4 slices medium Roma tomato

1. Lightly grease four silicone muffin cups.

2. In a small bowl, whisk together eggs, salt, and pepper.

3. Preheat air fryer at 350°F for 3 minutes.

4. Pour whisked eggs into muffin cups. Distribute bacon and cheese among cups. Top each with a tomato slice.

5. Place cups in air fryer basket and cook 9 minutes. Transfer to a plate to cool and serve warm.

PER SERVING Calories: 92 | Fat: 5.9 g | Protein: 7.4 g | Sodium: 202 mg | Fiber: 0.2 g | Carbohydrates: 1.0 g | Sugar: 0.5 g

Breakfast Tarts

Puff pastry can be found in the freezer section of your grocery store. Thaw it out, slice it, add your favorite toppings, air-fry, and then enjoy this meal for a scrumptious "brinner" (brunch plus dinner) served with a light salad or some fresh fruit!

HANDS-ON TIME: 15 minutes
COOK TIME: 26 minutes

INGREDIENTS | YIELDS 6 TARTS

¼ pound lean ground pork
¼ teaspoon rubbed sage
¼ teaspoon brown sugar
Pinch cayenne pepper
Pinch ground nutmeg
¼ teaspoon salt
1 tablespoon all-purpose flour
1 sheet puff pastry, thawed to room temperature
1 large egg, whisked
4 large eggs, scrambled
½ cup shredded Cheddar cheese

1. In a large skillet over medium-high heat, cook pork 2 minutes, chopping it as the pork cooks. Add sage, sugar, cayenne pepper, nutmeg, and salt. Continue to stir-fry 2–3 minutes until pork is no longer pink.

2. Scatter flour over a flat, clean surface. Unfold puff pastry sheet on the floured surface. Cut into six equal rectangles. Brush each rectangle perimeter with whisked egg.

3. Top each rectangle with even amounts pork mixture, scrambled eggs, and shredded cheese.

4. Preheat air fryer at 350°F for 3 minutes.

5. Place two tarts at a time in lightly greased air fryer basket. Cook 7 minutes. Repeat with remaining tarts. Serve warm.

PER SERVING Calories: 206 | Fat: 11.9 g | Protein: 15.9 g | Sodium: 269 mg | Fiber: 0.2 g | Carbohydrates: 5.5 g | Sugar: 0.8 g

Frooty French Toast Sticks

If you don't have Froot Loops, crush up any cereal that you have on hand or buy miniature boxes and let the kids and your guests choose their own coating! Dip in maple syrup or flavored syrup or even just serve with a side of fresh fruit. These are easy, quick, and will bring smiles to the faces of everyone around!

HANDS-ON TIME: 10 minutes
COOK TIME: 20 minutes

INGREDIENTS | YIELDS 16 STICKS

1 large egg
⅓ cup whole milk
Pinch salt
½ teaspoon ground cinnamon
1 cup crushed Froot Loops cereal
4 slices hearty sandwich bread, cut into 4 sticks per slice
¼ cup pure maple syrup

How to Make Nonconventional "Crumbs"

Whether you are crushing cereal, cookies, crackers, or chips, there is a fine science to it. Well, not really. Place the items in a plastic bag and either smoosh them with your fingers or use a mallet to gently crush them. Make sure that the air has been let out of the plastic bag or that you don't seal it up completely, otherwise you might create a pillow and make a crumb explosion!

1. In a small bowl, whisk together egg, milk, salt, and cinnamon. Place cereal crumbs in a separate shallow dish.

2. Preheat air fryer at 375°F for 3 minutes.

3. Dip bread sticks in egg mixture, then dredge in cereal crumbs.

4. Place four sticks in air fryer basket. Cook 3 minutes. Flip sticks. Cook an additional 2 minutes. Repeat with remaining sticks.

5. Transfer to a plate and serve warm with maple syrup for dipping.

PER SERVING Calories: 57 | Fat: 0.8 g | Protein: 1.5 g | Sodium: 76 mg | Fiber: 0.6 g | Carbohydrates: 11.1 g | Sugar: 5.3 g

Breakfast Egg Rolls

Egg-roll wrappers are amazing cooked in the air fryer because they receive convection heat from all around, creating crispness with each bite. Filled with breakfast goodies, these rolls are a great way to start the day, either sitting down at the table or for an on-the-go experience!

HANDS-ON TIME: 15 minutes
COOK TIME: 9 minutes

INGREDIENTS | YIELDS 6 EGG ROLLS

6 egg-roll wrappers

4 large eggs, scrambled

6 slices cooked bacon, crumbled

1 medium Roma tomato, seeded and diced small

1 teaspoon freshly ground black pepper

½ cup shredded Monterey jack cheese

1 tablespoon butter, melted

The Difference Between Egg-Roll Wrappers and Wonton Wrappers

Both egg-roll and wonton wrappers are paper-thin sheets of dough. Wonton wrappers are smaller and come in squares or circles meant for dumplings, ravioli, and probably a million other great ideas. Egg-roll wrappers are meant for sweet and savory rolls only limited by your imagination. Although these are easily purchased at most grocers, there are many homemade recipes online if you choose to go the extra step.

1. Place egg-roll wrappers on a cutting board. Evenly distribute scrambled eggs, bacon, tomato, pepper, and cheese over each wrapper. Fold ½" of sides of egg-roll wrapper over the mixture. Roll length to form an egg roll and place seam side down in lightly greased air fryer basket. Repeat with remaining wrappers.

2. Preheat air fryer at 325°F for 3 minutes.

3. Cook egg rolls 3 minutes. Lightly brush the tops of egg rolls with melted butter. Cook an additional 6 minutes.

4. Transfer to a plate. Serve warm.

PER SERVING Calories: 261 | Fat: 12.9 g | Protein: 13.6 g | Sodium: 492 mg | Fiber: 0.8 g | Carbohydrates: 20.1 g | Sugar: 0.9 g

Baked Oatmeal

This breakfast treat is not only full of flavor; its oats have a low glycemic index and are slow to digest, improving your satiety. Slice and serve as is or scoop out a portion to a bowl and pour your preferred milk around the baked oatmeal.

HANDS-ON TIME: 10 minutes
COOK TIME: 8 minutes

INGREDIENTS | SERVES 4

1½ cups quick-cooking oats

⅓ cup packed light brown sugar

1 large egg

1 teaspoon fresh orange zest

1 tablespoon freshly squeezed orange juice

2 tablespoons whole milk

2 tablespoons pure maple syrup

2 tablespoons unsalted butter, melted

¼ cup raisins

Pinch ground nutmeg

Pinch salt

¼ cup pecan pieces

1. Preheat air fryer at 325°F for 3 minutes.

2. In a medium bowl, combine all the ingredients. Transfer mixture to a greased cake barrel (accessory).

3. Place pan in fryer basket and cook 8 minutes.

4. Transfer to a cooling rack for 5 minutes. Slice and serve warm.

PER SERVING Calories: 363 | Fat: 13.0 g | Protein: 6.9 g | Sodium: 66 mg | Fiber: 4.2 g | Carbohydrates: 55.4 g | Sugar: 31.3 g

Peanut Butter and Banana Baked Oatmeal to Go

If Elvis had eaten oatmeal, this peanut butter and banana combination would have been his choice. But to truly mimic his favorite sandwich, add a strip or two of crumbled bacon into the oatmeal mixture before baking.

HANDS-ON TIME: 10 minutes
COOK TIME: 11 minutes

INGREDIENTS | YIELDS 6 OATMEAL MUFFINS

1½ cups quick-cooking oats
½ cup packed light brown sugar
1 large egg
¼ cup whole milk
2 tablespoons unsalted butter, melted
¼ cup creamy peanut butter
1 small banana, smashed with the back of a fork
Pinch ground cinnamon
Pinch salt

1. Preheat air fryer at 325°F for 3 minutes.

2. In a medium bowl, combine all the ingredients. Transfer mixture to six greased silicone muffin cups.

3. Place cups in fryer basket and cook 11 minutes.

4. Transfer to a cooling rack and serve warm or chilled.

PER SERVING Calories: 277 | Fat: 11.0 g | Protein: 6.7 g | Sodium: 48 mg | Fiber: 3.0 g | Carbohydrates: 38.5 g | Sugar: 21.7 g

Mushroom and Cheddar Strata

Although there isn't a crust, the strata contains pieces of bread to give a starchy feel. Add the eggs and milk and you've almost created a savory bread pudding for a warm, filling breakfast.

HANDS-ON TIME: 10 minutes
COOK TIME: 14 minutes

INGREDIENTS | SERVES 2

5 large eggs
¼ cup whole milk
¼ teaspoon salt
¼ teaspoon freshly ground black pepper
1 teaspoon Dijon mustard
¼ cup minced sweet yellow onion
¼ cup finely chopped white mushrooms
⅓ cup grated Cheddar cheese
2 slices sandwich bread, diced into ½" cubes

1. Preheat air fryer at 325°F for 3 minutes.

2. In a medium bowl, whisk eggs and milk. Stir in remaining ingredients. Pour into lightly greased cake barrel (accessory).

3. Cook 14 minutes. Transfer to a cooling rack for 5 minutes. Slice and serve warm.

PER SERVING Calories: 367 | Fat: 18.4 g | Protein: 24.6 g | Sodium: 812 mg | Fiber: 1.3 g | Carbohydrates: 20.0 g | Sugar: 4.8 g

Dutch Baby Pancake with Fresh Blackberries

Sometimes called a German pancake or a Dutch puff, this hybrid of a pancake and a popover is a tasty breakfast and can be served with toppings only limited by your imagination. Serve a chilled mimosa with this treat for a special brunch on a slow morning.

HANDS-ON TIME: 10 minutes
COOK TIME: 10 minutes

INGREDIENTS | YIELDS 1 LARGE PANCAKE

¼ cup all-purpose flour

¼ cup whole milk

1 large egg

1 tablespoon sugar

½ teaspoon vanilla extract

¼ teaspoon salt

¼ teaspoon ground cinnamon

1 tablespoon unsalted butter

1 tablespoon powdered sugar

¼ cup fresh blackberries

1 tablespoon pure maple syrup

1. In a medium bowl, combine flour, milk, egg, sugar, vanilla, salt, and cinnamon.

2. Preheat air fryer at 400°F for 3 minutes with pizza pan (accessory) in the air fryer. After preheating, add butter and push it to coat pan as it melts.

3. Add batter to pan. Cook 10 minutes. The pancake will be puffed up when done but will fall immediately after it comes out of the air fryer.

4. Transfer pancake to a plate. Sprinkle with powdered sugar. Add blackberries and drizzle with maple syrup. Serve warm.

PER SERVING Calories: 460 | Fat: 17.0 g | Protein: 11.6 g | Sodium: 681 mg | Fiber: 1.2 g | Carbohydrates: 61.8 g | Sugar: 36.0 g

Blackberries for Health

The magnesium in blackberries can do amazing things for respiratory relief but can also help create stronger bones. This powerful mineral plays an important role in the absorption of calcium, and a diet rich in magnesium ensures strong bones.

Dutch Baby Pancake with Peach Coulis

This Dutch Baby Pancake with Peach Coulis is bursting with flavor and sweetness. A truly great way to start your day.

HANDS-ON TIME: 10 minutes
COOK TIME: 13 minutes

INGREDIENTS | YIELDS 1 LARGE PANCAKE

Peach Coulis

1 small peach, peeled, pitted, and sliced
2 tablespoons pure maple syrup
¼ teaspoon ground cinnamon
2 tablespoons water

Dutch Baby Pancake

¼ cup all-purpose flour
¼ cup whole milk
1 large egg
1 tablespoon sugar
½ teaspoon vanilla extract
¼ teaspoon salt
Pinch ground nutmeg
1 tablespoon unsalted butter
1 tablespoon powdered sugar
2 tablespoons whipped cream

1. In a small saucepan, combine coulis ingredients. Bring to a rolling boil. Reduce heat and simmer 3 minutes until peaches are tender. Transfer to a small food processor and blend until smooth. Set aside.

2. In a medium bowl, combine flour, milk, egg, sugar, vanilla, salt, and nutmeg.

3. Preheat air fryer at 400°F for 3 minutes with pizza pan (accessory) in the air fryer. After preheating, add butter and push it to coat pan as it melts.

4. Add batter to pan. Cook 10 minutes. The pancake with be puffed up when done but will fall immediately after it comes out of the air fryer.

5. Transfer pancake to a plate. Sprinkle with powdered sugar. Add Peach Coulis and top with whipped cream. Serve warm.

PER SERVING Calories: 577 | Fat: 18.5 g | Protein: 13.0 g | Sodium: 683 mg | Fiber: 3.2 g | Carbohydrates: 88.4 g | Sugar: 59.5 g

What Is a Coulis?

A coulis is a French sauce made from fruits or vegetables and can be sweet or savory. Cooked with seasonings or sweeteners and then strained or puréed, this simple sauce can be served with seafood, meats, or desserts and adds another level of fresh flavor.

Crab and Goat Cheese Frittata

This crustless creation is naturally gluten-free and will have your taste buds dancing for joy. This frittata is a flavor powerhouse with the sweetness from the beautiful lump crab, the creaminess of the goat cheese, the intense pungent bite of the horseradish, and the freshness of the mint and lemon juice.

HANDS-ON TIME: 10 minutes
COOK TIME: 14 minutes

INGREDIENTS | SERVES 2

5 large eggs
¼ teaspoon salt
¼ teaspoon freshly ground black pepper
1 teaspoon prepared horseradish
¼ cup minced sweet yellow onion
¼ cup lump crabmeat, picked over and any shells discarded
⅓ cup crumbled goat cheese
2 tablespoons chopped fresh mint
¼ teaspoon lemon juice

1. Preheat air fryer at 325°F for 3 minutes.

2. In a medium bowl, whisk eggs. Stir in remaining ingredients. Pour into lightly greased cake barrel (accessory).

3. Cook 14 minutes. Transfer to a cooling rack for 5 minutes. Slice and serve warm.

PER SERVING Calories: 331 | Fat: 21.0 g | Protein: 26.7 g | Sodium: 721 mg | Fiber: 0.6 g | Carbohydrates: 3.6 g | Sugar: 1.6 g

Chicken and Broccoli Frittata

After eating a rotisserie chicken for dinner, you could use the leftovers in this frittata. Also, use what vegetables you have on hand. If you don't have a bell pepper, use an onion. If you don't have Cheddar cheese, use Swiss, mozzarella, or Monterey jack. It changes the flavor profile, but it all tastes good.

HANDS-ON TIME: 10 minutes
COOK TIME: 14 minutes

INGREDIENTS | SERVES 2

5 large eggs
¼ teaspoon salt
¼ teaspoon freshly ground black pepper
¼ cup seeded and minced red bell pepper
¼ cup chopped cooked chicken
¼ cup chopped fresh broccoli florets
⅓ cup shredded Cheddar cheese
¼ teaspoon lemon juice

1. Preheat air fryer at 325°F for 3 minutes.

2. In a medium bowl, whisk eggs. Stir in remaining ingredients. Pour into lightly greased cake barrel (accessory).

3. Cook 14 minutes. Transfer to a cooling rack for 5 minutes. Slice and serve warm.

PER SERVING Calories: 297 | Fat: 17.5 g | Protein: 25.8 g | Sodium: 608 mg | Fiber: 0.8 g | Carbohydrates: 3.3 g | Sugar: 1.5 g

Breakfast Quesadillas Fixins Bar

This breakfast is perfect for a houseful of guests that wander into the kitchen at different times. Have all of the fixins ready and let them choose for a quick, made-to-order morning delight! Just multiply this recipe for the larger or hungrier groups!

HANDS-ON TIME: 10 minutes
COOK TIME: 16 minutes

INGREDIENTS | SERVES 4

½ pound cooked bacon, crumbled
6 large eggs, scrambled
1 cup cooked ¼" ham cubes
2 medium Roma tomatoes, seeded and diced
1 cup shredded Cheddar cheese
1 cup shredded Swiss cheese
8 (6") flour tortillas

1. Preheat air fryer at 350°F for 3 minutes.

2. Set out bacon, eggs, ham, tomatoes, and cheeses in separate dishes on the counter.

3. Place a tortilla in the bottom of the round cake barrel (accessory). Layer preferred ingredients evenly over tortilla. Top with second tortilla. Cook 4 minutes and transfer to a plate. Repeat three more times with remaining tortillas and fixins.

4. Let cool 3 minutes. Slice and serve.

PER SERVING Calories: 828 | Fat: 46.8 g | Protein: 55.4 g | Sodium: 2,173 mg | Fiber: 1.9 g | Carbohydrates: 35.4 g | Sugar: 3.5 g

Loaded Avocado Toast

There is a reason that everyone's been talking about avocado toast. It is delicious! Now load it up with other goodies, like fresh tomatoes and creamy goat cheese, and you won't want to eat anything else for breakfast...ever!

HANDS-ON TIME: 10 minutes
COOK TIME: 10 minutes

INGREDIENTS | SERVES 2

1 medium avocado, peeled and pitted
1 clove garlic, minced
¼ teaspoon lime juice
Pinch salt
2 slices whole-wheat bread
2 medium Campari tomatoes, sliced
¼ teaspoon freshly ground black pepper
4 tablespoons crumbled goat cheese

1. In a small bowl, using the back of a fork, press and combine avocado, garlic, lime juice, and salt until smooth.

2. Preheat air fryer at 350°F for 3 minutes.

3. Spread avocado mixture over bread. Add tomato slices. Sprinkle with pepper and top with goat cheese.

4. Place 1 piece topped bread in air fryer basket. Cook 5 minutes. Transfer to a plate. Repeat with remaining bread and serve warm.

PER SERVING Calories: 270 | Fat: 14.4 g | Protein: 9.6 g | Sodium: 287 mg | Fiber: 8.1 g | Carbohydrates: 25.1 g | Sugar: 4.9 g

Cubano Strata

After cooking a pork shoulder or butt for those barbecue sandwiches, set aside some of the meat before adding the sauce. You'll have enough for this breakfast tribute to the tasty and amazing Cuban sandwich.

HANDS-ON TIME: 10 minutes
COOK TIME: 14 minutes

INGREDIENTS | SERVES 2

5 large eggs
¼ teaspoon salt
¼ teaspoon freshly ground black pepper
1 teaspoon yellow mustard
1 tablespoon dill pickle relish
¼ cup small-diced cooked ham
¼ cup shredded cooked pork
⅓ cup grated Swiss cheese
2 slices sandwich bread, diced

1. Preheat air fryer at 325°F for 3 minutes.

2. In a medium bowl, whisk eggs. Stir in remaining ingredients. Pour into lightly greased cake barrel (accessory).

3. Cook 14 minutes. Transfer to a cooling rack for 5 minutes. Slice and serve warm.

PER SERVING Calories: 416 | Fat: 21.5 g | Protein: 31.2 g | Sodium: 990 mg | Fiber: 1.1 g | Carbohydrates: 18.9 g | Sugar: 2.4 g

Bacony Brunch Frittata

There's nothing more indulgent than wearing your pajamas all day, eating off a tray in bed, and binge-watching that series you've been meaning to get to. Well, make a date with yourself, sleep in late, and enjoy this tasty frittata.

HANDS-ON TIME: 10 minutes
COOK TIME: 14 minutes

INGREDIENTS | SERVES 2

5 large eggs
¼ teaspoon salt
¼ teaspoon freshly ground black pepper
½ cup baby spinach
¼ cup minced sweet yellow onion
4 slices cooked bacon, crumbled
1 medium Roma tomato, diced
¼ cup grated mozzarella cheese

1. Preheat air fryer at 325°F for 3 minutes.

2. In a medium bowl, whisk eggs. Stir in remaining ingredients. Pour into lightly greased cake barrel (accessory).

3. Cook 14 minutes. Transfer to a cooling rack for 5 minutes. Slice and serve warm.

PER SERVING Calories: 343 | Fat: 21.5 g | Protein: 27.3 g | Sodium: 950 mg | Fiber: 1.0 g | Carbohydrates: 5.1 g | Sugar: 2.3 g

CHAPTER 3

Breads and Baked Goods

Chocolate-Espresso Muffins

When you need your chocolate and coffee all in one and you need it to go, grab one of these muffins and hit the road. Sweet, rich, and quick are just what some mornings call for!

HANDS-ON TIME: 10 minutes
COOK TIME: 7 minutes

INGREDIENTS | SERVES 6

½ cup all-purpose flour
¼ cup unsweetened cocoa powder
2 teaspoons instant espresso powder
1 teaspoon baking powder
½ teaspoon baking soda
¼ cup sugar
Pinch salt
½ teaspoon vanilla extract
3 tablespoons unsalted butter, melted
2 large eggs
2 tablespoons whole milk

1. In a large bowl, combine flour, cocoa powder, espresso powder, baking powder, baking soda, sugar, and salt.

2. In a medium bowl, combine vanilla, butter, eggs, and milk.

3. Preheat air fryer at 375°F for 3 minutes.

4. Pour wet ingredients from the medium bowl into the large bowl of dry ingredients. Gently combine ingredients. Do not overmix. Spoon mixture into six lightly greased silicone cupcake liners.

5. Cook 7 minutes. Transfer silicone muffins to a cooling rack. Serve warm or cooled.

PER SERVING Calories: 158 | Fat: 7.5 g | Protein: 4.1 g | Sodium: 237 mg | Fiber: 1.6 g | Carbohydrates: 19.2 g | Sugar: 8.8 g

Chocolate-Strawberry Muffins

Inspired by chocolate-covered strawberries, these muffins are just the ticket when you're craving a doughnut but want to skip the over-the-top calorie count. For a variation, use dark, unsweetened cocoa. It will yield a rich blackish color, and there is definitely a flavor difference.

HANDS-ON TIME: 10 minutes
COOK TIME: 7 minutes

INGREDIENTS | SERVES 6

½ cup all-purpose flour
¼ cup unsweetened cocoa powder
½ teaspoon baking soda
¼ cup sugar
Pinch salt
½ teaspoon vanilla extract
3 tablespoons butter, melted
2 large eggs
2 tablespoons whole milk
¼ cup minced strawberries

1. In a large bowl, combine flour, cocoa powder, baking soda, sugar, and salt.

2. In a medium bowl, combine vanilla, butter, eggs, milk, and strawberries.

3. Preheat air fryer at 375°F for 3 minutes.

4. Pour wet ingredients from the medium bowl into the large bowl of dry ingredients. Gently combine ingredients. Do not overmix. Spoon mixture into six lightly greased silicone cupcake liners.

5. Cook 7 minutes. Transfer silicone muffins to a cooling rack. Serve warm or cooled.

PER SERVING Calories: 158 | Fat: 7.5 g | Protein: 4.1 g | Sodium: 156 mg | Fiber: 1.7 g | Carbohydrates: 19.3 g | Sugar: 9.1 g

No-Knead Crusty Bread

Crispy on the outside and soft on the inside, this crusty bread will rival any artisanal bread you can buy at the store. Just combine ingredients and allow to rise overnight. There is no kneading required in the making of this simple bread, and the results are very tasty!

HANDS-ON TIME: 10 minutes
COOK TIME: 40 minutes

INGREDIENTS | SERVES 6

1 teaspoon active dry yeast
1 cup warm water
2½ cups all-purpose flour
1½ teaspoons salt
2 tablespoons water
1 teaspoon olive oil

1. In a large bowl add yeast and warm water. Stir until yeast is dissolved. Add flour and salt and stir until a dough forms. It will look messy and loose, not a perfect ball, and this is good. Seal top of bowl with plastic wrap and let sit on the kitchen counter 10 hours.

2. Preheat air fryer at 400°F for 10 minutes with round cake barrel (accessory) in the air fryer as well. Place 2 tablespoons water in bottom drip pan after preheating the device.

3. Flour your hands and carefully form the dough into a ball but don't overmix it. Place ball into heated cake barrel. Lightly press down on top of ball to slightly flatten. Cover dish with aluminum foil. Cook 30 minutes.

4. Remove foil and lightly brush top of bread with olive oil. Cook an additional 10 minutes. Transfer to a cooling rack.

5. Serve warm or at room temperature.

PER SERVING Calories: 198 | Fat: 1.1 g | Protein: 5.7 g | Sodium: 582 mg | Fiber: 1.6 g | Carbohydrates: 40.0 g | Sugar: 0.1 g

Artisanal Olive Bread

For lovers of the humble and briny olive, this is your bread. This Mediterranean-style crusty loaf is perfect with steamed mussels, a bowl of pasta, or even sliced for a fresh mozzarella and tomato sandwich (crisped and melted to perfection in your air fryer)!

HANDS-ON TIME: 10 minutes
COOK TIME: 40 minutes

INGREDIENTS | SERVES 6

1 teaspoon active dry yeast

1 cup warm water

2½ cups all-purpose flour

1½ teaspoons salt

¼ cup finely diced pitted Kalamata olives

1 tablespoon chopped fresh dill

2 tablespoons water

1 teaspoon olive oil

1. In a large bowl add yeast and warm water. Stir until yeast is dissolved. Add flour, salt, olives, and dill. Stir until a dough forms. It will look messy and loose, not a perfect ball, and this is good. Seal top of bowl with plastic wrap and let sit on the kitchen counter 10 hours.

2. Preheat air fryer at 400°F for 10 minutes with round cake barrel (accessory) in the air fryer as well. Place 2 tablespoons water in bottom drip pan after preheating the device.

3. Flour your hands and carefully form the dough into a ball but don't overmix it. Place ball into heated cake barrel. Lightly press down on top of ball to slightly flatten. Cover dish with aluminum foil. Cook 30 minutes.

4. Remove foil and lightly brush top of bread with olive oil. Cook an additional 10 minutes. Transfer to a cooling rack.

5. Serve warm or at room temperature.

PER SERVING Calories: 217 | Fat: 3.0 g | Protein: 5.8 g | Sodium: 685 mg | Fiber: 1.8 g | Carbohydrates: 40.6 g | Sugar: 0.1 g

Yeast Rolls

These yeasty dinner rolls are just like Grandma used to make. Give them the time to rise and allow the yeast to do its thing. Also, if you are feeling creative, form these into whatever shapes you'd like.

HANDS-ON TIME: 15 minutes
COOK TIME: 18 minutes

INGREDIENTS | YIELDS 8 ROLLS

1 teaspoon active dry yeast

¼ cup warm water

2 cups all-purpose flour

1 teaspoon salt

1 tablespoon sugar

1 large egg

½ cup whole milk

3 tablespoons butter, melted and divided

1 teaspoon olive oil

1. In a large bowl add yeast and water. Stir until yeast is dissolved. Stir in flour, salt, and sugar. Add egg, milk, and 1 tablespoon melted butter. Use a fork to combine until a dough starts to form. Transfer dough to a floured flat, clean surface. Knead dough 5 minutes. Form into a ball.

2. Brush olive oil on a medium bowl. Add dough. Cover with a damp cloth and set aside 1 hour.

3. Punch down dough and transfer to a floured flat, clean surface.

4. Preheat air fryer at 375°F for 3 minutes.

5. Separate dough into eight sections. Roll each section into a ball. Place four balls in lightly greased pizza pan (accessory). Cook 7 minutes. Brush 1 tablespoon melted butter on tops of rolls. Cook an additional 2 minutes. Repeat with remaining rolls and butter.

6. Transfer to a cooling rack. Serve warm.

PER SERVING Calories: 177 | Fat: 5.2 g | Protein: 4.7 g | Sodium: 307 mg | Fiber: 1.0 g | Carbohydrates: 26.4 g | Sugar: 2.4 g

Cheddar Dinner Rolls

Let's face it, Cheddar cheese goes with almost any dish, but you can get creative with other cheese varieties as well in these rolls. Swiss cheese would complement a ham meal. Feta cheese would be nice with a Greek salad. And try blue cheese with a steak dish for a sharp contrast.

HANDS-ON TIME: 15 minutes
COOK TIME: 18 minutes

INGREDIENTS | YIELDS 8 ROLLS

1 teaspoon active dry yeast

¼ cup warm water

2 cups all-purpose flour

1 teaspoon salt

1 tablespoon Italian seasoning

2 teaspoons sugar

1 large egg

⅓ cup whole milk

¼ cup shredded Cheddar cheese

3 tablespoons butter, melted and divided

1 teaspoon olive oil

1. In a large bowl add yeast and water. Stir until yeast is dissolved. Stir in flour, salt, seasoning, and sugar. Add egg, milk, cheese, and 1 tablespoon melted butter. Use a fork to combine until a dough starts to form. Transfer dough to a floured flat, clean surface. Knead dough 5 minutes. Form into a ball.

2. Brush olive oil on a medium bowl. Add dough. Cover with a damp cloth and set aside 1 hour.

3. Punch down dough and transfer to a floured flat, clean surface.

4. Preheat air fryer at 375°F for 3 minutes.

5. Separate dough into eight sections. Roll each section into a ball. Place four balls in lightly greased pizza pan (accessory). Cook 7 minutes. Brush 1 tablespoon melted butter on tops of rolls. Cook an additional 2 minutes. Repeat with remaining rolls and butter.

6. Transfer to a cooling rack. Serve warm.

PER SERVING Calories: 186 | Fat: 6.1 g | Protein: 5.4 g | Sodium: 327 mg | Fiber: 1.0 g | Carbohydrates: 25.7 g | Sugar: 1.7 g

Soft Pretzel Breadsticks

*Make these easy pretzel breadsticks for your next craft beer tasting party! They
are equally great served with your next sausage and cabbage meal.*

HANDS-ON TIME: 10 minutes
COOK TIME: 13 minutes

INGREDIENTS | YIELDS 10 BREADSTICKS

½ cup warm water

2 teaspoons white sugar

1½ teaspoons packed brown sugar

1 teaspoon active dry yeast

2 tablespoons vegetable oil

2 cups all-purpose flour

1 tablespoon olive oil

6 cups water

1 cup baking soda

1 teaspoon salt

1 large egg, whisked

2 teaspoons coarse salt

1. In a large bowl, add warm water, white sugar, and brown sugar. Stir until sugars are dissolved. Add yeast. Let stand 5 minutes. Incorporate vegetable oil and flour into liquid.

2. Flip sticky dough onto a floured flat, clean work surface. Knead dough 3 minutes. Brush olive oil on large bowl and add dough. Cover bowl with a damp cloth and leave alone 1 hour.

3. Punch down dough. Divide into ten sections. Roll each section into a breadstick 6" long.

4. In a large pot, bring 6 cups water, baking soda, and salt to a boil. Working in batches of five, add pretzel sticks to water and allow to boil about 30 seconds each batch. Using a slotted spoon, remove pretzels from water and set aside on a plate. Brush sticks with whisked egg.

5. Preheat air fryer at 375°F for 3 minutes.

6. Place five pretzel sticks in lightly greased air fryer basket and cook 6 minutes. Transfer to a plate and garnish with half of the coarse salt. Repeat. Serve warm.

PER SERVING Calories: 129 | Fat: 3.2 g | Protein: 3.4 g | Sodium: 1,193 mg | Fiber: 0.8 g | Carbohydrates: 20.1 g | Sugar: 1.6 g

Creamed Corn Buttermilk Corn Bread

Have you ever bitten into a piece of dry corn bread and just thought you didn't like it? Well, try again. The addition of the creamed corn and onion lends a moisture to this bread that will make you come back for more.

HANDS-ON TIME: 10 minutes
COOK TIME: 15 minutes

INGREDIENTS | SERVES 4

1 large egg
1 cup self-rising buttermilk cornmeal mix
½ cup creamed corn
½ cup diced sweet onion
½ cup buttermilk
½ teaspoon sugar
Pinch salt
⅛ teaspoon freshly ground black pepper

1. Lightly grease pizza pan (accessory).

2. In a large bowl, combine egg, cornmeal, creamed corn, onion, buttermilk, sugar, salt, and pepper. Do not overmix. Transfer mixture to greased pan.

3. Preheat air fryer at 350°F for 3 minutes.

4. Cook 15 minutes or until inserted toothpick comes out clean. Let cool 5 minutes. Flip onto a plate and slice. Serve warm.

PER SERVING Calories: 169 | Fat: 2.7 g | Protein: 6.1 g | Sodium: 550 mg | Fiber: 2.8 g | Carbohydrates: 31.4 g | Sugar: 4.1 g

Orange Spiced Pumpkin Bread

Oranges and pumpkin go together not just because their colors match but because the sweet citrus flavor plays nicely with the savory pumpkin.

HANDS-ON TIME: 10 minutes
COOK TIME: 20 minutes

INGREDIENTS | SERVES 6

1½ cups all-purpose flour
1 teaspoon baking soda
1 cup sugar
2 teaspoons pumpkin pie spice
¼ teaspoon salt
½ cup pumpkin purée
2 large eggs
1 teaspoon fresh orange zest
1 tablespoon freshly squeezed orange juice
¼ cup crushed walnuts

1. In a medium bowl, combine all the ingredients.

2. Preheat air fryer at 375°F for 3 minutes.

3. Spread mixture in lightly greased pizza pan (accessory). Cook 20 minutes.

4. Remove from air fryer and let cool 10 minutes to set. Serve warm.

PER SERVING Calories: 308 | Fat: 4.8 g | Protein: 6.3 g | Sodium: 332 mg | Fiber: 1.9 g | Carbohydrates: 60.4 g | Sugar: 34.5 g

Corn Dog Bread

This is a lazy man's corn dog with all the same great flavors. Couple this with a tall glass of iced fresh lemonade and you'll feel like you're at the amusement park!

HANDS-ON TIME: 10 minutes
COOK TIME: 20 minutes

INGREDIENTS | SERVES 4

½ cup all-purpose flour
½ cup cornmeal
2 teaspoons baking powder
½ teaspoon salt
Pinch cayenne pepper
1 large egg
½ cup whole milk
2 tablespoons honey
3 tablespoons butter, melted
⅓ cup diced sweet onion
3 beef franks, sliced into ¼" slices

1. Lightly grease a round cake barrel (accessory).

2. In a medium bowl, combine flour, cornmeal, baking powder, salt, and cayenne pepper.

3. In a small bowl, whisk together egg, milk, honey, and butter. Pour into flour mixture and stir slowly. Do not overmix. Fold in onion and beef franks.

4. Preheat air fryer at 375°F for 3 minutes.

5. Pour mixture into cake barrel and seal top with a piece of aluminum foil. Cook 10 minutes. Remove foil and cook an additional 10 minutes.

6. Remove from air fryer and let cool 10 minutes to set. Serve warm.

PER SERVING Calories: 395 | Fat: 19.4 g | Protein: 10.0 g | Sodium: 874 mg | Fiber: 1.5 g | Carbohydrates: 40.6 g | Sugar: 11.6 g

Cheesy Ham Palmiers

These buttery, bready goodies are loaded with that comforting duo of ham and cheese. Great as an appetizer, snack, breakfast, side dish...well, you get the picture. These are just great!

HANDS-ON TIME: 15 minutes
COOK TIME: 24 minutes

INGREDIENTS | SERVES 6

4 ounces cream cheese, at room temperature

¼ cup shredded Swiss cheese

1 teaspoon Dijon mustard

3 ounces deli ham, finely chopped

1 teaspoon fresh thyme leaves

¼ teaspoon salt

½ teaspoon freshly ground black pepper

1 tablespoon all-purpose flour

1 sheet phyllo dough, thawed to room temperature

1 tablespoon butter, melted

1. In a medium bowl, combine cream cheese, Swiss cheese, mustard, ham, thyme, salt, and pepper.

2. Sprinkle flour over a flat, clean surface. Place phyllo sheet over scattered flour. Brush butter over sheet. Flip dough.

3. Evenly spread cheese mixture over sheet. Carefully roll long end toward the middle of sheet. Stop at the halfway point. Roll opposite length toward the center so that both rolls meet in the middle. Refrigerate 30 minutes.

4. Slice double log into eighteen equal slices.

5. Preheat air fryer at 350°F for 3 minutes.

6. Place six palmiers in lightly greased air fryer basket. Cook 8 minutes. Repeat with remaining palmiers.

7. Transfer cooked palmiers to a cooling rack. Serve warm.

PER SERVING Calories: 137 | Fat: 9.9 g | Protein: 5.2 g | Sodium: 366 mg | Fiber: 0.4 g | Carbohydrates: 4.4 g | Sugar: 0.7 g

Dilly Dinner Puff Rolls

Light and buttery, the phyllo dough helps accent the very distinct and mildly bitter addition of dill. These puff rolls are amazing paired with salmon, crab cakes, seared scallops, and even a crisp summer salad.

HANDS-ON TIME: 15 minutes
COOK TIME: 18 minutes

INGREDIENTS | YIELDS 10 ROLLS

1 tablespoon all-purpose flour
1 sheet phyllo dough, thawed to room temperature
1 tablespoon butter, melted
2 tablespoons grated Parmesan cheese
1 teaspoon garlic salt
2 teaspoons chopped fresh dill

1. Sprinkle flour over a flat, clean surface. Place phyllo sheet over scattered flour. Brush butter over sheet.

2. Evenly scatter cheese, garlic salt, and dill over phyllo sheet. From short end to short end, roll into a log. Refrigerate 30 minutes. Slice log into ten equal slices.

3. Preheat air fryer at 350°F for 3 minutes.

4. Place four puff rolls in lightly greased air fryer basket. Cook 6 minutes. Repeat with remaining puff rolls. Transfer cooked puff rolls to a cooling rack. Serve warm.

PER SERVING Calories: 19 | Fat: 1.4 g | Protein: 0.4 g | Sodium: 223 mg | Fiber: 0.0 g | Carbohydrates: 1.1 g | Sugar: 0.0 g

Hush Puppies

Your guests will be very pleased with this recipe for a perfect accompaniment to a fish fry. Add a side of coleslaw and make sure you have a lot of ketchup or tartar sauce and sweet tea to go along with this meal.

HANDS-ON TIME: 5 minutes
COOK TIME: 10 minutes

INGREDIENTS | YIELDS 8 HUSH PUPPIES

⅔ cup self-rising buttermilk cornmeal
2 tablespoons all-purpose flour
¼ teaspoon baking soda
Pinch salt
4 tablespoons minced yellow onion
⅓ cup buttermilk
1 large egg
3 tablespoons butter, melted

1. Preheat air fryer at 350°F for 3 minutes.

2. In a medium bowl, combine cornmeal, flour, baking soda, salt, onion, buttermilk, and egg.

3. Scoop and form batter into eight hush puppies, approximately 2 tablespoons each, and place in lightly greased pizza pan (accessory). It's all right if the hush puppies are touching.

4. Cook 10 minutes. Brush tops with melted butter. Separate the hush puppies and transfer to a plate. Serve warm.

PER SERVING Calories: 95 | Fat: 5.1 g | Protein: 2.4 g | Sodium: 204 mg | Fiber: 0.8 g | Carbohydrates: 9.7 g | Sugar: 0.8 g

Buckwheat Quick Bread

If you are serving a meal out of your cast-iron pan, this buckwheat quick bread will fit right in with its rustic and rich flavor. The addition of the honey adds just enough sweetness to counter the flavor of buckwheat, still making this a savory bread option.

HANDS-ON TIME: 5 minutes
COOK TIME: 7 minutes

INGREDIENTS | SERVES 6

1 cup buckwheat flour
1½ teaspoons baking powder
⅛ teaspoon garlic powder
½ teaspoon salt
3 tablespoons butter, melted
½ cup whole milk
1 tablespoon honey

1. In a medium bowl, combine all the ingredients.

2. Preheat air fryer at 375°F for 3 minutes.

3. Spread mixture in lightly greased pizza pan (accessory). Cook 7 minutes.

4. Remove from air fryer and let cool 10 minutes to set. Serve warm.

PER SERVING Calories: 141 | Fat: 6.5 g | Protein: 3.3 g | Sodium: 327 mg | Fiber: 2.0 g | Carbohydrates: 18.3 g | Sugar: 4.4 g

Banana Nut Bread

Banana bread has the ability to awaken memories of Grandma. You can bring back a little nostalgia and also get rid of that lone ripe banana in 25 minutes from start to finish!

HANDS-ON TIME: 10 minutes
COOK TIME: 15 minutes

INGREDIENTS | SERVES 6

1 cup all-purpose flour
1 teaspoon baking powder
¼ teaspoon baking soda
⅓ cup sugar
¼ teaspoon ground cinnamon
¼ teaspoon salt
⅓ cup mashed banana (about 1 large banana)
1 large egg
1 tablespoon whole milk
1 teaspoon vanilla extract
¼ cup pecan pieces

1. In a medium bowl, combine all the ingredients.

2. Preheat air fryer at 375°F for 3 minutes.

3. Spread mixture in lightly greased pizza pan (accessory). Cook 15 minutes.

4. Remove from air fryer and let cool 10 minutes to set. Serve warm.

PER SERVING Calories: 186 | Fat: 4.1 g | Protein: 4.0 g | Sodium: 243 mg | Fiber: 1.7 g | Carbohydrates: 33.4 g | Sugar: 14.4 g

Bacon and Cheese Biscuit Bites

Serve these biscuit bites alongside your favorite eggs, a bowl of grits, and a thick slice of tomato for a good ol' down-home Georgia breakfast. Your family will scream for these savory and fluffy biscuits every weekend.

HANDS-ON TIME: 10 minutes
COOK TIME: 12 minutes

INGREDIENTS | YIELDS 9 BISCUITS

⅓ cup all-purpose flour

¼ teaspoon salt

¼ teaspoon baking powder

½ cup cooked, crumbled bacon

2 ounces cream cheese, at room temperature

¼ cup shredded sharp Cheddar cheese

1 teaspoon chopped chives

2 tablespoons buttermilk

½ teaspoon vegetable oil

1. In a medium bowl, combine flour, salt, and baking powder.

2. In a small bowl, combine remaining ingredients and stir until smooth. Add ingredients from small bowl to dry ingredients in medium bowl. Do not overmix.

3. Preheat air fryer at 325°F for 3 minutes.

4. Form mixture into nine (1") balls and add to pizza pan (accessory). It's all right if the biscuits are touching. Cook 12 minutes.

5. Transfer to a plate. Serve warm.

PER SERVING Calories: 102 | Fat: 6.5 g | Protein: 5.2 g | Sodium: 296 mg | Fiber: 0.1 g | Carbohydrates: 4.2 g | Sugar: 0.4 g

Zucchini Chocolate Chip Bread

This recipe is essential when your garden is overflowing with zucchini. Because this bread has a similar taste to banana bread, your picky eaters will never know the difference, especially with the addition of chocolate chips. Who can resist that?!

HANDS-ON TIME: 10 minutes
COOK TIME: 15 minutes

INGREDIENTS | SERVES 6

1 cup all-purpose flour
1 teaspoon baking powder
¼ teaspoon baking soda
½ cup sugar
¼ teaspoon ground cinnamon
¼ teaspoon salt
⅓ cup grated zucchini
1 large egg
1 tablespoon whole milk
1 teaspoon vanilla extract
¼ cup chocolate chips

1. In a medium bowl, combine all the ingredients.

2. Preheat air fryer at 375°F for 3 minutes.

3. Spread mixture in lightly greased pizza pan (accessory). Cook 15 minutes.

4. Remove from air fryer and let cool 10 minutes to set. Serve warm.

PER SERVING Calories: 193 | Fat: 3.1 g | Protein: 3.7 g | Sodium: 245 mg | Fiber: 1.1 g | Carbohydrates: 38.2 g | Sugar: 21.2 g

Pull-Apart Buttermilk Biscuits

When cooking, biscuits actually fluff up higher when placed beside each other. So crowd that pan. Your taller, fluffy biscuits will reward you.

HANDS-ON TIME: 10 minutes
COOK TIME: 15 minutes

INGREDIENTS | YIELDS 10 BISCUITS

2 cups all-purpose flour
2 teaspoons baking powder
1 teaspoon salt
2 tablespoons butter, melted
1 cup buttermilk

1. In a medium bowl, combine flour, baking powder, and salt. Add butter and buttermilk until a sticky dough forms.

2. Preheat air fryer at 350°F for 3 minutes.

3. Flour your hands and form mixture evenly into ten Ping-Pong–sized balls. Add balls to lightly greased pizza pan (accessory) so that they are touching. Cook 15 minutes.

4. Transfer to a plate. Serve warm.

PER SERVING Calories: 125 | Fat: 2.8 g | Protein: 3.6 g | Sodium: 356 mg | Fiber: 0.7 g | Carbohydrates: 20.6 g | Sugar: 1.4 g

Garlic-Butter Cloverleafs

Cloverleafs are made by placing three balls of dough in one muffin cup. They rise up together during the cooking process, achieving cute little clover-shaped rolls. These cloverleafs are quick to bake and make a great addition to a meat and potatoes meal.

HANDS-ON TIME: 10 minutes
COOK TIME: 6 minutes

INGREDIENTS | YIELDS 4 CLOVERLEAFS

1 cup all-purpose flour
1½ teaspoons baking powder
¾ teaspoon salt
3 cloves garlic, minced
4 tablespoons whole milk
3 tablespoons butter, melted and divided

1. In a small bowl, combine flour, baking powder, and salt. Add garlic, milk, and 1 tablespoon butter until a sticky dough forms.

2. Preheat air fryer at 350°F for 3 minutes.

3. Lightly grease four silicone muffin cups.

4. Flour your hands and form mixture into twelve balls of equal size. Add three balls to each muffin cup. Place muffin cups in air fryer basket. Cook 3 minutes. Brush tops of cloverleafs with remaining 2 tablespoons butter. Cook an additional 3 minutes.

5. Transfer to a plate. Serve warm.

PER SERVING Calories: 203 | Fat: 8.7 g | Protein: 3.9 g | Sodium: 626 mg | Fiber: 0.9 g | Carbohydrates: 25.8 g | Sugar: 0.9 g

Smoked Salmon Rolls

Although homemade dough can certainly be used for this recipe, those tubes of refrigerated dough make life easier. These Smoked Salmon Rolls can be prepared and baked within 25 minutes, and the tomatoes, red onion, capers, and fresh dill make these amazingly fresh-tasting.

HANDS-ON TIME: 10 minutes
COOK TIME: 15 minutes

INGREDIENTS | SERVES 4

1 (13.8-ounce) can refrigerated pizza dough

4 ounces cream cheese, at room temperature

8 ounces smoked salmon

2 medium Roma tomatoes, seeded and diced small

¼ cup diced red onion

2 tablespoons capers

1 tablespoon chopped fresh dill

1. Press out pizza dough into its rectangle shape. Spread cream cheese over dough. Evenly distribute salmon, tomatoes, onion, capers, and dill.

2. Preheat air fryer at 400°F for 3 minutes.

3. Roll small end of dough to small end tightly into a roll. Slice into eight even portions.

4. Place slices cut side up in lightly buttered round cake barrel (accessory). Cover with aluminum foil.

5. Cook 12 minutes. Uncover and cook an additional 3 minutes.

6. Transfer cake barrel to a cooling rack and let rest 10 minutes. Pull apart and serve warm.

PER SERVING Calories: 413 | Fat: 13.6 g | Protein: 20.1 g | Sodium: 1,911 mg | Fiber: 2.2 g | Carbohydrates: 50.2 g | Sugar: 8.2 g

Cranberry-Orange Cinnamon Rolls

When you have guests over, these cinnamon rolls hit all of those fall flavors and don't keep you in the kitchen long. You can change up the cranberries with other dried fruits, such as raisins, dates, or cherries.

HANDS-ON TIME: 10 minutes
COOK TIME: 15 minutes

INGREDIENTS | YIELDS 8 CINNAMON ROLLS

Cinnamon Rolls

1 (13.8-ounce) can refrigerated pizza dough
3 tablespoons unsalted butter, melted
⅓ cup sugar
1 teaspoon ground cinnamon
1 tablespoon fresh orange zest
¼ cup chopped baking cranberries

Orange Glaze

3 tablespoons powdered sugar
2–3 teaspoons freshly squeezed orange juice

What Are Baking Cranberries?

Baking cranberries can be found in the baking aisle of the grocery store in the same area with all of the chocolate chips. If your store doesn't carry them, head over to the raisin section and find dried cranberries. When you get home, dice up the amount your recipe calls for and you now have baking cranberries!

1. Press out pizza dough into its rectangle shape. Brush with melted butter. Sprinkle evenly with sugar, cinnamon, and orange zest. Scatter cranberries over dough.

2. Preheat air fryer at 400°F for 3 minutes.

3. Roll small end of dough to small end tightly in a roll. Slice into eight even portions.

4. Place slices cut side up in lightly buttered round cake barrel (accessory). Cover with aluminum foil.

5. Cook 12 minutes. Uncover and cook an additional 3 minutes.

6. Transfer cake barrel to a cooling rack and let rest 10 minutes.

7. In a small bowl, whisk together glaze ingredients and drizzle over cinnamon rolls. Pull apart and serve warm.

PER SERVING Calories: 215 | Fat: 5.6 g | Protein: 3.8 g | Sodium: 286 mg | Fiber: 1.2 g | Carbohydrates: 38.3 g | Sugar: 16.9 g

Celebration Cinnamon Rolls

When your little one is celebrating a birthday, can you think of a better way to start the day? Sweets and rainbow sprinkles are the best equation to create smiles. You can also tailor the sprinkle colors to match different holidays for a fun surprise!

HANDS-ON TIME: 10 minutes
COOK TIME: 15 minutes

INGREDIENTS | YIELDS 8 CINNAMON ROLLS

Cinnamon Rolls

1 (13.8-ounce) can refrigerated pizza dough
3 tablespoons unsalted butter, melted
¼ cup sugar
2 tablespoons rainbow sprinkles
1 teaspoon ground cinnamon
¼ cup raisins

Glaze

3 tablespoons powdered sugar
2–3 teaspoons whole milk
1 tablespoon rainbow sprinkles

1. Press out pizza dough into its rectangle shape. Brush dough with melted butter. Sprinkle evenly with sugar, rainbow sprinkles, and cinnamon. Scatter raisins over dough.

2. Preheat air fryer at 400°F for 3 minutes.

3. Roll small end of dough to small end tightly in a roll. Slice into eight even portions.

4. Place slices cut side up in lightly buttered round cake barrel (accessory). Cover with aluminum foil.

5. Cook 12 minutes. Uncover and cook an additional 3 minutes.

6. Transfer cake barrel to a cooling rack and let rest 10 minutes.

7. In a small bowl, whisk together powdered sugar and milk. Drizzle over cinnamon rolls. Garnish with rainbow sprinkles.

PER SERVING Calories: 228 | Fat: 6.5 g | Protein: 4.0 g | Sodium: 287 mg | Fiber: 1.1 g | Carbohydrates: 41.5 g | Sugar: 19.8 g

Lemon-Raspberry Swirls

The sweetness of the raspberry preserves is enhanced by the lemon zest and juice in the glaze. Try different combinations, such as orange and blackberry jam or lime and strawberry jelly. These swirls can be enjoyed as a breakfast, snack, or dessert!

HANDS-ON TIME: 10 minutes
COOK TIME: 15 minutes

INGREDIENTS | SERVES 4

Swirls

1 (13.8-ounce) can refrigerated pizza dough

3 tablespoons unsalted butter, melted

⅓ cup raspberry preserves

1 tablespoon fresh lemon zest

Glaze

3 tablespoons powdered sugar

2–3 teaspoons fresh lemon juice

1. Press out pizza dough into its rectangle shape. Brush with melted butter. Spread raspberry preserves over dough. Sprinkle evenly with lemon zest.

2. Preheat air fryer at 400°F for 3 minutes.

3. Roll small end of dough to small end tightly in a roll. Slice into eight even portions.

4. Place slices cut side up in lightly buttered round cake barrel (accessory). Cover with aluminum foil.

5. Cook 12 minutes. Uncover and cook an additional 3 minutes.

6. Transfer cake barrel to a cooling rack and let rest 10 minutes.

7. In a small bowl, whisk together powdered sugar and lemon juice. Drizzle over raspberry swirls. Pull apart and serve warm.

PER SERVING Calories: 415 | Fat: 11.1 g | Protein: 7.8 g | Sodium: 581 mg | Fiber: 2.0 g | Carbohydrates: 71.5 g | Sugar: 25.0 g

CHAPTER 4

Appetizers and Snacks

Bite-Sized Blooming Onions

These little guys are somewhat tedious in the prep, but your guests will flip over the cuteness factor! The reward in praise is worth your careful knife skills. Serve these warm with dipping sauce.

HANDS-ON TIME: 20 minutes
COOK TIME: 14 minutes

INGREDIENTS | SERVES 5

10 ounces raw yellow pearl onions (about 20)
½ cup all-purpose flour
1 teaspoon salt, plus more for sprinkling
½ teaspoon ground dry mustard
½ teaspoon chili powder
1 large egg
½ cup whole milk
1 cup panko bread crumbs, crushed fine
½ cup cornmeal

1. Shallowly cut the root end off of each onion so it can sit flat but the sections remain attached. Peel and discard the skins. Using a sharp knife, gently slice about three-quarters of the way down through the onion into fifths, as if you were cutting a pie, revealing a total of ten sections, keeping the base intact. Soak the onions in a bowl of ice water 30 minutes to help spread the sections. Transfer onions to a paper towel and remove excess water.

2. Add flour, salt, mustard, and chili powder to a small bowl.

3. In a separate small bowl, whisk together egg and milk.

4. Combine bread crumbs and cornmeal in a shallow dish.

5. Preheat air fryer at 375°F for 3 minutes.

6. Roll onions in flour and spice mixture. Shake off excess flour. Dredge onions in egg mixture. Shake off excess. Roll in bread crumb mixture. Transfer to a plate. Repeat with remaining onions.

7. Add half of onions to fryer basket. Cook 7 minutes. Transfer to a plate and repeat with remaining onions. Sprinkle with salt. Serve warm.

PER SERVING Calories: 192 | Fat: 2.1 g | Protein: 5.4 g | Sodium: 416 mg | Fiber: 1.7 g | Carbohydrates: 36.0 g | Sugar: 4.5 g

Mini Scotch Eggs

Your partygoers will fall in love with these Mini Scotch Eggs. Quail eggs can be found at some specialty grocers as well as Asian markets. These eggs have a similar taste to chicken eggs but are slightly richer due to the bigger yolk-to-white ratio.

HANDS-ON TIME: 15 minutes
COOK TIME: 10 minutes

INGREDIENTS | SERVES 4

12 quail eggs
1 cup ice
1 cup water
½ pound lean ground pork
1 teaspoon fresh thyme leaves
¼ teaspoon salt
¼ teaspoon freshly ground black pepper
1 large egg
½ cup panko bread crumbs

1. Preheat air fryer at 250°F for 3 minutes.

2. Place eggs in air fryer basket. Cook 4 minutes.

3. Add ice and water to a medium bowl. Transfer eggs to this water bath immediately to stop the cooking process. After 5 minutes, peel eggs.

4. In a medium bowl, combine pork, thyme, salt, and pepper. Form a thin layer of pork around each egg.

5. Preheat air fryer at 375°F for 3 minutes.

6. In a small bowl, whisk large egg. In another bowl, add bread crumbs.

7. Dip covered eggs in whisked egg and then dredge in bread crumbs.

8. Place eggs in air fryer basket. Cook 3 minutes. Turn. Cook an additional 3 minutes. Serve warm.

PER SERVING Calories: 168 | Fat: 5.8 g | Protein: 17.7 g | Sodium: 250 mg | Fiber: 0.1 g | Carbohydrates: 8.3 g | Sugar: 0.5 g

Pimiento Cheese–Stuffed Jalapeños

This mild, creamy mixture is great stuffed in spicy jalapeño boats. Because the peppers are seeded, most of the heat is removed. If you like things spicy, mix the seeds in with the pimiento cheese to heat things up.

HANDS-ON TIME: 10 minutes
COOK TIME: 16 minutes

INGREDIENTS | SERVES 4

6 medium jalapeño peppers
½ cup pimiento cheese

How to Make Pimiento Cheese

Although prepared pimiento cheese can be purchased in the deli section of most grocery stores, making it couldn't be any easier! Simply combine the following ingredients and then refrigerate covered until ready to use. Combine: 16 ounces finely shredded sharp Cheddar cheese, 1 (4-ounce) jar pimientos including juice, ½ cup mayonnaise, ¼ teaspoon salt, and ¼ teaspoon freshly ground black pepper. Stir. Refrigerate 15 minutes.

1. Cut jalapeño peppers lengthwise and discard seeds. (If you like the heat, stir the seeds into the pimiento cheese.)

2. Press equal amounts pimiento cheese into each jalapeño half.

3. Preheat air fryer at 350°F for 3 minutes.

4. Lay six stuffed peppers into air fryer basket. Cook 8 minutes. Transfer cooked peppers to a serving plate. Repeat with remaining peppers.

5. Transfer to a serving plate and serve warm.

PER SERVING Calories: 71 | Fat: 5.2 g | Protein: 4.1 g | Sodium: 160 mg | Fiber: 0.6 g | Carbohydrates: 1.7 g | Sugar: 1.0 g

Jalapeño Popper Bombs

Cheesy, spicy, bready…yummy! These Jalapeño Popper Bombs have all the flavor deep-fried poppers have but without all the oil and with less cheese. The dough helps tone down the pepper heat, making these appetizers enjoyable for all your guests.

HANDS-ON TIME: 10 minutes
COOK TIME: 12 minutes

INGREDIENTS | SERVES 3

⅓ cup all-purpose flour

¼ teaspoon salt

¼ teaspoon baking powder

2 tablespoons diced jalapeño pepper, seeds removed

2 ounces cream cheese, at room temperature

1 tablespoon shredded Monterey jack cheese

2 tablespoons shredded Cheddar cheese

2 tablespoons whole milk

½ teaspoon olive oil

1. In a medium bowl, combine flour, salt, and baking powder.

2. In a small bowl, combine remaining ingredients.

3. Pour mixture from small bowl into dry ingredients in medium bowl.

4. Preheat air fryer at 325°F for 3 minutes.

5. Form mixture into nine (1") balls. Place in lightly greased pizza pan (accessory). It's all right if the poppers are touching. Cook 12 minutes.

6. Transfer to a plate. Serve warm.

PER SERVING Calories: 155 | Fat: 8.7 g | Protein: 4.6 g | Sodium: 350 mg | Fiber: 0.5 g | Carbohydrates: 12.3 g | Sugar: 1.3 g

Cheddar Biscuit–Breaded Green Olives

You'll become obsessed with this new discovery. Cheddar dough wrapped around briny green olives? Yes! Try this recipe with black olives too!

HANDS-ON TIME: 15 minutes
COOK TIME: 8 minutes

INGREDIENTS | SERVES 5

⅔ cup all-purpose flour
½ teaspoon baking powder
½ cup finely grated sharp Cheddar cheese
4 tablespoons butter, melted
25 pimiento-stuffed standard Manzanilla green olives

1. In a food processor, pulse flour, baking powder, cheese, and melted butter until a doughy ball forms.

2. Drain olives and pat dry with a paper towel.

3. Form just enough flour mixture around an olive to cover it. Roll between your hands to form a smooth ball. Repeat with remaining olives.

4. Preheat air fryer at 375°F for 3 minutes.

5. Place olives in lightly greased air fryer basket. Cook 3 minutes. Gently shake. Cook an additional 3 minutes. Gently shake. Cook an additional 2 minutes. Check to see if lightly browned. Give more time if needed; otherwise, transfer to a serving dish and let rest 5 minutes before serving warm.

PER SERVING Calories: 207 | Fat: 14.0 g | Protein: 4.7 g | Sodium: 332 mg | Fiber: 0.9 g | Carbohydrates: 13.5 g | Sugar: 0.2 g

Fried Feta-Dill-Breaded Kalamata Olives

The familiar combination of feta, dill, and Kalamata olives is concentrated in this one little bite of joy. The crispy exterior dough is perfected in the air fryer. Serve these olives as an appetizer, a snack, or even thrown into a fresh Greek salad!

HANDS-ON TIME: 15 minutes
COOK TIME: 8 minutes

INGREDIENTS | SERVES 5

⅔ cup all-purpose flour
½ teaspoon baking powder
½ cup crumbled feta cheese
½ teaspoon dried dill
4 tablespoons butter, melted
25 pitted standard Kalamata olives

1. In a food processor, pulse flour, baking powder, feta cheese, dill, and melted butter until a doughy ball forms.

2. Drain olives and pat dry with a paper towel.

3. Form just enough flour mixture around an olive to cover it. Roll between your hands to form a smooth ball. Repeat with remaining olives.

4. Preheat air fryer at 375°F for 3 minutes.

5. Place olives in lightly greased air fryer basket. Cook 3 minutes. Gently shake. Cook an additional 3 minutes. Gently shake. Cook an additional 2 minutes. Check to see if lightly browned. Give more time if needed; otherwise, transfer to a serving dish and let rest 5 minutes before serving warm.

PER SERVING Calories: 225 | Fat: 16.7 g | Protein: 4.0 g | Sodium: 475 mg | Fiber: 0.5 g | Carbohydrates: 13.5 g | Sugar: 0.7 g

Buffalo-Honey Chicken Wings

The sweetness of the honey helps temper the heat from the buffalo sauce, making this a mild combination perfect for the entire family. You may want to make a double batch because these wings disappear in no time.

HANDS-ON TIME: 15 minutes
COOK TIME: 44 minutes

INGREDIENTS | SERVES 6

1 tablespoon water

2 pounds chicken wings, split at the joint, tips removed

1 tablespoon butter

½ cup buffalo sauce

2 tablespoons honey

How to Separate Chicken Wings

Some grocery stores will have the wings already broken down for the consumer; however, a lot of times you will have to purchase whole wings. To separate, stretch the wing out. There will be two cuts to each wing, yielding three parts—the drumette, the wingette, and the tip. Using kitchen shears or a sharp knife, cut the portions at the joints. The tip is typically not used in making chicken wings. Refrigerate or freeze these and use later to make broth or to season soups.

1. Place 1 tablespoon water in the bottom of the air fryer to ensure minimum smoke from fat drippings.

2. Preheat air fryer at 250°F for 3 minutes.

3. Place half of wings in air fryer basket. Cook 6 minutes. Flip wings. Cook an additional 6 minutes.

4. While wings are cooking, combine butter, wing sauce, and honey in a large bowl. The chicken wings will melt the butter, so don't worry about melting it beforehand.

5. Raise temperature on air fryer to 400°F. Flip wings and cook 5 minutes. Flip wings and cook an additional 5 minutes. Transfer to bowl with sauce and toss.

6. Repeat process with remaining wings and transfer all to a serving dish.

PER SERVING Calories: 368 | Fat: 22.9 g | Protein: 31.0 g | Sodium: 741 mg | Fiber: 0.0 g | Carbohydrates: 5.8 g | Sugar: 5.8 g

Peanut Butter and Strawberry Jelly Wings

This classic combination of peanut butter and jelly is a natural complement to the humble chicken wing. You could also try jalapeño jelly garnished with fresh cilantro for a Mexican twist, or fig jam garnished with some goat cheese crumbles.

HANDS-ON TIME: 15 minutes
COOK TIME: 44 minutes

INGREDIENTS | SERVES 6

1 tablespoon water

2 pounds chicken wings, split at the joint, tips removed

2 teaspoons butter

¼ cup creamy peanut butter

½ cup strawberry jelly

2 tablespoons apple cider vinegar

1 teaspoon hot sauce

1. Place 1 tablespoon water in the bottom of the air fryer to ensure minimum smoke from fat drippings.

2. Preheat air fryer at 250°F for 3 minutes.

3. Place half of wings in air fryer basket. Cook 6 minutes. Flip wings. Cook an additional 6 minutes.

4. While wings are cooking, combine butter, peanut butter, jelly, vinegar, and hot sauce in a large bowl. The chicken wings will melt the butter, so don't worry about melting it beforehand.

5. Raise temperature on air fryer to 400°F. Flip wings and cook 5 minutes. Flip wings and cook an additional 5 minutes. Transfer to bowl with sauce and toss.

6. Repeat process with remaining wings and transfer all to a serving dish.

PER SERVING Calories: 480 | Fat: 27.6 g | Protein: 33.4 g | Sodium: 142 mg | Fiber: 0.8 g | Carbohydrates: 20.8 g | Sugar: 14.1 g

Thai Sweet Chili Wings

The crispy skin on these wings from air frying is amazing with the sticky goodness of the sauce. Although you can purchase a similar sauce in the ethnic aisle of your grocery store, you'll find a homemade recipe in Chapter 15.

HANDS-ON TIME: 15 minutes
COOK TIME: 44 minutes

INGREDIENTS | SERVES 6

1 tablespoon water
2 pounds chicken wings, split at the joint, tips removed
½ cup Sweet Chili Sauce (see Chapter 15)

1. Place 1 tablespoon water in the bottom of the air fryer to ensure minimum smoke from fat drippings.

2. Preheat air fryer at 250°F for 3 minutes.

3. Place half of wings in air fryer basket. Cook 6 minutes. Flip wings. Cook an additional 6 minutes.

4. While wings are cooking, add sauce to a large bowl.

5. Raise temperature on air fryer to 400°F. Flip wings and cook 5 minutes. Flip wings and cook an additional 5 minutes. Transfer to bowl with sauce and toss.

6. Repeat process with remaining wings and transfer all to a serving dish.

PER SERVING Calories: 472 | Fat: 21.1 g | Protein: 31.1 g | Sodium: 238 mg | Fiber: 0.0 g | Carbohydrates: 35.2 g | Sugar: 33.6 g

Salmon Croquettes

Traditionally, croquettes are a fried delicacy, as the word croquette *comes from the French word* croquer, *which means "to crunch" or "to be crunchy." However, with the air fryer, you'll get all the crispness without the unhealthy cooking style. Serve these with your favorite dipping sauce.*

HANDS-ON TIME: 15 minutes
COOK TIME: 24 minutes

INGREDIENTS | SERVES 4

1 (14.75-ounce) can wild-caught salmon, drained

⅓ cup mayonnaise

1 tablespoon minced celery

2 teaspoons dried dill, divided

1 teaspoon lime juice

½ cup panko bread crumbs, divided

1 large egg

1 teaspoon prepared horseradish

¼ cup cornmeal

1 teaspoon salt

The Difference Between Yellow and White Cornmeal

You may be asking, what is the difference between white and yellow cornmeal? The answer is simple. Yellow cornmeal comes from yellow corn. White cornmeal is ground from white corn. Boom. They are completely interchangeable in recipes and have the same flavor.

1. In a medium bowl, combine salmon, mayonnaise, celery, 1 teaspoon dill, lime juice, ¼ cup bread crumbs, egg, and horseradish.

2. In a shallow dish, combine ¼ cup bread crumbs, cornmeal, remaining dill, and salt.

3. Preheat air fryer at 375°F for 3 minutes.

4. Form 2 tablespoons salmon mixture into sixteen tots or egg shapes. Roll in bread crumb mixture. Continue with remainder of salmon.

5. Place eight tots in lightly greased air fryer basket. Cook 4 minutes. Gently turn tots a third of the way around. Cook an additional 4 minutes. Gently turn tots another third. Cook an additional 4 minutes. Transfer to a serving dish. Repeat with remaining tots. Let rest 5 minutes before serving warm.

PER SERVING Calories: 395 | Fat: 20.1 g | Protein: 31.6 g | Sodium: 1,154 mg | Fiber: 0.5 g | Carbohydrates: 18.6 g | Sugar: 1.0 g

Pepperoni Pizza Bites

Dip these scrumptious little Pepperoni Pizza Bites in a warm marinara sauce as an after-school snack or as quick game-day food! The salty pepperoni and melty mozzarella create a winning combination for anyone, and they are so easy to make.

HANDS-ON TIME: 10 minutes
COOK TIME: 12 minutes

INGREDIENTS | SERVES 2

⅓ cup all-purpose flour
¼ teaspoon salt
¼ teaspoon baking powder
½ cup small-diced pepperoni
2 ounces cream cheese, at room temperature
¼ cup shredded mozzarella cheese
½ teaspoon Italian seasoning
2 tablespoons whole milk
1 teaspoon olive oil

1. In a small bowl, combine flour, salt, and baking powder.

2. In a medium bowl, combine remaining ingredients until smooth. Add dry ingredients until well combined.

3. Preheat air fryer at 325°F for 5 minutes.

4. Form mixture into nine (1") balls and add to pizza pan (accessory). It's all right if the pizza bites are touching. Cook 12 minutes.

5. Transfer to a plate. Serve warm.

PER SERVING Calories: 366 | Fat: 22.8 g | Protein: 13.1 g | Sodium: 987 mg | Fiber: 0.6 g | Carbohydrates: 18.2 g | Sugar: 1.9 g

Broccoli Snackers

The slightly browned edges give this sometimes-hated vegetable a new taste and texture. Add a little dipping sauce for those hard-to-win-over folks, and this may become a new favorite snack!

HANDS-ON TIME: 10 minutes
COOK TIME: 12 minutes

INGREDIENTS | SERVES 4

1 large head of broccoli, chopped into florets
1 tablespoon olive oil
½ teaspoon salt

1. Preheat air fryer at 350°F for 3 minutes.

2. In a large bowl, toss broccoli florets with olive oil.

3. Place half of broccoli in fryer basket. Cook 3 minutes. Shake. Cook an additional 3 minutes. Transfer to a serving bowl. Season with salt.

4. Repeat with remaining broccoli and serve warm.

PER SERVING Calories: 81 | Fat: 3.4 g | Protein: 4.3 g | Sodium: 340 mg | Fiber: 4.0 g | Carbohydrates: 10.1 g | Sugar: 2.6 g

Bite-Sized Pork Egg Rolls

These little guys may be a bit tedious to make, but the end result is so worth the time. One way to cut hands-on time is by purchasing already-shredded cabbage and carrots. These are usually labeled "coleslaw mix" and can be found next to the packaged salads in the produce section.

HANDS-ON TIME: 30 minutes
COOK TIME: 24 minutes

INGREDIENTS | SERVES 10

½ pound lean ground pork

2 cups coleslaw mix (shredded cabbage and carrots)

3 scallions, trimmed and minced

1 tablespoon hoisin sauce

1 tablespoon soy sauce

¼ teaspoon sriracha

½ teaspoon lime juice

30 wonton wrappers

2 teaspoons olive oil

Slimmed-Down Egg Rolls

If you are counting calories, substitute the pork with ground turkey or ground chicken. The egg rolls will still be fabulous. Other fillings that can be added are sprouts, canned bamboo shoots, and shiitake mushrooms.

1. In a large skillet, heat ground pork over medium-high heat. Stir-fry 5–6 minutes until no longer pink. Add coleslaw mix and stir into pork. Add scallions, hoisin sauce, soy sauce, sriracha, and lime juice. Stir-fry an additional 2 minutes. Remove from heat and let rest 5 minutes off the burner.

2. Place a wonton wrapper on a cutting board. Place a small bowl of water near the board. Spoon approximately 2 teaspoons mixture in a line in the middle of the wrapper. Dip your finger into the water and lightly run it around the perimeter of the wonton wrapper. Fold ¼" of the perimeter of wonton toward the middle. Roll up the length to form an egg roll. Repeat for each wonton wrapper.

3. Preheat air fryer at 325°F for 3 minutes.

4. Place half of the egg rolls in the air fryer basket. Cook 3 minutes. Lightly brush the tops of egg rolls with olive oil. Cook an additional 5 minutes. Repeat with second batch.

5. Transfer to a plate. Serve warm.

PER SERVING Calories: 106 | Fat: 1.2 g | Protein: 7.5 g | Sodium: 268 mg | Fiber: 0.9 g | Carbohydrates: 15.7 g | Sugar: 1.0 g

Green Chili Crispy Wonton Squares

Crunchy on the outside and smooth and gooey on the inside, these squares burst with flavor in each bite. Queso fresco, a creamy and mild Mexican cheese, can be found in most grocers in blocks and wedges.

HANDS-ON TIME: 15 minutes
COOK TIME: 35 minutes

INGREDIENTS | SERVES 6

30 wonton wrappers
1 cup refried beans
2 (4-ounce) cans diced green chilies
1 cup grated queso fresco

1. Place a wonton wrapper on a cutting board. Place approximately 1½ teaspoons beans in the middle of wrapper. Add approximately 1½ teaspoons green chilies and approximately 1½ teaspoons queso fresco.

2. Place a small bowl of water near the working area. Dip your finger in the water bowl and run it around the perimeter of the wonton. Bring all corners to the center and press the straight edges together. Set aside. Repeat with remaining wontons.

3. Preheat air fryer at 325°F for 3 minutes.

4. Place six wontons in air fryer basket. Cook 7 minutes. Transfer to a plate and cook the remaining batches. Serve warm.

PER SERVING Calories: 220 | Fat: 4.8 g | Protein: 9.7 g | Sodium: 680 mg | Fiber: 3.9 g | Carbohydrates: 31.7 g | Sugar: 2.0 g

Brie and Red Pepper Jelly Triangles

This is an upgrade on that block of cream cheese topped with red pepper jelly that you see served with crackers at many house parties. These triangles contain all of the flavors in one neat and pretty delicious bite!

HANDS-ON TIME: 10 minutes
COOK TIME: 16 minutes

INGREDIENTS | SERVES 4

20 wonton wrappers

10 teaspoons Brie cheese

10 teaspoons red pepper jelly

40 almond slivers

1 tablespoon olive oil

Can You Eat the White Rind Surrounding Brie?

The soft rind surrounding Brie is absolutely edible. It actually comes down to personal preference whether you want to eat it or not. When heated to warm and soften the Brie, the rind is even more appetizing.

1. Place a wonton wrapper on a cutting board. Place approximately ½ teaspoon Brie and then ½ teaspoon red pepper jelly in the middle of wrapper. Place 2 almond slivers on top.

2. Place a small bowl of water near the working area. Dip your finger in the water bowl and run it around the perimeter of the wonton. Fold one corner to the opposite corner, forming a triangle. Press down edges to seal. Set aside. Repeat with remaining wontons.

3. Preheat air fryer at 325°F for 3 minutes.

4. Place half of the triangles in the air fryer basket. Cook 3 minutes. Lightly brush the tops of triangles with olive oil. Cook an additional 5 minutes. Repeat with second batch.

5. Transfer to a plate. Serve warm.

PER SERVING Calories: 239 | Fat: 8.9 g | Protein: 6.9 g | Sodium: 292 mg | Fiber: 1.6 g | Carbohydrates: 32.2 g | Sugar: 7.8 g

Reuben Pizza for One

If you are a Reuben lover, then this is your pizza. With all of the flavors from the classic Reuben sandwich, it ensures that you never want your pizza any other way.

HANDS-ON TIME: 10 minutes
COOK TIME: 17 minutes

INGREDIENTS | YIELDS 1 PERSONAL PIZZA

¼ pound fresh pizza dough, about the size of a tennis ball

¼ teaspoon caraway seeds

2 tablespoons Thousand Island dressing (or Russian dressing)

¼ cup chopped corned beef

¼ cup shredded Swiss cheese

¼ cup sauerkraut, drained

1. Preheat air fryer at 200°F for 6 minutes.

2. Press out dough to fit pizza pan (accessory). Sprinkle caraway seeds evenly over dough. Cook 7 minutes.

3. Turn up the heat to 275°F.

4. Remove basket and spread dressing over dough, leaving ¼" outer crust uncovered. Evenly add corned beef. Sprinkle cheese over meat. Cook an additional 10 minutes.

5. Gently transfer pizza to a cutting board. Evenly add sauerkraut. Cut into six slices and serve.

PER SERVING Calories: 848 | Fat: 42.5 g | Protein: 41.3 g | Sodium: 2,409 mg | Fiber: 3.1 g | Carbohydrates: 62.7 g | Sugar: 12.8 g

Personal Pepperoni and Mushroom Pizza

This recipe is for one, with the suggestion of adding pepperoni and mushrooms. However, you can double or quadruple this recipe and get family members involved in adding their favorite toppings to their individual pizzas.

HANDS-ON TIME: 10 minutes
COOK TIME: 17 minutes

INGREDIENTS | YIELDS 1 PERSONAL PIZZA

¼ pound fresh pizza dough, about the size of a tennis ball

2 tablespoons marinara or pizza sauce

6 slices pepperoni

¼ cup sliced white mushrooms

¼ cup grated mozzarella cheese

1. Preheat air fryer at 200°F for 6 minutes.

2. Press out dough to fit pizza pan (accessory). Cook 7 minutes.

3. Turn up the heat to 275°F. Remove basket and spread sauce over dough, leaving ¼" outer crust uncovered. Add pepperoni slices and mushrooms. Sprinkle cheese over both. Cook an additional 10 minutes.

4. Gently transfer pizza to a cutting board. Cut into six slices and serve.

PER SERVING Calories: 554 | Fat: 16.3 g | Protein: 21.9 g | Sodium: 2,154 mg | Fiber: 6.7 g | Carbohydrates: 75.1 g | Sugar: 22.1 g

Everything Bagel–Fried Chickpeas

This recipe seasons chickpeas with the popular everything bagel spice mix. Crispy and crunchy once cooked, these chickpeas make a great snack!

HANDS-ON TIME: 5 minutes
COOK TIME: 16 minutes

INGREDIENTS | SERVES 4

1 (15-ounce) can chickpeas/garbanzo beans, drained and rinsed
2 teaspoons olive oil
1 tablespoon everything bagel seasoning mix (see sidebar)

Homemade Everything Bagel Spice Mix

Everything bagel spice mix is starting to show up in spice aisles at most grocery stores. However, if you cannot find any, simply mix the following ingredients and then store in an airtight container. Combine: 2 tablespoons poppy seeds, 2 tablespoons sesame seeds (preferably a mix of white and black), 2 tablespoons dried minced garlic, 2 tablespoons dried minced onion, and 2 teaspoons coarse sea salt.

1. Preheat air fryer at 350°F for 3 minutes.

2. In a small bowl, toss chickpeas in olive oil. Add to fryer basket.

3. Place in air fryer basket and cook 5 minutes. Shake. Cook an additional 5 minutes. Shake. Cook an additional 6 minutes.

4. Transfer to a small bowl and toss with seasoning mix. Let cool and serve.

PER SERVING Calories: 122 | Fat: 3.2 g | Protein: 4.5 g | Sodium: 374 mg | Fiber: 4.0 g | Carbohydrates: 14.5 g | Sugar: 2.5 g

Five Spice Crunchy Edamame

The sweet flavor of the edamame pairs nicely with the spices in Chinese five spice. Crispy on the outside and slightly tender on the inside, these snackable bites deliver a healthy dose of fiber, vitamins, and minerals.

HANDS-ON TIME: 5 minutes
COOK TIME: 16 minutes

INGREDIENTS | SERVES 4

1 cup ready-to-eat edamame, shelled
1 tablespoon sesame oil
1 teaspoon five spice powder
½ teaspoon salt

1. Preheat air fryer at 350°F for 3 minutes.

2. In a small bowl, toss edamame in sesame oil. Add to fryer basket.

3. Place in air fryer basket and cook 5 minutes. Shake. Cook an additional 5 minutes. Shake. Cook an additional 6 minutes.

4. Transfer to a small bowl and toss with five spice powder and salt. Let cool and serve.

PER SERVING Calories: 77 | Fat: 4.8 g | Protein: 4.2 g | Sodium: 292 mg | Fiber: 2.0 g | Carbohydrates: 3.9 g | Sugar: 0.8 g

BBQ Cauliflower Bites

The flavor of this dish can change depending on which barbecue sauce you choose—spicy or sweet, Korean or St. Louis style. The cauliflower takes on the flavor of whatever you pair it with, all the while delivering your body a healthy punch of vitamin C!

HANDS-ON TIME: 10 minutes
COOK TIME: 12 minutes

INGREDIENTS | SERVES 4

1 large head cauliflower, chopped into florets, core removed
2 teaspoons olive oil
¼ cup barbecue sauce of your choice

1. Preheat air fryer at 350°F for 3 minutes.

2. In a large bowl, toss cauliflower florets with olive oil.

3. Place half of cauliflower in fryer basket. Cook 3 minutes. Shake. Cook an additional 3 minutes.

4. Transfer to a medium bowl and toss with half the barbecue sauce. Repeat with remaining cauliflower.

5. Transfer to a serving bowl and serve warm.

PER SERVING Calories: 102 | Fat: 2.6 g | Protein: 4.2 g | Sodium: 246 mg | Fiber: 4.4 g | Carbohydrates: 17.7 g | Sugar: 10.0 g

Mozzarella Sticklets

This is a mini version of those deep-fried delights found on many appetizer menus—minus the oil. Serve these mini sticks with toothpicks and a warm marinara sauce.

HANDS-ON TIME: 15 minutes
COOK TIME: 10 minutes

INGREDIENTS | SERVES 6

2 tablespoons all-purpose flour
1 large egg
1 tablespoon whole milk
½ cup plain bread crumbs
¼ teaspoon salt
¼ teaspoon Italian seasoning
10 mozzarella sticks, each cut into thirds
2 teaspoons olive oil

1. In a small bowl, add flour.

2. In another small bowl, whisk together egg and milk.

3. Combine bread crumbs, salt, and Italian seasoning in a shallow dish.

4. Roll a mozzarella sticklet in flour, then dredge in egg mixture, and then roll in bread crumb mixture. Shake off excess between each step. Set aside on a plate and repeat with remaining mozzarella. Place in freezer 10 minutes.

5. Preheat air fryer at 400°F for 3 minutes.

6. Place half of mozzarella sticklets in fryer basket. Cook 2 minutes. Shake. Lightly brush with olive oil. Cook an additional 2 minutes. Shake. Cook an additional 1 minute. Transfer to a serving dish.

7. Repeat with remaining sticklets and serve warm.

PER SERVING Calories: 181 | Fat: 9.5 g | Protein: 13.6 g | Sodium: 451 mg | Fiber: 0.4 g | Carbohydrates: 8.6 g | Sugar: 1.1 g

Goat Cheese and Prosciutto–Stuffed Mushrooms

Your taste buds will applaud once they taste the creamy goat cheese mixed with the saltiness of the prosciutto, all stuffed in earthy mushrooms. The combination is explosive, and the preparation is so simple.

HANDS-ON TIME: 10 minutes
COOK TIME: 20 minutes

INGREDIENTS | SERVES 4

¼ cup crumbled goat cheese

1 tablespoon minced onion

1 teaspoon lemon juice

½ teaspoon salt

½ teaspoon freshly ground black pepper

16 ounces baby bella (cremini) mushrooms, stems removed

2 tablespoons panko bread crumbs

2 tablespoons butter, melted

2 ounces prosciutto, torn into small pieces

¼ cup julienned fresh basil

What Is Julienned?

To julienne is simply to cut something into thin, uniform matchsticks. A sharp knife is key to creating clean cuts. Most mandolines also have a julienne function, which makes life much easier when trying to achieve consistently thin vegetables.

1. In a medium bowl, combine goat cheese, onion, lemon juice, salt, and pepper.

2. Preheat air fryer at 350°F for 3 minutes.

3. Evenly stuff goat cheese mixture into mushroom caps. Distribute bread crumbs over stuffed mushrooms. Slowly pour melted butter over bread crumbs.

4. Place half of mushrooms in fryer basket. Cook 10 minutes. Transfer to serving plate. Repeat with remaining mushrooms.

5. Sprinkle with prosciutto and basil. Serve warm.

PER SERVING Calories: 155 | Fat: 10.7 g | Protein: 7.7 g | Sodium: 390 mg | Fiber: 0.8 g | Carbohydrates: 8.0 g | Sugar: 2.1 g

CHAPTER 5

Chips and Fries

Curly Fries

To obtain these cute Curly Fries, you'll need a spiralizer. The spiralizer will cut the entire potato into curls; once completed, cut the curls in 3" lengths to obtain "fries."

HANDS-ON TIME: 10 minutes
COOK TIME: 13 minutes

INGREDIENTS | SERVES 2

2 medium Russet potatoes, scrubbed and spiraled into curls, then cut into 3" lengths

3 teaspoons salt, divided

2 teaspoons olive oil

¼ teaspoon freshly ground black pepper

1. Place fries in a medium saucepan. Cover fries with water. Add 1 teaspoon salt. Bring to a boil. Boil 2–3 minutes. Drain.

2. Preheat air fryer at 400°F for 3 minutes.

3. Toss fries with olive oil and 1 teaspoon salt. Place fries in fryer basket and cook 4 minutes. Shake basket. Cook an additional 4 minutes. Shake. Season with pepper and remaining teaspoon salt. Cook an additional 5 minutes.

4. Transfer fries to a plate and serve warm.

PER SERVING Calories: 146 | Fat: 4.5 g | Protein: 2.3 g | Sodium: 2,618 mg | Fiber: 2.5 g | Carbohydrates: 24.8 g | Sugar: 1.1 g

Thyme and Garlic Beet Chips

There is no need to peel your beets; simply scrub them and trim the ends. The skin is edible. Also, don't be afraid to try the beautiful varieties for a colorful bowl of beet chips. They come in yellow, orange, and even striped.

HANDS-ON TIME: 10 minutes
COOK TIME: 14 minutes

INGREDIENTS | SERVES 4

2 medium beets, scrubbed, ends trimmed, and sliced into ⅛"-thin circles

1 tablespoon olive oil

½ teaspoon salt, divided

¼ teaspoon garlic salt

1 teaspoon minced fresh thyme leaves

1. In a small bowl, toss beets with oil and ¼ teaspoon salt.

2. Preheat air fryer at 400°F for 3 minutes.

3. Place beets in fryer basket and cook 5 minutes. Shake basket. Cook 5 minutes more. Shake. Cook an additional 4 minutes.

4. Transfer to a serving bowl and garnish with remaining salt, garlic salt, and thyme. Serve when ready.

PER SERVING Calories: 47 | Fat: 3.3 g | Protein: 0.7 g | Sodium: 444 mg | Fiber: 1.2 g | Carbohydrates: 4.0 g | Sugar: 2.8 g

Home Fries

These cubed, crispy Home Fries are accented with browned onions and simply dressed with olive oil, salt, pepper, and fresh parsley.

HANDS-ON TIME: 10 minutes
COOK TIME: 21 minutes

INGREDIENTS | SERVES 2

2 medium Russet potatoes, scrubbed and cut into 1" cubes

4 teaspoons salt, divided

3 teaspoons olive oil, divided

¼ teaspoon freshly ground black pepper

1 small yellow onion, peeled and thinly sliced into half moons

¼ cup chopped fresh parsley

What Does It Mean to Caramelize Onions?

Onions contain natural sugars that when heated start to brown or caramelize. But there is a point of contention among chefs when recipes ask you to "caramelize" the onions for 5–10 minutes. Yes, the onions are starting to caramelize, but stopping at this cooking point is called "blonding" the onions. To be considered true caramelization, the procedure takes 30–40 minutes. And there is an art. They have to be cared for: not crowded in the skillet, not heated too quickly, and given a deglazing or two with some water, broth, wine, or even whiskey during the process!

1. Place potato cubes in a medium saucepan and cover with water. Add 1 teaspoon salt. Bring to a boil and boil 2–3 minutes. Drain.

2. Preheat air fryer at 400°F for 3 minutes.

3. Place potato cubes in a medium bowl and toss with 2 teaspoons olive oil and 1 teaspoon salt. Place potatoes in fryer basket and cook 4 minutes. Shake basket. Cook an additional 4 minutes. Shake. Season with pepper and 1 teaspoon salt. Cook an additional 4 minutes.

4. Transfer potatoes to a plate and keep warm.

5. While fries are cooking, place onions, 1 teaspoon olive oil, and 1 teaspoon salt in a medium skillet over medium heat. Cook 5–6 minutes until onions are tender and starting to brown.

6. Combine cooked potatoes and onions in a medium serving dish. Garnish with chopped parsley. Serve warm.

PER SERVING Calories: 194 | Fat: 6.7 g | Protein: 3.2 g | Sodium: 2,656 mg | Fiber: 3.6 g | Carbohydrates: 31.3 g | Sugar: 2.7 g

Spicy Yuca Fries

Don't let the thick waxy, barklike exterior of the yuca root, or cassava, scare you off. There is a beautiful starchy tuber under that ugliness. Higher in vitamin C and fiber than the common potato, the yuca has a similar starch level and makes an excellent substitution for typical French fries.

HANDS-ON TIME: 10 minutes
COOK TIME: 18 minutes

INGREDIENTS | SERVES 2

1 pound yuca, or cassava, peeled and cut lengthwise into ¼" fries
2 teaspoons salt, divided
2 teaspoons olive oil
¼ teaspoon cayenne pepper
¼ teaspoon chili powder

The Difference Between Yuca and Yucca

Yucca (pronounced YUHK-uh) is a shrub in the agave family; it is ornamental and not meant for eating. Yuca (pronounced YOO-kuh) is a starchy root that can be eaten and is sometimes processed into flour. You will often see the latter spelled incorrectly with two c's—so now you know!

1. Place yuca fries in a medium saucepan. Cover fries with water. Add 1 teaspoon salt. Bring to a boil and boil 5 minutes. Drain.

2. Preheat air fryer at 400°F for 3 minutes.

3. Toss fries with olive oil and place fries in fryer basket and cook 4 minutes. Shake basket. Cook an additional 4 minutes. Shake. Season with remaining salt, cayenne pepper, and chili powder. Cook an additional 5 minutes.

4. Transfer fries to a plate and serve warm.

PER SERVING Calories: 330 | Fat: 4.8 g | Protein: 2.5 g | Sodium: 1,313 mg | Fiber: 3.4 g | Carbohydrates: 69.4 g | Sugar: 3.1 g

Disco Fries

Disco Fries are similar to poutine, but poutine has gravy over the fries and is topped with cheese curds. Disco Fries traditionally have Cheddar cheese or mozzarella, but this recipe throws in an upscale twist with gravy and some creamy goat cheese crumbles.

HANDS-ON TIME: 10 minutes
COOK TIME: 18 minutes

INGREDIENTS | SERVES 2

2 medium Russet potatoes, scrubbed and cut lengthwise into ¼" fries

2 teaspoons olive oil

3 teaspoons salt, divided

½ cup brown gravy, warmed (see sidebar)

4 tablespoons crumbled goat cheese

How to Make Brown Gravy

Brown gravy can be purchased already jarred or made from meat drippings. But what if you are making Disco Fries and aren't cooking meat but still want a homemade version? In a small saucepan over medium-high heat, melt 3 tablespoons unsalted butter. Whisk in 3 tablespoons all-purpose flour. Slowly whisk in 1 cup beef broth, 1 teaspoon Worcestershire sauce, and ½ teaspoon garlic salt until sauce thickens. If sauce is too thick, add a tablespoon at a time of beef broth or water until desired consistency.

1. Place fries in a medium saucepan. Cover fries with water. Add olive oil and 1 teaspoon salt. Bring to a boil. Boil 3 minutes until fork-tender but still somewhat firm. Drain.

2. Preheat air fryer at 400°F for 3 minutes.

3. Toss fries with 1 teaspoon salt. Place fries in fryer basket and cook 5 minutes. Shake basket. Cook an additional 5 minutes. Shake. Season with remaining teaspoon salt. Cook an additional 5 minutes.

4. Transfer to a plate and top with gravy and crumbled goat cheese. Serve warm.

PER SERVING Calories: 233 | Fat: 8.9 g | Protein: 6.6 g | Sodium: 2,979 mg | Fiber: 2.7 g | Carbohydrates: 30.4 g | Sugar: 2.2 g

Gingered Sweet Potato Fries

All the flavor of Thanksgiving without the extra sweet addition of gooey marshmallow, these fries take care of your sweet tooth without going completely off the rails. Plus, sweet potatoes are a great source of vitamins A and C!

HANDS-ON TIME: 10 minutes
COOK TIME: 15 minutes

INGREDIENTS | SERVES 2

1 large sweet potato, peeled, and cut lengthwise into ¼" fries
1 tablespoon olive oil
¼ teaspoon salt
½ teaspoon ground ginger
2 teaspoons brown sugar

1. Preheat air fryer at 375°F for 3 minutes.

2. In a medium bowl, toss fries with olive oil and salt. Place fries in fryer basket and cook 5 minutes. Shake basket. Cook an additional 5 minutes. Shake. Cook an additional 5 minutes.

3. Transfer to a serving bowl and toss with ginger and sugar. Serve warm.

PER SERVING Calories: 133 | Fat: 6.6 g | Protein: 1.1 g | Sodium: 327 mg | Fiber: 2.0 g | Carbohydrates: 17.9 g | Sugar: 7.2 g

Crispy French Fries

By boiling the potatoes prior to air frying, the center becomes tender and the exterior gets that nice crunch from the air fryer. There's no need for going out to satisfy that French fry craving when this healthier alternative is so easy to achieve.

HANDS-ON TIME: 10 minutes
COOK TIME: 18 minutes

INGREDIENTS | SERVES 4

2 medium Russet potatoes, scrubbed and cut lengthwise into ¼" fries
3 teaspoons salt, divided
2 teaspoons olive oil

1. Place fries in a medium saucepan. Cover fries with water. Add 1 teaspoon salt. Bring to a boil. Boil 3 minutes until fork-tender. Drain.

2. Preheat air fryer at 400°F for 3 minutes.

3. In a medium bowl, toss fries with olive oil and 1 teaspoon salt. Place fries in fryer basket and cook 5 minutes. Shake basket. Cook an additional 5 minutes. Shake. Season with remaining teaspoon salt. Cook an additional 5 minutes.

4. Transfer fries to a plate and serve warm.

PER SERVING Calories: 78 | Fat: 2.2 g | Protein: 1.3 g | Sodium: 1,325 mg | Fiber: 1.4 g | Carbohydrates: 13.7 g | Sugar: 0.6 g

Jicama Fries

Jicama is a tuber that can be eaten raw or diced into salads. Several grocers carry them already peeled and cut into fries. The chili powder and paprika play nicely with the natural sweetness of the jicama.

HANDS-ON TIME: 10 minutes
COOK TIME: 15 minutes

INGREDIENTS | SERVES 2

1 medium jicama, peeled and sliced into ¼" fries
1 tablespoon olive oil
½ teaspoon chili powder
½ teaspoon smoked paprika
½ teaspoon salt

What Is a Jicama?

Jicama (pronounced HEE-cahmah) is a round and slightly flattened tuber also referred to as a Mexican yam bean or a Mexican turnip. The flesh has a texture similar to a pear or apple but isn't quite as sweet. Peeled jicama is not only good as these air-fried fries; it also lends a great flavor julienned in salads or just spiralized with a little salt and/or smoked paprika sprinkled on for a snack.

1. Preheat air fryer at 400°F for 3 minutes.

2. In a medium bowl, toss jicama fries with olive oil, chili powder, paprika, and salt. Place fries in fryer basket and cook 5 minutes. Shake basket. Cook an additional 5 minutes. Shake. Cook an additional 5 minutes.

3. Transfer to a serving bowl and serve warm.

PER SERVING Calories: 162 | Fat: 6.9 g | Protein: 2.1 g | Sodium: 610 mg | Fiber: 13.4 g | Carbohydrates: 23.9 g | Sugar: 4.9 g

Herbed Zucchini Fries

These breaded, crispy zucchini fries are crave-worthy and will have you buying a bagful of zucchini just so you can keep making them. A healthy alternative to the drive-through French fries, this treat is delicious!

HANDS-ON TIME: 10 minutes
COOK TIME: 20 minutes

INGREDIENTS | SERVES 2

1 large zucchini, cut in half crosswise, then lengthwise into ¼" fries
1 teaspoon salt
½ cup buttermilk
¾ cup plain bread crumbs
1 tablespoon Italian seasoning

1. Scatter zucchini pieces evenly over a paper towel. Sprinkle with salt. Let sit 10 minutes to pull out the moisture. Pat with paper towels.

2. Preheat air fryer at 375°F for 3 minutes.

3. Place buttermilk in a shallow dish. Combine bread crumbs and Italian seasoning in a separate shallow dish.

4. Dip zucchini in buttermilk. Dredge in bread crumb mixture.

5. Place half of zucchini pieces in fryer basket and cook 5 minutes. Flip fries. Cook an additional 5 minutes.

6. Transfer to a serving dish. Repeat with remaining zucchini fries and serve warm.

PER SERVING Calories: 173 | Fat: 2.5 g | Protein: 8.0 g | Sodium: 1,156 mg | Fiber: 3.0 g | Carbohydrates: 29.4 g | Sugar: 8.5 g

Savory Sweet Potato Fries

The savory spices of onion powder and smoked paprika play well with the natural sugars in the sweet potato. Both crisp and tender, these fries are a healthy snack option or tasty side for a juicy burger!

HANDS-ON TIME: 10 minutes
COOK TIME: 15 minutes

INGREDIENTS | SERVES 2

1 large sweet potato, peeled, and cut lengthwise into ¼" fries
1 tablespoon olive oil
¼ teaspoon salt
¼ teaspoon onion powder
¼ teaspoon smoked paprika

1. Preheat air fryer at 375°F for 3 minutes.

2. In a medium bowl, toss fries with olive oil, salt, onion powder, and paprika. Place fries in fryer basket and cook 5 minutes. Shake basket. Cook an additional 5 minutes. Shake. Cook an additional 5 minutes.

3. Transfer to a serving bowl. Serve warm.

PER SERVING Calories: 116 | Fat: 6.6 g | Protein: 1.1 g | Sodium: 326 mg | Fiber: 2.1 g | Carbohydrates: 13.5 g | Sugar: 2.8 g

Butternut Squash Fries

If you can't find butternut squash fries precut, simply use a vegetable peeler to remove the skin, slice squash lengthwise, and use a spoon to scrape out and discard the seeds, then cut flesh into ¼" fries.

HANDS-ON TIME: 10 minutes
COOK TIME: 15 minutes

INGREDIENTS | SERVES 2

20 ounces butternut squash fries, precut or home-cut, or about 1 large squash
1 tablespoon olive oil
½ teaspoon cinnamon
½ teaspoon ground ginger
Pinch cayenne pepper
½ teaspoon salt

1. Preheat air fryer at 375°F for 3 minutes.

2. In a medium bowl, toss fries with olive oil, cinnamon, ground ginger, cayenne pepper, and salt. Place fries in fryer basket and cook 5 minutes. Shake basket. Cook an additional 5 minutes. Shake. Cook an additional 5 minutes.

3. Transfer to a serving bowl and serve warm.

PER SERVING Calories: 190 | Fat: 6.8 g | Protein: 2.9 g | Sodium: 592 mg | Fiber: 6.1 g | Carbohydrates: 34.0 g | Sugar: 6.3 g

Nacho Cheese Avocado Fries

Don't knock this one till you've tried it. The crushed nacho cheese tortilla chips are a natural flavor complement to the avocado and make these fries amazing.

HANDS-ON TIME: 10 minutes
COOK TIME: 10 minutes

INGREDIENTS | YIELDS 12 AVOCADO FRIES

1 medium avocado, a bit firm
1 large egg
2 tablespoons whole milk
1 cup crushed nacho cheese tortilla chip crumbs

1. Cut avocado in half lengthwise. Remove pit. While still in the skin, gently score each half into 6 "fries." Use a soup spoon to gently scrape the avocado away from the skin.

2. Whisk together egg and milk in a small bowl. Scatter tortilla chip crumbs in a shallow dish.

3. Preheat air fryer at 375°F for 3 minutes.

4. Dip avocado slices into egg mixture. Dredge in chip crumbs to coat. Place half of avocado slices into air fryer basket. Cook 5 minutes.

5. Transfer to serving plate. Repeat with remaining avocado slices. Serve warm.

PER SERVING Calories: 53 | Fat: 3.3 g | Protein: 1.3 g | Sodium: 46 mg | Fiber: 1.1 g | Carbohydrates: 4.5 g | Sugar: 0.2 g

Alabama Dill Pickle Chips

An Alabama original, these briny little crispy coins are amazing, especially dipped in some Comeback Sauce (see Chapter 15), which will have you comin' back for more!

HANDS-ON TIME: 10 minutes
COOK TIME: 16 minutes

INGREDIENTS | SERVES 4

1 (16-ounce) jar dill pickle chips, drained
2 large eggs
¼ cup whole milk
1 teaspoon Worcestershire sauce
½ cup plain bread crumbs
½ cup cornmeal
1 teaspoon garlic powder
1 teaspoon salt

1. Pat pickle chips dry between paper towels.

2. Whisk together eggs, milk, and Worcestershire sauce in a small bowl.

3. Combine bread crumbs, cornmeal, garlic powder, and salt in a shallow dish.

4. Preheat air fryer at 400°F for 3 minutes.

5. Dip pickle slices in egg mixture. Dredge in cornmeal mixture, shaking off any excess.

6. Add half of pickle slices to fryer basket and cook 4 minutes. Shake and flip pickles. Cook an additional 4 minutes.

7. Transfer to a plate. Repeat with remaining pickles.

PER SERVING Calories: 149 | Fat: 2.9 g | Protein: 5.9 g | Sodium: 1,356 mg | Fiber: 2.0 g | Carbohydrates: 23.9 g | Sugar: 2.8 g

Cajun-Fried Sweet Pickle Chips

This is a sweet and spicy twist on the classic dill pickle version. Read the seasoning labels on your Cajun seasoning, as some can deliver quite a punch in the heat department.

HANDS-ON TIME: 10 minutes
COOK TIME: 16 minutes

INGREDIENTS | SERVES 4

1 (16-ounce) jar sweet pickle chips, drained
2 large eggs
¼ cup whole milk
½ cup plain bread crumbs
¼ cup cornmeal
¼ teaspoon salt
2 tablespoons Cajun seasoning

1. Pat pickles dry between paper towels.

2. In a small bowl, whisk together eggs and milk.

3. Combine bread crumbs, cornmeal, salt, and Cajun seasoning in a shallow dish.

4. Preheat air fryer at 400°F for 3 minutes.

5. Dip pickle slices in egg mixture. Dredge in cornmeal mixture, shaking off any excess.

6. Add half of pickle slices to fryer basket and cook 4 minutes. Shake and flip pickles. Cook an additional 4 minutes.

7. Transfer to a plate. Repeat with remaining pickles.

PER SERVING Calories: 143 | Fat: 2.8 g | Protein: 5.7 g | Sodium: 2,119 mg | Fiber: 1.9 g | Carbohydrates: 22.9 g | Sugar: 2.4 g

Parmesan Potato Chips

Slicing the potato paper-thin and consistently is the key to perfect potato chips. The air fryer will brown the edges, but keep checking them toward the end of the cooking time. They can go from brown to burned quickly!

HANDS-ON TIME: 10 minutes
COOK TIME: 17 minutes

INGREDIENTS | SERVES 2

1 medium Russet potato, scrubbed and sliced into ⅛"-thick circles

2 teaspoons olive oil

1 teaspoon salt, divided

4 teaspoons grated Parmesan cheese, divided

1. In a small bowl, toss potato circles with olive oil and ½ teaspoon salt.

2. Preheat air fryer at 400°F for 3 minutes.

3. Place chips in fryer basket and cook 6 minutes. Shake basket. Cook an additional 5 minutes. Shake. Add 2 teaspoons Parmesan cheese and cook 6 minutes.

4. Transfer to a serving bowl and garnish with remaining salt and Parmesan cheese. Let rest 15 minutes before serving.

PER SERVING Calories: 116 | Fat: 5.4 g | Protein: 2.5 g | Sodium: 1,400 mg | Fiber: 1.4 g | Carbohydrates: 14.3 g | Sugar: 0.6 g

Chili-Lime Corn Chips

When you're craving chips and salsa, giving in doesn't have to be a diet killer. Make your own chips using corn tortillas. They are seasoned and crispy and not deep-fried. Try these with Pico Guacamole (see Chapter 15).

HANDS-ON TIME: 10 minutes
COOK TIME: 15 minutes

INGREDIENTS | SERVES 4

1 tablespoon olive oil

1 tablespoon fresh lime juice

6 (6") corn tortillas, each cut into 6 triangles

½ teaspoon chili powder

½ teaspoon salt

1. Preheat air fryer at 400°F for 3 minutes.

2. In a small bowl, whisk together olive oil and lime juice. Brush over tortilla triangles. Toss with chili powder.

3. Place a third of the triangles in the air fryer basket. Cook 3 minutes. Flip and season with salt. Cook an additional 2 minutes, then transfer to a serving bowl. Repeat with remaining two batches.

4. Let chips cool 5 minutes before serving.

PER SERVING Calories: 109 | Fat: 4.3 g | Protein: 2.1 g | Sodium: 316 mg | Fiber: 2.4 g | Carbohydrates: 16.6 g | Sugar: 0.4 g

Itty-Bitty Potato Chips

Fingerling potatoes, which are long and narrow, are the perfect earthy and mild potato for these Itty-Bitty Potato Chips. Thinly and uniformly slice these little tubers and in minutes you'll enjoy some guilt-free potato chips!

HANDS-ON TIME: 10 minutes
COOK TIME: 16 minutes

INGREDIENTS | SERVES 2

2 cups thinly sliced fingerling potatoes
2 teaspoons olive oil
½ teaspoon salt
¼ teaspoon freshly ground black pepper

1. In a small bowl, toss potato slices with olive oil, salt, and pepper.

2. Preheat air fryer at 400°F for 3 minutes.

3. Place potatoes in fryer basket and cook 3 minutes. Shake basket. Cook an additional 3 minutes. Shake. Cook 5 minutes more. Shake. Cook an additional 5 minutes.

4. Transfer to a serving bowl and let rest 15 minutes. Serve when ready.

PER SERVING Calories: 158 | Fat: 4.5 g | Protein: 3.2 g | Sodium: 588 mg | Fiber: 2.0 g | Carbohydrates: 27.3 g | Sugar: 0.9 g

Cinnamon-Sugar Plantain Chips

Unlike similar-looking bananas, unripe green plantains are what you need for this recipe. They are firm and easier to slice. The ripe ones are stickier, yielding a messy product.

HANDS-ON TIME: 10 minutes
COOK TIME: 12 minutes

INGREDIENTS | SERVES 4

2 medium unripe green plantains, peeled and thinly sliced
2 teaspoons olive oil
1 teaspoon sugar
½ teaspoon ground cinnamon
Pinch salt

1. In a medium bowl, toss plantains with olive oil.

2. Preheat air fryer at 400°F for 3 minutes.

3. Place chips in fryer basket and cook 4 minutes. Shake basket. Cook an additional 4 minutes. Shake. Cook 4 minutes more.

4. Transfer to a serving bowl and toss with sugar, cinnamon, and salt. Serve warm.

PER SERVING Calories: 133 | Fat: 2.4 g | Protein: 1.2 g | Sodium: 39 mg | Fiber: 2.2 g | Carbohydrates: 29.9 g | Sugar: 14.5 g

Carrot Chips

Although you can use whatever cooking oil you prefer, with these Carrot Chips, the coconut oil provides a great flavor accent for the carrots.

HANDS-ON TIME: 10 minutes
COOK TIME: 12 minutes

INGREDIENTS | SERVES 4

2 large carrots, peeled and sliced into paper-thin circles
2 teaspoons coconut oil, melted
¼ teaspoon ground cumin
¼ teaspoon smoked paprika
¼ teaspoon salt
⅛ teaspoon freshly ground black pepper

1. In a medium bowl, toss carrots in coconut oil. Season with cumin, paprika, salt, and pepper.

2. Preheat air fryer at 400°F for 3 minutes.

3. Place chips in fryer basket and cook 12 minutes, shaking every 3 minutes.

4. Transfer to a bowl. Let rest 10 minutes before serving.

PER SERVING Calories: 34 | Fat: 2.2 g | Protein: 0.4 g | Sodium: 170 mg | Fiber: 1.1 g | Carbohydrates: 3.7 g | Sugar: 1.7 g

Sesame Parsnip Chips

Parsnips are the white carrot-looking produce you have probably passed by in the store a million times. They are related to the carrot but have a sweeter and a bit of a peppery flavor. Parsnips are often used as potato replacements in soups and stews.

HANDS-ON TIME: 10 minutes
COOK TIME: 14 minutes

INGREDIENTS | SERVES 2

1 large parsnip, peeled and sliced into ⅛"-thick circles
1 tablespoon sesame oil
½ teaspoon salt, divided

1. In a small bowl, toss parsnip slices with sesame oil and ¼ teaspoon salt.

2. Preheat air fryer at 400°F for 3 minutes.

3. Place parsnips in fryer basket and cook 5 minutes. Shake basket. Cook an additional 5 minutes. Shake. Cook an additional 4 minutes.

4. Transfer to a serving bowl and garnish with remaining salt. Serve when ready.

PER SERVING Calories: 97 | Fat: 6.6 g | Protein: 0.6 g | Sodium: 585 mg | Fiber: 2.4 g | Carbohydrates: 9.0 g | Sugar: 2.4 g

Ranch Corn Chips

Air-fry your own healthy chips tossed in some dry ranch seasoning mix and enjoy this guilt-free snack with a side of Pico Guacamole (see Chapter 15)!

HANDS-ON TIME: 10 minutes
COOK TIME: 15 minutes

INGREDIENTS | SERVES 4

6 (6") corn tortillas, each cut into 6 triangles
1 tablespoon olive oil
1 teaspoon dry ranch seasoning mix
½ teaspoon salt, divided

1. Preheat air fryer at 400°F for 3 minutes.

2. Brush olive oil over tortilla triangles. Toss with dry ranch-seasoning mix. Sprinkle with ¼ teaspoon salt.

3. Place a third of the chips in the air fryer basket. Cook 3 minutes. Flip chips. Cook an additional 2 minutes. Repeat with remaining two batches.

4. Season chips with remaining salt as they come out of the fryer basket. Let cool 5 minutes before serving.

PER SERVING Calories: 110 | Fat: 4.2 g | Protein: 2.1 g | Sodium: 374 mg | Fiber: 2.3 g | Carbohydrates: 16.6 g | Sugar: 0.3 g

Sesame Tortilla Chips

When you want some Asian flair added to your tortilla chips, a little sesame oil and seeds can help achieve this. The addition of the honey sweetens these just enough but does not overpower.

HANDS-ON TIME: 10 minutes
COOK TIME: 18 minutes

INGREDIENTS | SERVES 4

2 teaspoons sesame oil
2 teaspoons honey
6 (6") flour tortillas, each cut into 6 triangles
2 teaspoons sesame seeds
1 teaspoon poppy seeds
½ teaspoon salt

1. Preheat air fryer at 400°F for 3 minutes.

2. In a small bowl, whisk together sesame oil and honey. Brush oil mixture over tortilla triangles. Toss with sesame seeds and poppy seeds.

3. Place a third of the chips in the air fryer basket. Cook 3 minutes. Flip chips. Cook an additional 3 minutes. Repeat with remaining two batches.

4. Season chips with salt as they come out of the fryer basket. Let cool 5 minutes before serving.

PER SERVING Calories: 167 | Fat: 5.0 g | Protein: 3.8 g | Sodium: 610 mg | Fiber: 1.3 g | Carbohydrates: 26.6 g | Sugar: 4.4 g

CHAPTER 6

Poultry Main Dishes

Prep-Day Chicken Thighs

Chicken thighs are not only easy on the wallet, but are also juicy and delicious. Make these and add them to salads or soups during the week, or just heat them up and eat them as is!

HANDS-ON TIME: 5 minutes
COOK TIME: 35 minutes

INGREDIENTS | SERVES 4

2 teaspoons olive oil

1¼ pounds boneless, skinless chicken thighs (approximately 6)

½ teaspoon salt

¼ teaspoon freshly ground black pepper

Are Chicken Thighs Fatty?

Although chicken thighs (the dark meat) contain more fat than the chicken breast (white meat), both are excellent sources of lean protein. One advantage of chicken thighs is that they are more economical than breasts. Another is that because of the fattier nature of the thighs, they are less likely to dry out than white meat during the cooking process. And as far as flavor? Well, chicken thighs win!

1. Brush oil lightly over chicken. Season with salt and pepper.

2. Preheat air fryer at 350°F for 3 minutes.

3. Add chicken to fryer basket and cook 35 minutes.

4. Using a meat thermometer, assure that the chicken is at least 165°F. Transfer to a serving plate and let rest 5 minutes.

5. Chop and store covered in the refrigerator for some of your week's recipes.

PER SERVING Calories: 207 | Fat: 9.9 g | Protein: 26.0 g | Sodium: 401 mg | Fiber: 0.0 g | Carbohydrates: 0.1 g | Sugar: 0.0 g

Salsa Chicken

This is absolutely the easiest, tastiest, and lowest-calorie meal you can prepare in minutes on the hour. Trust your own heat-o-meter when choosing your salsa, or make some fruit salsas instead.

HANDS-ON TIME: 5 minutes
COOK TIME: 30 minutes

INGREDIENTS | SERVES 2

1 pound boneless, skinless chicken thighs (approximately 4)
1 cup salsa of your choice

Easy Salsa Recipe
For a quick, fresh salsa, combine the following ingredients in a container and refrigerate covered until ready to use, up to 3 days. Combine 5 Roma tomatoes (seeded and diced), ¼ cup peeled and diced red onion, 3 peeled and minced garlic cloves, ¼ cup chopped fresh cilantro, 1 tablespoon fresh lime juice, ½ teaspoon salt, and 1 small diced jalapeño (optional).

1. Preheat air fryer at 350°F for 3 minutes.

2. Place chicken thighs in square cake barrel (accessory). Cover with salsa.

3. Cook 30 minutes. Using a meat thermometer, assure that the chicken is at least 165°F. Add another minute to the cooking time if necessary.

4. Transfer to a serving plate and let rest 5 minutes. Serve warm.

PER SERVING Calories: 341 | Fat: 12.5 g | Protein: 43.3 g | Sodium: 671 mg | Fiber: 1.6 g | Carbohydrates: 8.1 g | Sugar: 0.0 g

Buttermilk Southern-Fried Chicken Legs

These fried chicken legs are crisp on the outside and juicy on the inside. The buttermilk lends a citric quality, adding flavor as well as the ability to tenderize the meat and create a crispier skin.

HANDS-ON TIME: 10 minutes
COOK TIME: 36 minutes

INGREDIENTS | SERVES 3

1½ pounds boneless, skinless chicken legs (approximately 5–6)
1 cup buttermilk
1 cup plain bread crumbs
1 teaspoon smoked paprika
1 teaspoon garlic powder
Pinch ground nutmeg
1 teaspoon salt
1 teaspoon freshly ground black pepper
3 tablespoons butter, melted

Does a Pinch of Nutmeg Really Make a Difference?

Yes, yes, yes! Don't just think about gingerbread and holiday cookies when considering using nutmeg. It is so aromatic and unique that just a dash in sauces, casseroles, and even soups will make your guests not only gasp in delight but start scratching their head wondering what that spice is… They just can't place it. If you ever think this, the likelihood is pretty strong that it's nutmeg!

1. In a medium bowl, place chicken legs and buttermilk and marinate in the refrigerator covered 30 minutes up to overnight.

2. Preheat air fryer at 350°F for 3 minutes.

3. Combine bread crumbs, paprika, garlic powder, nutmeg, salt, and pepper in a shallow dish. Shake excess buttermilk off chicken legs and dredge in bread crumb mixture. Set aside.

4. Add half of chicken to lightly greased fryer basket and cook 10 minutes.

5. Brush lightly with melted butter. Flip chicken. Brush other side lightly with butter. Increase temperature to 400°F. Cook an additional 8 minutes. Using a meat thermometer, assure that the chicken is at least 165°F.

6. Transfer to a serving plate. Repeat cooking process with remaining chicken and serve warm.

PER SERVING Calories: 661 | Fat: 28.3 g | Protein: 71.2 g | Sodium: 904 mg | Fiber: 1.2 g | Carbohydrates: 18.0 g | Sugar: 3.8 g

BBQ-Breaded Chicken Legs

By using barbecue sauce instead of egg wash to hold on to the bread crumb coating, you let these chicken legs retain all of the flavor but still get a "fried" exterior coating. Don't forget to serve a little extra sauce on the side for dipping!

HANDS-ON TIME: 10 minutes
COOK TIME: 36 minutes

INGREDIENTS | SERVES 3

1½ pounds chicken legs (approximately 5–6)

1 cup barbecue sauce of your choice

1 cup plain bread crumbs

1 teaspoon salt

3 tablespoons butter, melted

1. In a medium bowl, toss chicken legs with barbecue sauce. Refrigerate covered 30 minutes or up to overnight.

2. Preheat air fryer at 350°F for 3 minutes.

3. Combine bread crumbs and salt in a shallow dish. Shake excess sauce off of chicken legs and dredge in bread crumb mixture. Set aside.

4. Lightly spray or brush fryer basket with oil. Add half of chicken to fryer basket and cook 10 minutes.

5. Brush chicken lightly with melted butter. Flip chicken. Brush other side lightly with butter. Increase temperature to 400°F. Cook an additional 8 minutes. Using a meat thermometer, assure that the chicken is at least 165°F.

6. Transfer chicken to a serving plate. Repeat cooking process with remaining chicken and serve warm.

PER SERVING Calories: 965 | Fat: 36.7 g | Protein: 92.7 g | Sodium: 1,875 mg | Fiber: 1.9 g | Carbohydrates: 48.6 g | Sugar: 25.5 g

Sesame Chicken Legs

The combination of soy sauce, honey, sriracha, and lime come together to lend a beautiful balance of Asian flavors. The toasted sesame seed garnish has a little nuttiness and gives another layer of crunch to these crispy chicken legs.

HANDS-ON TIME: 5 minutes
COOK TIME: 36 minutes

INGREDIENTS | SERVES 3

¼ cup soy sauce

¼ cup honey

1 tablespoon sriracha

Juice of 1 small lime

1½ pounds chicken legs (approximately 5–6)

1 cup plain bread crumbs

1 teaspoon salt

3 tablespoons butter, melted

2 tablespoons toasted sesame seeds

How to Toast Sesame Seeds

Although sesame seeds are sometimes sold already toasted, if you can only get plain ones, it is easy to toast them on your own. Simply place seeds in a dry skillet over medium-high heat. Using a wooden spatula, continuously push seeds around the skillet 2–4 minutes until golden brown. Immediately transfer to a bowl, as over-cooking them will create a bitter flavor.

1. In a medium bowl, combine soy sauce, honey, sriracha, and lime juice. Toss chicken legs in sauce. Refrigerate covered 30 minutes up to overnight.

2. Preheat air fryer at 350°F for 3 minutes.

3. Combine bread crumbs and salt in a shallow dish. Shake excess sauce off chicken legs and dredge in bread crumb mixture. Set aside.

4. Lightly spray or brush fryer basket with oil. Add half of chicken to fryer basket and cook 10 minutes.

5. Brush lightly with melted butter. Flip chicken. Brush other side lightly with butter. Increase temperature to 400°F. Cook an additional 8 minutes. Using a meat thermometer, assure that the chicken is at least 165°F.

6. Transfer to a serving plate. Repeat cooking process with remaining chicken.

7. Garnish with toasted sesame seeds and serve warm.

PER SERVING Calories: 862 | Fat: 36.6 g | Protein: 92.7 g | Sodium: 1,270 mg | Fiber: 1.2 g | Carbohydrates: 23.9 g | Sugar: 4.1 g

Ritzy Chicken Meatballs

Ground chicken can tend to be a little dry, but with the onions and the buttery nature of the Ritz crackers, these meatballs are juicy and delicious.

HANDS-ON TIME: 10 minutes
COOK TIME: 16 minutes

INGREDIENTS | SERVES 2

1 pound ground chicken

1 large egg

¾ cup crushed Ritz crackers

¼ cup finely diced yellow onion

1 teaspoon Italian seasoning

1 teaspoon salt

½ teaspoon freshly ground black pepper

¼ cup chopped fresh parsley

1. Preheat air fryer at 350°F for 3 minutes.

2. In a medium bowl, combine chicken, egg, crackers, onion, Italian seasoning, salt, and pepper. Form into eighteen meatballs, about 2 tablespoons each.

3. Add half of meatballs to fryer basket and cook 6 minutes. Flip meatballs. Cook an additional 2 minutes. Transfer to serving dish.

4. Repeat with remaining meatballs and garnish with chopped parsley.

PER SERVING Calories: 452 | Fat: 22.4 g | Protein: 37.4 g | Sodium: 1,572 mg | Fiber: 1.4 g | Carbohydrates: 21.8 g | Sugar: 3.4 g

Mexican Chicken Burgers

Flavored with cumin and chili powder, these burgers get their moisture from the red onion and diced green chilies. They're great served alone, or you can melt queso fresco atop the patties, add a slice of tomato and some Sriracha Mayonnaise (see Chapter 15), and eat on a bun.

HANDS-ON TIME: 10 minutes
COOK TIME: 26 minutes

INGREDIENTS | SERVES 4

1 pound ground chicken

2 tablespoons minced red onion

1 large egg white

¼ cup panko bread crumbs

2 tablespoons canned diced green chilies

1 tablespoon chili powder

½ teaspoon ground cumin

Pinch salt

1. Preheat air fryer at 350°F for 3 minutes.

2. In a medium bowl, combine all the ingredients and form into four patties, making a slight indentation in the middle of each burger.

3. Add two patties to lightly greased fryer basket and cook 6 minutes. Flip burgers and cook an additional 7 minutes or until desired doneness. Repeat with remaining burgers.

4. Transfer to a serving plate and serve warm.

PER SERVING Calories: 207 | Fat: 9.3 g | Protein: 22.1 g | Sodium: 216 mg | Fiber: 1.2 g | Carbohydrates: 7.9 g | Sugar: 1.0 g

Italian Stuffed Chicken Breasts

*The air fryer and breading give this chicken a beautiful coating
and ensure that the chicken remains tender.*

HANDS-ON TIME: 10 minutes
COOK TIME: 18 minutes

INGREDIENTS | SERVES 4

1 large egg
1½ cups whole milk
1 cup plain bread crumbs
1 tablespoon Italian seasoning
2 boneless, skinless chicken breasts
(approximately 1 pound)
¼ teaspoon salt
¼ teaspoon freshly ground black pepper
2 tablespoons cream cheese
2 teaspoons Dijon mustard
4 slices jarred roasted red peppers
4 (1-ounce) slices deli ham
2 tablespoons butter, melted

1. In a medium bowl, whisk together egg and milk.

2. In a shallow dish, combine bread crumbs and Italian seasoning.

3. Between two pieces of parchment paper, pound chicken breasts to ¼" thickness. Season with salt and pepper.

4. Spread a layer of half the cream cheese and then half the mustard on each chicken breast. Add 2 pepper slices and 2 ham slices on each. Roll tightly from short end to short end.

5. Preheat air fryer at 375°F for 3 minutes.

6. Carefully dip chicken rolls in egg mixture. Dredge in bread crumbs. Shake off any excess.

7. Add rolled chicken to air fryer basket. Cook 10 minutes. Brush tops with melted butter. Cook an additional 8 minutes.

8. Transfer to a cutting board. Let rest 5 minutes. Slice each breast into four rounds and serve warm.

PER SERVING Calories: 362 | Fat: 15.4 g | Protein: 34.5 g | Sodium: 1,147 mg | Fiber: 1.5 g | Carbohydrates: 18.5 g | Sugar: 3.1 g

Wild Rice and Pesto–Stuffed Chicken Breasts

You can buy jarred pesto off the shelves of most grocery stores, but the recipe in Chapter 15 is delicious and so easy to make. This recipe is excellent served with a side salad and a crisp, chilled glass of Pinot Grigio.

HANDS-ON TIME: 10 minutes
COOK TIME: 18 minutes

INGREDIENTS | SERVES 2

1 large egg
1½ cups whole milk
1 cup plain bread crumbs
1 tablespoon dried basil
2 boneless, skinless chicken breasts (approximately 1 pound)
¼ teaspoon salt
¼ teaspoon freshly ground black pepper
¼ cup Traditional Pesto (see Chapter 15)
¼ cup cooked wild rice
2 tablespoons butter, melted

1. In a medium bowl, whisk together egg and milk.

2. In a shallow dish, combine bread crumbs and dried basil.

3. Between two pieces of parchment paper, pound chicken breasts to ¼" thickness. Season with salt and pepper.

4. Spread a layer of half the Traditional Pesto on each chicken breast. Add half the rice to each. Roll tightly from short end to short end.

5. Preheat air fryer at 375°F for 3 minutes.

6. Carefully dip chicken rolls in egg mixture. Dredge in bread crumbs. Shake off any excess.

7. Add rolled chicken to air fryer basket. Cook 10 minutes. Brush tops with melted butter. Cook an additional 8 minutes.

8. Transfer to a cutting board. Let rest 5 minutes. Slice each breast into four rounds and serve warm.

PER SERVING Calories: 362 | Fat: 29.3 g | Protein: 21.5 g | Sodium: 747 mg | Fiber: 3.5 g | Carbohydrates: 42.8 g | Sugar: 6.3 g

Honey Mustard Chicken Bites

Marinating these chicken bites in the honey mustard and then using some of the unused sauce for dipping doubles up on the sweet and savory flavor combination.

HANDS-ON TIME: 10 minutes
COOK TIME: 18 minutes

INGREDIENTS | SERVES 2

1 large egg
2 tablespoons honey
2 tablespoons Dijon mustard
1 teaspoon apple cider vinegar
2 boneless, skinless chicken breasts (approximately 1 pound), cut into 1" cubes
1 cup plain bread crumbs
1 teaspoon salt
1 teaspoon freshly ground black pepper

1. In a medium bowl, whisk together egg, honey, mustard, and vinegar. Toss in chicken cubes. Refrigerate covered 30 minutes or up to overnight.

2. Preheat air fryer at 350°F for 3 minutes.

3. In a shallow dish, combine bread crumbs, salt, and pepper. Shake excess marinade off each piece of chicken and then dredge in bread crumb mixture.

4. Add chicken cubes in two batches to air fryer basket. Cook 4 minutes. Shake gently. Cook an additional 5 minutes. Check the chicken using a meat thermometer to ensure the internal temperature is at least 165°F.

5. Transfer chicken to a serving plate and serve warm.

PER SERVING Calories: 413 | Fat: 8.6 g | Protein: 54.0 g | Sodium: 1,334 mg | Fiber: 1.4 g | Carbohydrates: 29.2 g | Sugar: 10.4 g

Sesame-Orange Chicken

This Sesame-Orange Chicken is healthy, time-saving, and affordable. To cut down on cost even more, you can use chicken thighs. They are equally as wonderful.

HANDS-ON TIME: 10 minutes
COOK TIME: 18 minutes

INGREDIENTS | SERVES 4

⅓ cup freshly squeezed orange juice

2 tablespoons sesame oil

¼ cup honey

2 tablespoons soy sauce

1 teaspoon peeled and minced fresh ginger

1 teaspoon sriracha

2 boneless, skinless chicken breasts (approximately 1 pound), cut into 1" cubes

1½ cups plain bread crumbs

1 teaspoon salt

4 cups cooked rice

¼ cup chopped fresh cilantro

The Easy Way to Peel Ginger

Fresh ginger can seem difficult to navigate, with its uneven surface and all the branches. Instead of taking your fingers' safety into the war zone, simply use the edge of a spoon to scrape the peel off of a fresh piece of gingerroot before you grate or mince it.

1. In a medium bowl, whisk together orange juice, oil, honey, soy sauce, ginger, and sriracha. Pour half of mixture into a small bowl and set aside.

2. Toss chicken cubes in the medium bowl with sauce mixture and refrigerate covered 30 minutes.

3. In a shallow dish, combine bread crumbs and salt. Shake excess marinade off each piece of chicken and then dredge in bread crumb mixture.

4. Preheat air fryer at 350°F for 3 minutes.

5. Add chicken bites in two batches to air fryer basket. Cook 4 minutes. Shake gently and flip chicken. Cook an additional 5 minutes. Check the chicken using a meat thermometer to ensure the internal temperature is at least 165°F.

6. Transfer to a serving plate and drizzle with remaining marinade.

7. Serve chicken warm over rice and garnish with cilantro.

PER SERVING Calories: 465 | Fat: 7.3 g | Protein: 30.7 g | Sodium: 821 mg | Fiber: 1.4 g | Carbohydrates: 68.4 g | Sugar: 14.5 g

Chicken Salad with Strawberries and Pecans

Whether you serve this on bread, in lettuce wraps, or straight off the spoon, the strawberries add such a fresh twist on this classic salad. The crunch from the pecans gives a textural element that adds another welcome surprise!

HANDS-ON TIME: 10 minutes
COOK TIME: 18 minutes

INGREDIENTS | SERVES 4

2 boneless, skinless chicken breasts (approximately 1 pound), cut into 1" cubes
1 teaspoon salt
¼ teaspoon freshly ground black pepper
¾ cup mayonnaise
1 tablespoon fresh lime juice
½ cup chopped pecans
½ cup finely chopped celery
½ cup diced strawberries

1. Preheat air fryer at 350°F for 3 minutes.

2. Season chicken with salt and pepper.

3. Add chicken cubes in two batches to air fryer basket. Cook 4 minutes. Shake gently and flip chicken. Cook an additional 5 minutes. Check the chicken using a meat thermometer to ensure the internal temperature is at least 165°F.

4. Transfer to a plate and cool.

5. Chop chicken and add to a medium bowl. Add remaining ingredients and combine well. Refrigerate covered until ready to eat.

PER SERVING Calories: 504 | Fat: 42.4 g | Protein: 26.0 g | Sodium: 1,028 mg | Fiber: 1.9 g | Carbohydrates: 4.4 g | Sugar: 1.9 g

Chicken Taco Bowl

Taco Tuesday just found a new recipe. Although there are mixed greens at the bottom of this loaded bowl, it is definitely a step up from a tired dinner salad. A drizzle of homemade Cilantro-Jalapeño Ranch Dip pulls everything together!

HANDS-ON TIME: 15 minutes
COOK TIME: 15 minutes

INGREDIENTS | SERVES 4

1 tablespoon avocado oil

1 teaspoon chili powder

½ teaspoon ground cumin

⅛ teaspoon garlic powder

⅛ teaspoon smoked paprika

⅛ teaspoon salt

Pinch cayenne pepper

1 pound boneless, skinless chicken thighs, thinly sliced into 1" strips

4 cups mixed greens

1 cup yellow corn kernels

1 cup black beans, rinsed and drained

1 large avocado, peeled, pitted, and diced

2 medium Roma tomatoes, seeded and diced

16 tortilla chips

½ cup Cilantro-Jalapeño Ranch Dip (see Chapter 15)

1. In a medium bowl, whisk together avocado oil, chili powder, cumin, garlic powder, paprika, salt, and cayenne pepper. Add chicken and toss. Refrigerate covered 30 minutes.

2. Preheat air fryer at 350°F for 3 minutes.

3. Add chicken to air fryer basket. Cook 6 minutes. Toss. Cook another 6 minutes. Toss. Cook 3 minutes more.

4. To assemble bowls, distribute mixed greens among four bowls. Top with chicken, corn, black beans, avocado, and tomatoes. Crush 4 chips over each bowl. Drizzle with Cilantro-Jalapeño Ranch Dip.

PER SERVING Calories: 858 | Fat: 60.5 g | Protein: 32.9 g | Sodium: 1,325 mg | Fiber: 9.8 g | Carbohydrates: 41.9 g | Sugar: 6.5 g

Benefits of Avocado Oil

Avocado oil, pressed from the pulp of avocados, is touted as having positive effects on heart health by reducing blood pressure and cholesterol due to its healthy fats. And don't just use this liquid gold in the kitchen. Because of its moisturizing oleic acid, try using it as a night cream after cleansing your face. Wash it off in the morning and tackle your day with glowing skin!

Chicken-Pimiento Puffs

These heavenly pockets are melt-in-your-mouth delicious. Serve either for dinner, as a snack, or as an appetizer for guests.

HANDS-ON TIME: 15 minutes
COOK TIME: 20 minutes

INGREDIENTS | SERVES 4

2 tablespoons all-purpose flour, divided
1 cup chopped cooked chicken
4 ounces mascarpone cheese
1 (2-ounce) jar pimientos, drained
1 teaspoon herbes de Provence
¼ cup diced sweet onion
½ teaspoon salt
¼ teaspoon freshly ground black pepper
2 sheets puff pastry, thawed to room temperature
1 large egg, whisked

What Are Pimientos?

Registering lowest on the Scoville scale (of the "heat" of peppers), the adorable little, mild, red, heart-shaped peppers called pimientos are most commonly stuffed in green olives or used in the Southern pimiento-cheese spread. They also make a nice surprise added to squash fritters or casseroles.

1. Use 1 tablespoon flour to sprinkle on a flat, clean surface. Set aside the other tablespoon for your hands when you start working with the dough, as well as for the surface if needed.

2. Preheat air fryer at 375°F for 3 minutes.

3. In a medium bowl, combine chicken, cheese, pimientos, herbes de Provence, onion, salt, and pepper.

4. Place a sheet of puff pastry on floured surface. Cut the sheet into six equal rectangles. Place 1 tablespoon of chicken mixture in the middle of each rectangle. Fold over short side to short side and lightly pinch the seam edges, using the tines of a fork to secure the seal. Repeat to create twelve puff pockets. Brush the tops of each with whisked egg.

5. Add three chicken puffs to lightly greased air fryer basket. Cook 5 minutes. Transfer to a plate. Repeat until all are cooked and serve warm.

PER SERVING Calories: 350 | Fat: 21.2 g | Protein: 19.0 g | Sodium: 630 mg | Fiber: 0.9 g | Carbohydrates: 18.3 g | Sugar: 2.0 g

Chicken Quesadillas

Due to its ability to evenly cook tortillas, the air fryer is the perfect appliance for quesadillas. These Chicken Quesadillas are tasty on their own but round out a meal when served with sour cream, guacamole, shredded lettuce, and a side of rice and black beans.

HANDS-ON TIME: 10 minutes
COOK TIME: 12 minutes

INGREDIENTS | SERVES 4

2 medium Roma tomatoes, seeded and diced

1 teaspoon chili powder

½ teaspoon salt

3 tablespoons butter, melted

8 (6") flour tortillas

2 cups shredded cooked chicken

2 cups grated Mexican cheese blend

1. In a small bowl, toss diced tomatoes with chili powder and salt. Set aside.

2. Preheat air fryer at 350°F for 3 minutes.

3. Lightly brush melted butter on one side of a tortilla. Place tortilla butter side down in air fryer basket. Layer ¼ of the shredded chicken on tortilla, followed by ¼ of the tomatoes and ¼ of the cheese. Top with second tortilla. Lightly butter top of tortilla.

4. Cook 3 minutes. Set aside and continue to make three more quesadillas.

5. Slice each quesadilla like a pie into six sections. Serve warm.

PER SERVING Calories: 608 | Fat: 30.5 g | Protein: 41.5 g | Sodium: 967 mg | Fiber: 2.1 g | Carbohydrates: 33.4 g | Sugar: 3.6 g

Chicken and Green Olive Pizzadillas

Pizza + quesadilla = pizzadilla! The interesting combination of ingredients coupled with the fresh amazing taste will make you come back for more!

HANDS-ON TIME: 10 minutes
COOK TIME: 12 minutes

INGREDIENTS | SERVES 4

2 cups shredded cooked chicken
1 teaspoon garlic powder
3 tablespoons butter, melted
8 (6") flour tortillas
1 cup Super Easy Romesco Sauce (see Chapter 15)
2 cups grated mozzarella cheese
1 cup sliced pitted green olives
2 teaspoons fresh thyme leaves

1. In a small bowl, toss chicken with garlic powder.

2. Preheat air fryer at 350°F for 3 minutes.

3. Lightly brush melted butter on one side of a tortilla. Place tortilla butter side down in air fryer basket. Spread ¼ of Super Easy Romesco Sauce on tortilla in basket. Layer ¼ of the chicken, ¼ of the cheese, ¼ of the olives, and ¼ of the thyme leaves. Top with second tortilla. Lightly butter top of tortilla. Cook 3 minutes. Set aside and continue to make the other three pizzadillas.

4. Slice each pizzadilla into six sections. Serve warm.

PER SERVING Calories: 724 | Fat: 40.5 g | Protein: 43.0 g | Sodium: 1,844 mg | Fiber: 4.3 g | Carbohydrates: 40.5 g | Sugar: 3.4 g

Asian Turkey Burgers

The sweetness of the orange marmalade is a natural complement to the Asian seasonings in these turkey burgers. You can serve them as is or on a bun with your favorite toppings.

HANDS-ON TIME: 10 minutes
COOK TIME: 26 minutes

INGREDIENTS | SERVES 4

1 pound ground turkey
1 scallion, trimmed and minced
1 large egg white
¼ cup panko bread crumbs
1 tablespoon orange marmalade
2 teaspoons sriracha
1 teaspoon soy sauce
1 teaspoon ground ginger
Pinch salt

1. Preheat air fryer at 350°F for 3 minutes.

2. In a medium bowl, combine all the ingredients and form four patties, making a slight indentation in the middle of each patty.

3. Add two patties to lightly greased fryer basket and cook 6 minutes. Flip burgers and cook an additional 7 minutes. Repeat with remaining burgers.

4. Transfer to a serving plate and serve warm.

PER SERVING Calories: 232 | Fat: 9.4 g | Protein: 25.5 g | Sodium: 267 mg | Fiber: 0.1 g | Carbohydrates: 9.4 g | Sugar: 3.9 g

Spicy Pretzel Chicken Nuggets

There's no need to add salt to this treat; the crushed pretzels lend a saltiness and a distinct flavor separate from plain bread crumbs. If you don't want the heat, skip the sriracha.

HANDS-ON TIME: 10 minutes
COOK TIME: 18 minutes

INGREDIENTS | SERVES 4

1 large egg

1 tablespoon sriracha

1 tablespoon yellow mustard

1 tablespoon mayonnaise

2 boneless, skinless chicken breasts (approximately 1 pound), cut into 1" cubes

1 cup panko bread crumbs

1 cup crushed pretzels

1. In a medium bowl, whisk together egg, sriracha, yellow mustard, and mayonnaise. Toss in chicken cubes. Refrigerate covered 30 minutes or up to overnight.

2. Preheat air fryer at 350°F for 3 minutes.

3. In a shallow dish, combine bread crumbs and crushed pretzels. Shake excess marinade off each piece of chicken and then dredge in bread crumb mixture.

4. Add half of chicken bites to air fryer basket. Cook 4 minutes. Shake gently. Cook an additional 5 minutes. Check the chicken using a meat thermometer to ensure the internal temperature is at least 165°F. Repeat with remaining chicken.

5. Transfer to a plate and serve warm.

PER SERVING Calories: 243 | Fat: 6.4 g | Protein: 27.8 g | Sodium: 490 mg | Fiber: 0.4 g | Carbohydrates: 18.9 g | Sugar: 1.1 g

Roasted Cornish Hen

A whole chicken is an everyday ordinary choice, but when it is miniaturized into a Cornish hen it becomes a sexy meal for two or a fancy dish for guests. You'll love this simple and delicious dish.

HANDS-ON TIME: 10 minutes
COOK TIME: 28 minutes

INGREDIENTS | SERVES 2

1 teaspoon salt
½ teaspoon freshly ground black pepper
½ teaspoon smoked paprika
½ teaspoon ground fennel powder
2 teaspoons olive oil
1 (approximately 2-pound) Cornish hen
½ medium lime, halved
2 cloves garlic, halved

What Exactly Are Cornish Hens?

Cornish hens are still chickens, just a particular variety originating from Cornwall, England. Sold younger than chickens and butchered at five weeks old, they are usually more tender. Ironically, although "hen" is in the name, they can be sold as male or female! Although they are higher in price, there is just something regal about being able to serve one guest their own whole or half bird.

1. In a small bowl, combine salt, pepper, paprika, and fennel powder.

2. Preheat air fryer at 350°F for 3 minutes.

3. Rub oil over and inside Cornish hen. Sprinkle hen with seasoning mixture. Stuff lime and garlic into the hen's cavity.

4. Place hen on air fryer basket. Cook 10 minutes. Flip hen. Cook 10 more minutes. Flip hen and cook an additional 8 minutes. Using a meat thermometer, check to ensure internal temperature is at least 165°F. If undercooked, cook an additional 2 minutes and check again until temperature is reached.

5. Transfer hen to a cutting board and let rest 5 minutes. Discard lime and garlic cloves. Cut down the spine of the hen to halve and serve warm.

PER SERVING Calories: 376 | Fat: 25.9 g | Protein: 28.8 g | Sodium: 1,244 mg | Fiber: 0.6 g | Carbohydrates: 0.9 g | Sugar: 0.1 g

Sage Turkey Legs

Big turkey legs are just fun. Serve with corn on the cob and a chunk of crunchy bread or anything else that can be picked up with your hands. The rubbed sage adds a piney element that conjures up memories of the holidays.

HANDS-ON TIME: 10 minutes
COOK TIME: 26 minutes

INGREDIENTS | SERVES 2

2 tablespoons Dijon mustard

2 tablespoons olive oil

1 tablespoon apple cider vinegar

½ teaspoon rubbed sage

½ teaspoon salt

¼ teaspoon freshly ground black pepper

2 medium turkey legs (about 1½ pounds total)

1. In a large plastic resealable bag, combine mustard, oil, vinegar, sage, salt, and pepper. Add turkey legs. Seal and massage mixture into legs. Refrigerate 30 minutes or up to overnight.

2. Preheat air fryer at 350°F for 3 minutes.

3. Place turkey legs in air fryer basket. Cook 8 minutes. Turn legs a third. Cook 9 minutes. Turn legs another third. Cook 9 more minutes. Using a meat thermometer, ensure that the internal temperature is at least 165°F.

4. Transfer to a plate and let rest 5 minutes. Serve warm.

PER SERVING Calories: 1,287 | Fat: 61.9 g | Protein: 153.4 g | Sodium: 795 mg | Fiber: 0.1 g | Carbohydrates: 1.6 g | Sugar: 0.0 g

Turkey Pizza Dogs

A perfect after-school snack or a weekend lunch, these dogs are so easy to make and just fun to eat. The melty mozzarella cheese and the fresh basil leaves mimic pizza toppings, and the crescent rolls are the "crust." Dip in the warmed Marinara Sauce and enjoy!

HANDS-ON TIME: 15 minutes
COOK TIME: 16 minutes

INGREDIENTS | SERVES 4

8 turkey hot dogs

½ cup shredded mozzarella cheese

16 fresh basil leaves

1 (8-count) package refrigerated uncooked crescent rolls

1 cup Marinara Sauce (see Chapter 15)

1. Using a paring knife, make a slit lengthwise in each hot dog without cutting through the dog and with leaving the ends intact. Stuff the opening with mozzarella cheese. Layer 2 basil leaves over the mozzarella cheese on each dog.

2. Preheat air fryer at 350°F for 3 minutes.

3. Unwrap crescent rolls. Place the long end of a roll over the stuffed section of a hot dog and roll the dough around the dog as you would normally roll the crescents. Repeat with each roll and dog.

4. Add four prepared hot dogs to lightly greased air fryer basket. Cook 8 minutes. Transfer cooked dogs to a serving plate and cook remaining dogs.

5. Serve with warmed Marinara Sauce for dipping.

PER SERVING Calories: 403 | Fat: 23.0 g | Protein: 16.2 g | Sodium: 1,510 mg | Fiber: 1.3 g | Carbohydrates: 31.1 g | Sugar: 8.7 g

CHAPTER 7

Beef and Bison Main Dishes

Chili-Seasoned Rib-Eye Steak

Cut from the rib area, the rib eye is beautifully marbled, and because of this extra fat, the taste is amazing. Because of the fat, be sure to add the tablespoon of water to the bottom of the air fryer. When the fat renders down, the water will help to avoid the fat drippings from smoking.

HANDS-ON TIME: 5 minutes
COOK TIME: 10 minutes

INGREDIENTS | SERVES 2

1 tablespoon water

½ teaspoon salt

¼ teaspoon freshly ground black pepper

¼ teaspoon garlic powder

¼ teaspoon chili powder

¼ teaspoon smoked paprika

1 (12-ounce) boneless rib-eye steak, 1" thick

1 tablespoon unsalted butter, cut into 2 pats

Is Resting Cooked Meat Necessary?

Resting meat is absolutely necessary if you prefer a juicy and flavorful dish. It not only cools the meat, but also reabsorbs the juices, which is key. If you cut the meat immediately after removing it from the heat, the juices will just pour out onto your cutting board. Those juices help flavor and keep the meat moist.

1. Preheat air fryer at 400°F for 3 minutes. Pour 1 tablespoon water into the bottom of the air fryer.

2. In a small bowl, combine salt, pepper, garlic powder, chili powder, and paprika.

3. Season rib eye on both sides with prepared dry rub. Place steak on fryer basket and cook 5 minutes. Flip steak and cook an additional 5 minutes. This should yield a medium-rare steak. Due to differences in steak sizes and doneness preferences, check steak with a meat thermometer to ensure preferred doneness.

4. Transfer steak to a cutting board and top with two pats of butter. Let rest 5 minutes before cutting and serving.

PER SERVING Calories: 592 | Fat: 46.2 g | Protein: 40.2 g | Sodium: 695 mg | Fiber: 0.3 g | Carbohydrates: 0.8 g | Sugar: 0.1 g

Cocoa-Chipotle Strip Steak

The air fryer is a simple way to yield a perfect steak with a seared exterior and a juicy interior. The cocoa powder, chipotle chili powder, and lime juice bring a little Mexico to your steak. Also try this with chicken, pork, and even salmon!

HANDS-ON TIME: 5 minutes
COOK TIME: 8 minutes

INGREDIENTS | SERVES 2

2 teaspoons unsweetened cocoa powder

1 teaspoon chipotle chili powder

1 tablespoon honey

½ teaspoon lime juice

Pinch salt

1 (¾-pound, 1½"-thick) strip steak

Substitute for Chili Chipotle Powder

Chili chipotle powder, or ancho chili powder, is simply dried ground peppers. Regular chili powder is a blend of spices, but if you are in a pinch, mix ¼ teaspoon of cayenne pepper with 2 teaspoons of chili powder for a quick substitute.

1. In a small bowl, combine cocoa powder, chili powder, honey, lime juice, and salt. Brush all over both sides of steak and refrigerate covered 30 minutes or up to overnight.

2. Preheat air fryer at 400°F for 3 minutes.

3. Place steak in air fryer basket and cook 4 minutes. Flip steak and cook an additional 4 minutes. This should yield a medium-rare steak. Due to differences in steak sizes and doneness preferences, check steak with a meat thermometer to ensure preferred doneness.

4. Transfer steak to a cutting board and let rest 5 minutes before cutting and serving.

PER SERVING Calories: 479 | Fat: 27.5 g | Protein: 37.4 g | Sodium: 201 mg | Fiber: 2.5 g | Carbohydrates: 12.6 g | Sugar: 8.8 g

Porcini-Rubbed Filets Mignons

Dried mushrooms can be found at most specialty grocers or online. Also, if you can't get your hands on porcinis, try other varieties, as they will fill in just nicely.

HANDS-ON TIME: 15 minutes
COOK TIME: 12 minutes

INGREDIENTS | SERVES 2

Porcini Dry Rub

¼ cup dried porcini mushrooms (about ½ ounce)

2 teaspoons sugar

2 teaspoons salt

2 teaspoons black peppercorns

1 teaspoon smoked paprika

1 teaspoon dried minced garlic

Steak

2 (1½"-thick) filet mignon steaks (about 1 pound total)

1 tablespoon unsalted butter, cut into 2 pats

1. Place Porcini Dry Rub ingredients in a small food processor or spice grinder. Pulse until powdered. Store in an airtight container until ready to use. This yields about ½ cup, so you will have leftover dry rub for future meals.

2. Preheat air fryer at 375°F for 3 minutes.

3. Season steaks on both sides with prepared dry rub. Place steaks in fryer basket and cook 4 minutes. Flip steaks and cook an additional 4 minutes. Flip steaks one more time and cook an additional 4 minutes. This should yield medium-rare steaks. Due to differences in steak sizes and doneness preferences, check steak with a meat thermometer to ensure preferred doneness.

4. Transfer steaks to a cutting board and top each with a pat of butter. Let rest 5 minutes before serving.

PER SERVING Calories: 431 | Fat: 19.3 g | Protein: 56.3 g | Sodium: 1,304 mg | Fiber: 0.9 g | Carbohydrates: 5.7 g | Sugar: 2.3 g

Cowboy Flank Steak

This flank steak is sure to put some giddyup in your step. And cowboys know that a little coffee in your steak rub lends a deep smokiness to the meat. (They also know not to squat while wearing spurs, so trust 'em; cowboys know things!)

HANDS-ON TIME: 5 minutes
COOK TIME: 19 minutes

INGREDIENTS | SERVES 4

¼ cup olive oil
½ teaspoon salt
½ teaspoon ground cumin
½ teaspoon chili powder
½ teaspoon garlic powder
½ teaspoon instant espresso powder
1 (1-pound) flank steak

What Is Instant Espresso Powder?

Found jarred in the coffee section, this powder is actually used by chefs more for its rich flavor than prepared as a drink. The coffee beans have been ground, brewed, dried, and then ground down into a fine powder. For a quick substitute, finely grind dark-roast coffee beans, but don't expect the same deep flavor.

1. In a medium bowl or gallon plastic resealable bag, combine olive oil, salt, cumin, chili powder, garlic powder, and espresso powder. Add flank steak, seal, and toss. Refrigerate 30 minutes or up to overnight.

2. Preheat air fryer at 325°F for 3 minutes.

3. Place steak on fryer basket and cook 10 minutes. Flip steak and cook an additional 9 minutes. This should yield a medium-rare steak. Due to differences in steak sizes and doneness preferences, check steak with a meat thermometer to ensure preferred doneness.

4. Transfer steak to a cutting board. Let rest 5 minutes before cutting. Slice thinly against the grain for maximum tenderness, then serve.

PER SERVING Calories: 253 | Fat: 14.5 g | Protein: 24.8 g | Sodium: 94 mg | Fiber: 0.0 g | Carbohydrates: 0.1 g | Sugar: 0.0 g

Beef Wellington

Beef Wellington is a beautiful filet mignon with Dijon mustard and mushroom duxelles wrapped neatly in puff pastry. You'll feel like there is a special little present on each plate.

HANDS-ON TIME: 15 minutes
COOK TIME: 27 minutes

INGREDIENTS | SERVES 2

2 cups chopped shiitake mushrooms (about 4 ounces)

¼ cup diced yellow onion

1 tablespoon fresh thyme leaves

4 teaspoons olive oil, divided

2 (1½"-thick) filet mignon steaks (about 1 pound)

4 ounces prosciutto (8 slices)

1 teaspoon Dijon mustard

¼ cup all-purpose flour, divided

1 large egg, whisked

1 sheet puff pastry, thawed to room temperature

What Are Mushroom Duxelles?

Traditionally found in Beef Wellington, mushroom duxelles is simply a paste made up of mushrooms, shallots or onions, herbs, and butter or oil. It is also amazing served at a party as an appetizer spread on toasted slices of French bread.

1. In a medium skillet over medium-high heat, stir-fry shiitakes, onion, thyme, and 2 teaspoons olive oil. Cook 3–4 minutes until onions are translucent and moisture has released from mushrooms. Let cool. Transfer to a small food processor and pulse until smooth.

2. In the same skillet, add remaining 2 teaspoons olive oil. Add steaks and sear all sides, 4–5 minutes until browned. Set aside to rest.

3. On a flat, clean surface, place a large piece of plastic wrap. In the middle of the wrap overlap 4 prosciutto slices, forming a square. Spread half of mushroom mixture, or duxelles, over prosciutto. Add a steak to the center. Brush top with ½ teaspoon Dijon mustard. Use the plastic wrap to help guide the prosciutto over steak, completely covering the steak. Roll tightly in the wrap and then twist ends of the wrap until a tight seal is formed. Repeat with remaining ingredients. Refrigerate 30 minutes to help set the forms.

4. Sprinkle some of the flour on flat, clean surface. The remaining flour can be used for your hands and the rolling pin. Place whisked egg in a small bowl nearby. Roll pastry sheet to ¼" thickness. Cut in half. Unwrap steaks and place one in the middle of each piece of puff pastry. Wrap steaks with puff pastry to cover. Cut away any excess pastry. Use egg to seal edges. Brush tops of Beef Wellingtons with egg.

5. Preheat air fryer at 350°F for 3 minutes.

Beef Wellington—continued

6. Place Beef Wellingtons seam side down in air fryer basket and cook 18 minutes. This should yield a medium-rare steak. Due to differences in steak sizes and doneness preferences, check steak with a meat thermometer to ensure preferred doneness.

7. Transfer Beef Wellingtons to plates. Let rest 5 minutes before serving.

PER SERVING Calories: 764 | Fat: 42.9 g | Protein: 72.8 g | Sodium: 477 mg | Fiber: 2.3 g | Carbohydrates: 18.2 g | Sugar: 2.4 g

Korean Gochujang Short Ribs

Gochujang, a fermented chili paste, is not quite as spicy as sriracha; it has a sweet and tangy component like ketchup. Slather it on some ribs with a few other spices, and these will be the best ribs you'll make this year!

HANDS-ON TIME: 10 minutes
COOK TIME: 16 minutes

INGREDIENTS | SERVES 2

¼ cup gochujang sauce
2 tablespoons rice vinegar
2 tablespoons honey
1 tablespoon soy sauce
1 teaspoon ground ginger
1 pound boneless beef short ribs
¼ cup chopped fresh cilantro

1. In a large plastic resealable bag, combine gochujang sauce, vinegar, honey, soy sauce, and ginger. Set aside 2 tablespoons of mixture in a small bowl.

2. Add short ribs to bag, seal, and massage mixture into ribs. Refrigerate 30 minutes up to overnight.

3. Preheat air fryer at 325°F for 3 minutes.

4. Place ribs in air fryer basket. Cook 8 minutes. Flip ribs and brush with extra sauce. Cook an additional 8 minutes.

5. Transfer ribs to a serving plate and garnish with fresh cilantro.

PER SERVING Calories: 404 | Fat: 22.0 g | Protein: 44.1 g | Sodium: 348 mg | Fiber: 0.8 g | Carbohydrates: 6.6 g | Sugar: 4.6 g

BBQ Short Ribs

Short ribs are taken from the shorter portion of the rib cage. Full of meat and fat, they make the best bites of the ribs. Warning: this is not elegant dining, so bring a stack of napkins!

HANDS-ON TIME: 10 minutes
COOK TIME: 16 minutes

INGREDIENTS | SERVES 2

¼ cup ketchup
1 teaspoon Worcestershire sauce
1 tablespoon pure maple syrup
1 teaspoon apple cider vinegar
1 teaspoon garlic powder
1 tablespoon smoked paprika
1 teaspoon sea salt
1 teaspoon freshly ground black pepper
½ teaspoon cayenne pepper
1 pound boneless beef short ribs

Measuring Maple Syrup Without the Mess

When measuring sticky liquids like maple syrup, honey, or molasses, warm up the measuring cup or spoon by rinsing it first with hot water. Your liquid won't stick to your cup, making cleanup much easier and the measurement more accurate!

1. In a large plastic resealable bag, combine ketchup, Worcestershire sauce, syrup, vinegar, garlic powder, paprika, salt, black pepper, and cayenne pepper. Set aside 2 tablespoons of mixture in a small bowl.

2. Add short ribs to bag, seal, and massage mixture into ribs. Refrigerate 30 minutes or up to overnight.

3. Preheat air fryer at 325°F for 3 minutes.

4. Place ribs in air fryer basket. Cook 8 minutes. Flip ribs and brush with extra sauce. Cook an additional 8 minutes.

5. Transfer ribs to a serving plate.

PER SERVING Calories: 385 | Fat: 20.5 g | Protein: 43.5 g | Sodium: 534 mg | Fiber: 0.6 g | Carbohydrates: 7.1 g | Sugar: 5.1 g

Summer Steak Salad

There is no need to spend big bucks at your local steakhouse, because this salad will quench your craving. Filled with succulent steak strips, bright greens, vibrant blue cheese, earthy nuts and seeds, and fresh blueberries, this salad is packed with flavor!

HANDS-ON TIME: 5 minutes
COOK TIME: 19 minutes

INGREDIENTS | SERVES 4

¼ cup olive oil

1 teaspoon salt

½ teaspoon freshly ground black pepper

1 (1-pound) flank steak

8 cups mixed greens

¼ cup balsamic vinaigrette

4 tablespoons crumbled blue cheese

4 tablespoons walnut pieces

4 tablespoons shelled sunflower seeds

1 cup blueberries

Why Cutting Across the Grain Is Important

In some cuts of meat the parallel-lined muscle fibers are bigger than in other cuts of meat. To just take a big bite out of the meat, you are dealing with these fibers and chewing and chewing. If you thinly slice the meat against the grain, you are cutting these fibers, leaving a tender piece of meat to enjoy instead of "chewing steak gum"!

1. In a medium bowl or gallon plastic resealable bag, combine olive oil, salt, and pepper. Add flank steak, seal, and toss. Refrigerate 30 minutes or up to overnight.

2. Preheat air fryer at 325°F for 3 minutes.

3. Place steak on fryer basket and cook 10 minutes. Flip steak and cook an additional 9 minutes. This should yield a medium-rare steak. Due to differences in steak sizes and doneness preferences, check steak with a meat thermometer to ensure preferred doneness.

4. Transfer steak to a cutting board. Let rest 5 minutes.

5. While steak is resting, add mixed greens to a large mixing bowl. Slowly drizzle in vinaigrette. Toss. Add more and toss again. Do this until greens are fully dressed. Transfer to four bowls.

6. Top each salad with blue cheese, walnuts, sunflower seeds, and blueberries.

7. Slice steak thinly across the grain for maximum tenderness. Top each salad with sliced steak. Serve immediately.

PER SERVING Calories: 427 | Fat: 26.0 g | Protein: 30.2 g | Sodium: 269 mg | Fiber: 3.7 g | Carbohydrates: 13.0 g | Sugar: 6.6 g

Steak Street Tacos

Because they're overflowing with flavor, you will think these street tacos came off a gourmet food truck. Cutting the air-fried flank steak against the grain causes this cheaper cut of meat to seem like it is the highest-priced beef from the butcher.

HANDS-ON TIME: 5 minutes
COOK TIME: 19 minutes

INGREDIENTS | SERVES 5

¼ cup olive oil
½ teaspoon salt
½ teaspoon ground cumin
1 (1-pound) flank steak
10 street tacos (4" mini flour tortillas)
1 cup shredded red cabbage
½ cup Sriracha Mayonnaise (see Chapter 15)
½ cup Pico Guacamole (see Chapter 15)

1. In a gallon plastic resealable bag, combine olive oil, salt, and cumin. Add flank steak, seal, and toss. Refrigerate 30 minutes.

2. Preheat air fryer at 325°F for 3 minutes.

3. Place steak on fryer basket and cook 10 minutes. Flip steak and cook an additional 9 minutes. This should yield a medium-rare steak. Due to differences in steak sizes and doneness preferences, check steak with a meat thermometer to ensure preferred doneness.

4. Transfer steak to a cutting board. Let rest 5 minutes before cutting. Slice thinly against the grain for maximum tenderness.

5. Build street tacos by adding steak slices to flour tortillas, along with red cabbage, Sriracha Mayonnaise, and Pico Guacamole. Serve immediately.

PER SERVING Calories: 526 | Fat: 33.7 g | Protein: 24.2 g | Sodium: 739 mg | Fiber: 3.5 g | Carbohydrates: 26.0 g | Sugar: 3.1 g

Hamburger Dogs

Turn the classic hamburger and hot dog on their heads by combining the two. This hot dog is actually seasoned ground beef in the shape of a hot dog and served in a hot dog bun. You can serve them with your favorite burger or hot dog toppings.

HANDS-ON TIME: 10 minutes
COOK TIME: 6 minutes

INGREDIENTS | SERVES 4

½ pound ground beef

¼ teaspoon Worcestershire sauce

1 large egg white

2 tablespoons plain bread crumbs

⅛ teaspoon chili powder

¼ teaspoon onion powder

¼ teaspoon salt

4 top-split hot dog buns

1. In a medium bowl, combine beef, Worcestershire sauce, egg white, bread crumbs, chili powder, onion powder, and salt. Form into four hot dog shapes. Roll them longer than usual because the beef will shrink some in cooking.

2. Preheat air fryer at 350°F for 3 minutes.

3. Place hamburger dogs in lightly greased air fryer basket. Cook 3 minutes. Flip. Cook an additional 3 minutes. Transfer to a paper towel–lined plate to soak up any grease.

4. Place Hamburger Dogs in buns and serve.

PER SERVING Calories: 212 | Fat: 5.1 g | Protein: 14.8 g | Sodium: 423 mg | Fiber: 1.1 g | Carbohydrates: 23.7 g | Sugar: 3.0 g

Bulgogi

Bulgogi, literally translated as "fire meat," is a Korean classic consisting of thin strips of marinated beef. The air fryer makes crispy edges on the beef strips, which lend added texture to this dish. The grated pear is the secret weapon and quintessential ingredient in Bulgogi.

HANDS-ON TIME: 15 minutes
COOK TIME: 12 minutes

INGREDIENTS | SERVES 2

2 tablespoons sesame oil

2 tablespoons grated pear

1 tablespoon soy sauce

1 tablespoon brown sugar

1 tablespoon gochujang

1 teaspoon ground ginger

1 clove garlic, minced

Pinch salt

6 scallions, trimmed, sliced, whites and greens separated

1 (12-ounce) rib-eye steak, 1" thick, thinly sliced

2 cups cooked rice

2 teaspoons toasted sesame seeds

1. In a gallon plastic resealable bag, combine oil, pear, soy sauce, sugar, gochujang, ginger, garlic, salt, and scallion whites. Add thinly sliced rib eye, seal, and toss. Refrigerate 30 minutes or up to overnight.

2. Preheat air fryer at 375°F for 3 minutes.

3. Place steak in air fryer basket and cook 12 minutes, stirring every 3 minutes. This should yield tender steak with crispy edges.

4. Serve steak over two bowls of rice. Garnish with scallion greens and toasted sesame seeds.

PER SERVING Calories: 627 | Fat: 30.0 g | Protein: 38.0 g | Sodium: 208 mg | Fiber: 1.1 g | Carbohydrates: 47.8 g | Sugar: 1.4 g

Steak and Peppers Quesadillas

The air fryer cooks this rib eye like a boss...a juicy center with a seared exterior. And those peppers and gooey cheese make these quesadillas simply delicious. Serve with some homemade Pico Guacamole (see Chapter 15) to finish it off!

HANDS-ON TIME: 15 minutes
COOK TIME: 29 minutes

INGREDIENTS | SERVES 4

1 (12-ounce) rib-eye steak, 1" thick
½ teaspoon salt
¼ teaspoon freshly ground black pepper
2 teaspoons olive oil
1 small red bell pepper, seeded and sliced
1 small green bell pepper, seeded and sliced
½ medium yellow onion, peeled and sliced
2 teaspoons chili powder
3 tablespoons butter, melted
8 (6") flour tortillas
2 cups grated Monterey jack cheese

1. Preheat air fryer at 400°F for 3 minutes.

2. Season rib eye on both sides with salt and pepper. Place steak in air fryer basket and cook 5 minutes. Flip steak and cook an additional 5 minutes. This should yield a medium-rare steak. Due to differences in steak sizes and doneness preferences, check steak with a meat thermometer to ensure preferred doneness.

3. Transfer steak to a cutting board and let rest 5 minutes.

4. While the steak is cooking and resting, sauté olive oil, bell peppers, onion, and chili powder in a skillet over medium-high heat 5–7 minutes until peppers are tender. Set aside. Thinly slice steak against the grain.

5. Reduce heat on air fryer to 350°F.

6. Lightly brush melted butter on one side of a tortilla. Place tortilla butter side down in air fryer basket. Layer ¼ of the steak on tortilla, followed with ¼ of the pepper and onion mixture, and ¼ of the cheese. Top with second tortilla. Lightly butter top of tortilla.

7. Cook 3 minutes. Set aside and continue to make remaining three quesadillas. Slice each quesadilla like a pie into six sections. Serve warm.

PER SERVING Calories: 701 | Fat: 44.1 g | Protein: 36.0 g | Sodium: 1,136 mg | Fiber: 3.1 g | Carbohydrates: 35.7 g | Sugar: 4.5 g

Brie and Fig Jam Sliders

Break out these upscale sliders for a family celebration or for your fancy guests! Fig jam and Brie go together like peanut butter and jelly. The peppery arugula elevates these sliders and will have you coming back for more...and more!

HANDS-ON TIME: 5 minutes
COOK TIME: 18 minutes

INGREDIENTS | SERVES 4

1 pound lean ground beef
½ teaspoon dried basil
½ teaspoon salt
8 tablespoons Brie cheese
8 slider buns
¼ cup fig jam
½ cup arugula

1. In a medium bowl, combine beef, basil, and salt. Form into eight balls.

2. Roll 1 tablespoon of Brie into a ball and press into the middle of a beef ball. Seal edges and gently press into a patty. Gently make a slight indentation in the middle of each patty, as the beef will rise during heating. Repeat with remaining beef and Brie.

3. Preheat air fryer at 350°F for 3 minutes.

4. Place four sliders in lightly greased air fryer basket or on the air fryer grill pan (accessory). Cook 4 minutes. Flip sliders and cook an additional 5 minutes or until desired doneness, which can be checked with a meat thermometer. Repeat with remaining sliders.

5. Transfer sliders to a plate and serve on buns spread with fig jam and topped with arugula.

PER SERVING Calories: 450 | Fat: 14.8 g | Protein: 30.8 g | Sodium: 749 mg | Fiber: 1.5 g | Carbohydrates: 42.4 g | Sugar: 13.5 g

Reuben Burgers

These burgers have all the classic flavors of a Reuben sandwich coupled with the juiciness of the simple hamburger. The air-fried corned beef takes the place of crispy bacon found on some burgers, and the caraway seeds give a nod to the traditional rye bread.

HANDS-ON TIME: 10 minutes
COOK TIME: 30 minutes

INGREDIENTS | SERVES 4

1 pound lean ground beef
2 tablespoons minced yellow onion
2 teaspoons caraway seeds
1 teaspoon salt
4 slices Swiss cheese
8 slices deli corned beef
½ cup Thousand Island dressing
4 hamburger buns
1 cup sauerkraut, drained

1. Preheat air fryer at 350°F for 3 minutes.

2. Combine ground beef, onion, caraway seeds, and salt. Form into four patties, making an indentation in the middle, as the beef will rise during heating.

3. Add two patties to lightly greased fryer basket and cook 6 minutes. Flip burgers and cook an additional 4 minutes. Add a slice of Swiss cheese to the top of the burgers and cook an additional 2 minutes.

4. Transfer to a serving plate. Repeat with remaining burgers. Remove when done and let them rest.

5. While burgers are resting, add corned beef to air fryer basket. Cook 3 minutes, flip, and cook an additional 3 minutes to achieve crispy edges.

6. Spread 2 tablespoons dressing on each bun. Place a burger on each bun and top each with ¼ cup sauerkraut and 2 slices crispy corned beef. Serve warm.

PER SERVING Calories: 553 | Fat: 25.9 g | Protein: 45.1 g | Sodium: 1,529 mg | Fiber: 2.8 g | Carbohydrates: 32.9 g | Sugar: 9.2 g

Porcini-Rubbed Filets Mignons (Chapter 7)

Pork Lettuce Cups (Chapter 8)

Cajun-Fried Sweet Pickle Chips (Chapter 5)

Individual Egg and Cheese Soufflés (Chapter 2)

Artisanal Olive Bread (Chapter 3)

Chicken Potpie (Chapter 13)

Disco Fries (Chapter 5)

Spicy Pretzel Chicken Nuggets (Chapter 6)

Sweet and Sour Pork (Chapter 8)

Lemon Cake (Chapter 14)

Red Wine Beef (Chapter 7)

Fried Corn on the Cob (Chapter 11)

Chili-Lime Corn Chips (Chapter 5)

Lobster Rolls (Chapter 12)

Chocolate-Cherry Cheesecake Crescents (Chapter 14)

Pimiento Cheese–Stuffed Jalapeños (Chapter 4)

Mixed Berry and Apple Crumble (Chapter 14)

Buttermilk Southern-Fried Chicken Legs (Chapter 6)

Brie, Fig, and Prosciutto Open-Faced Sandwiches (Chapter 12)

Confetti Cake (Chapter 14)

Salmon Croquettes (Chapter 4)

Bite-Sized Blooming Onions (Chapter 4)

Steak Street Tacos (Chapter 7)

Zucchini Chocolate Chip Bread (Chapter 3)

Red Wine Beef

Although this meal is simply made, the Dijon mustard and red wine lend a little acidic bite that will be appreciated with the robust beef. Serve with potatoes and green beans.

HANDS-ON TIME: 5 minutes
COOK TIME: 15 minutes

INGREDIENTS | SERVES 4

1 teaspoon Dijon mustard

½ teaspoon salt

¼ cup dry red wine

¼ cup tomato paste

1 pound beef stew cubes

What Kind of Wine Should You Buy for Cooking?

If a recipe calls for dry red wine, using a red blend, a Merlot, Cabernet, Pinot Noir, or Shiraz all fit the bill. The best rule for you as chef is to choose a wine that you enjoy to drink. Because you won't be using the entire bottle, there are leftovers for the cook, so buy what you like! Or if you don't like wine, vegetable or chicken broth is a good substitute for white wine, and beef broth can substitute for red wine.

1. In a medium bowl, combine mustard, salt, wine, and tomato paste. Add in beef cubes and toss to combine. Add to bottom of cake barrel (accessory).

2. Preheat air fryer at 350°F for 3 minutes.

3. Place barrel in air fryer basket. Cook 12–15 minutes, stirring twice during cooking.

4. Remove barrel from air fryer and let rest 10 minutes. Spoon into bowls and serve warm.

PER SERVING Calories: 237 | Fat: 7.2 g | Protein: 25.2 g | Sodium: 396 mg | Fiber: 0.7 g | Carbohydrates: 3.6 g | Sugar: 2.1 g

Hoisin Beef Meatballs

Hoisin has an incredibly rich flavor, hitting both sweet and salty tastes. These are fantastic straight out of the air fryer but even better served over rice garnished with scallion greens and eaten with a pair of chopsticks.

HANDS-ON TIME: 10 minutes
COOK TIME: 16 minutes

INGREDIENTS | SERVES 4

1 pound lean ground beef

1 large egg

½ cup panko bread crumbs

4 scallions trimmed and diced, greens and whites separated

2 tablespoons hoisin sauce

1 tablespoon soy sauce

½ teaspoon ground white pepper

What Is White Pepper?

White and black pepper are not only different in color, they are also different in flavor and preparation. Black pepper is made from berries that aren't ripe but are smoked, creating a black color. White pepper is created from ripe berries by removing the skin and soaking the berries. Removing the skin removes some of the flavor, which is why black pepper has a deeper flavor. White pepper is more subtle and is also good for white sauces, where the black pepper would inconveniently show itself.

1. Preheat air fryer at 350°F for 3 minutes.

2. In a medium bowl, combine beef, egg, bread crumbs, white parts of scallions, hoisin sauce, soy sauce, and pepper. Form into eighteen meatballs, about 2 tablespoons each.

3. Add half of meatballs to fryer basket and cook 6 minutes. Flip meatballs. Cook an additional 2 minutes. Transfer to serving dish.

4. Repeat with remaining meatballs.

5. Transfer meatballs to a serving dish. Garnish with scallion greens.

PER SERVING Calories: 266 | Fat: 10.0 g | Protein: 25.1 g | Sodium: 450 mg | Fiber: 0.5 g | Carbohydrates: 14.4 g | Sugar: 2.9 g

Cherry-Sage Beefburgers

The sweetness from the cherry preserves against the strong and savory sage creates a flavor combo that will make you squeal with delight. Serve these burgers as is or with your favorite toppings on an artisanal hamburger bun or in a fresh lettuce wrap.

HANDS-ON TIME: 10 minutes
COOK TIME: 24 minutes

INGREDIENTS | SERVES 4

1 pound ground beef
2 tablespoons minced yellow onion
1 large egg white
¼ cup panko bread crumbs
1 tablespoon cherry preserves
1 tablespoon chopped fresh sage leaves
Pinch salt

1. Preheat air fryer at 350°F for 3 minutes.

2. In a medium bowl, combine all the ingredients and form into four patties, making a slight indentation in the middle, as the beef will rise during heating.

3. Add two patties to lightly greased fryer basket and cook 6 minutes. Flip burgers and cook an additional 6 minutes or until desired doneness. Repeat with remaining burgers.

4. Transfer to a plate and serve.

PER SERVING Calories: 223 | Fat: 8.5 g | Protein: 23.1 g | Sodium: 120 mg | Fiber: 0.3 g | Carbohydrates: 9.3 g | Sugar: 3.0 g

Kraut Dogs

When you want that grill flavor but don't have the time, break out your air fryer, and within minutes you will be on your very own personal picnic. Add some sauerkraut and a little beer mustard and you'll feel like you're at Oktoberfest!

HANDS-ON TIME: 5 minutes
COOK TIME: 5 minutes

INGREDIENTS | SERVES 2

4 beef hot dogs
4 hot dog buns
½ cup sauerkraut, drained
2 tablespoons beer mustard (or Dijon)

1. Preheat air fryer at 400°F for 3 minutes.

2. Add hot dogs to air fryer basket. Cook 4 minutes.

3. Remove hot dogs and put in hot dog buns. Place back into the basket. Cook 1 additional minute.

4. Transfer hot dogs to a plate and garnish with sauerkraut and mustard. Serve warm.

PER SERVING Calories: 580 | Fat: 28.5 g | Protein: 21.0 g | Sodium: 1,721 mg | Fiber: 2.7 g | Carbohydrates: 47.4 g | Sugar: 7.2 g

Bison Rib-Eye Steak

Bison is an excellent source of protein, especially good for those following a low-fat, high-protein diet. Leaner and a bit sweeter than beef, bison also has a shorter cooking time. It is imperative that you don't overcook this high-quality meat, as it starts to toughen beyond medium-rare.

HANDS-ON TIME: 5 minutes
COOK TIME: 7 minutes

INGREDIENTS | SERVES 1

½ teaspoon salt
¼ teaspoon freshly ground black pepper
⅛ teaspoon smoked paprika
⅛ teaspoon garlic powder
1 (8-ounce) bison rib-eye steak, 1" thick

1. In a small bowl, combine salt, pepper, paprika, and garlic powder.

2. Preheat air fryer at 400°F for 3 minutes.

3. Season rib eye with prepared dry rub on both sides. Place in air fryer basket and cook 4 minutes. Flip steak and cook an additional 3 minutes. Check steak with a meat thermometer to ensure doneness satisfaction.

4. Transfer steak to a cutting board and let rest 5 minutes before serving.

PER SERVING Calories: 303 | Fat: 8.4 g | Protein: 50.3 g | Sodium: 1,250 mg | Fiber: 0.3 g | Carbohydrates: 0.8 g | Sugar: 0.0 g

Bison and Blue Cheese Wraps

Naturally lean, bison is a great substitute for beef. Because it is more robust in taste, the blue cheese kicks up the flavor even more with its sharp and pungent flavor. Tempered with lettuce and tomatoes, these wraps cover all the bases.

HANDS-ON TIME: 10 minutes
COOK TIME: 7 minutes

INGREDIENTS | SERVES 2

1 (8-ounce) bison rib-eye steak, 1" thick
½ teaspoon salt
¼ teaspoon freshly ground black pepper
4 tablespoons crumbled blue cheese
½ cup shredded lettuce
2 medium Roma tomatoes, seeded and diced
4 (6") flour tortillas

1. Preheat air fryer at 400°F for 3 minutes.

2. Season rib eye on both sides with salt and pepper. Place in air fryer basket and cook 4 minutes. Flip steak and cook an additional 3 minutes. Check steak with a meat thermometer to ensure doneness preference.

3. Transfer steak to a cutting board and let rest 5 minutes before cutting. Thinly slice steak against the grain.

4. Divide steak, blue cheese, lettuce, and tomatoes evenly among tortillas and roll each into a wrap. Serve.

PER SERVING Calories: 399 | Fat: 12.2 g | Protein: 34.2 g | Sodium: 1,247 mg | Fiber: 2.5 g | Carbohydrates: 34.2 g | Sugar: 4.1 g

The Benefits of Bison Meat

Bison will soon become your favorite red meat. It is so flavor-rich and dense, and it's lean! Also, while the demand is still quite low in comparison to beef, you will find most bison to be wild fed because they are still considered "wild game" and are able to roam in their natural habitats, eating what they were intended to eat. Bison is a good source of B vitamins, iron, zinc, and selenium.

Jalapeño Bison Meatballs

These bison meatballs are made tender and juicy with the jalapeño jelly and onion. Serve this dish with some mashed potatoes and fresh vegetables plus an extra dollop of the jalapeño jelly in which to drag your meatballs around for extra flavor.

HANDS-ON TIME: 10 minutes
COOK TIME: 16 minutes

INGREDIENTS | SERVES 4

1 pound ground bison
1 large egg
2 tablespoons jalapeño jelly
½ cup plain bread crumbs
¼ cup finely diced yellow onion
2 tablespoons chopped fresh mint, divided
1 teaspoon salt
½ teaspoon freshly ground black pepper

Containing Mint Plants

Although herbs are a luxury to grow in the summer and they lend freshness to meals, mint needs to be tended to closely. It is hearty and can spread fast, taking over your garden. Mint is an ideal herb to grow in a container. The container holds the plant to borders, still allowing you to reap its flavor and nutritional benefits.

1. In a medium bowl, combine bison, egg, jalapeño jelly, bread crumbs, onion, 1 tablespoon chopped mint, salt, and pepper. Form into eighteen meatballs, about 2 tablespoons each.

2. Preheat air fryer at 350°F for 3 minutes.

3. Add half of meatballs to fryer basket and cook 6 minutes. Flip meatballs. Cook an additional 2 minutes. Transfer to serving dish.

4. Repeat with remaining meatballs.

5. Transfer meatballs to a serving dish. Garnish with remaining chopped mint leaves.

PER SERVING Calories: 301 | Fat: 13.0 g | Protein: 24.3 g | Sodium: 711 mg | Fiber: 0.9 g | Carbohydrates: 15.5 g | Sugar: 5.8 g

CHAPTER 8

Pork and Lamb Main Dishes

Simple Pork Loin Roast

The air fryer definitely does justice to a succulent pork loin roast. The interior meat is so very juicy, and the convection-style cooking does wonders to crisp up the skin. Because of varying sizes of loin roasts, be sure to check the roast with a meat thermometer near the end of the cooking cycle.

HANDS-ON TIME: 10 minutes
COOK TIME: 40 minutes

INGREDIENTS | SERVES 4

1 (2-pound) boneless pork loin roast
3 cloves garlic, halved
1 tablespoon olive oil
1 teaspoon dried rosemary
1 teaspoon salt
½ teaspoon freshly ground black pepper

1. Preheat air fryer at 350°F for 3 minutes.

2. Cut six random slits, about 1" deep, in top of pork loin. Push a garlic half in each slit.

3. In a small bowl, whisk together olive oil, rosemary, salt, and pepper. Massage into loin on all sides.

4. Place pork in air fryer basket. Cook 20 minutes. Flip. Cook 20 minutes more. The internal temperature should be at least 145°F when checked with a meat thermometer.

5. Let pork rest on a cutting board 5 minutes before slicing and serving warm.

PER SERVING Calories: 444 | Fat: 23.2 g | Protein: 42.5 g | Sodium: 713 mg | Fiber: 0.2 g | Carbohydrates: 0.4 g | Sugar: 0.0 g

German Mustard Pork Loin Chops

There are actually many varieties of mustard in Germany but generally only a handful of choices on the shelves of American grocery stores. They can range from mild to quite spicy. So take a quick peek at the labels and choose one that is right for your taste buds.

HANDS-ON TIME: 5 minutes
COOK TIME: 11 minutes

INGREDIENTS | SERVES 3

3 boneless center-cut pork loin chops, each approximately 1" thick (about 1 pound total)

1 teaspoon salt

½ teaspoon freshly ground black pepper

6 teaspoons German mustard

1. Preheat air fryer at 350°F for 3 minutes.

2. Season both sides of pork chops with salt and pepper. Brush the top of each chop with 2 teaspoons mustard.

3. Place pork on lightly greased air fryer basket with mustard side up. Cook 4 minutes. Flip. Cook 4 minutes more. Flip. Cook an additional 3 minutes. The internal temperature should be at least 145°F when checked with a meat thermometer.

4. Let pork rest on a cutting board 5 minutes before serving warm.

PER SERVING Calories: 313 | Fat: 8.9 g | Protein: 53.7 g | Sodium: 1,696 mg | Fiber: 0.2 g | Carbohydrates: 1.6 g | Sugar: 0.0 g

Salt and Vinegar Potato Chip Pork Loin Chops

There are only a few ingredients in this recipe because the potato chip crumbs hit the salt, vinegar, and starchy elements found in a traditional breading. If you're adventurous, you can pick out a different variety of chip each time you make this recipe!

HANDS-ON TIME: 5 minutes
COOK TIME: 11 minutes

INGREDIENTS | SERVES 3

1 cup crushed salt and vinegar potato chips
1 teaspoon dried thyme
2 tablespoons butter, melted
3 boneless center-cut pork loin chops, each approximately 1" thick (about 1 pound total)

1. In a medium bowl, combine crushed chips, thyme, and melted butter.

2. Preheat air fryer at 350°F for 3 minutes.

3. Press chip mixture evenly over the top of each pork chop.

4. Place chops on lightly greased air fryer basket with chip side up. Cook 11 minutes. The internal temperature should be at least 145°F when checked with a meat thermometer.

5. Let pork rest on a cutting board 5 minutes before serving warm.

PER SERVING Calories: 306 | Fat: 15.0 g | Protein: 35.7 g | Sodium: 156 mg | Fiber: 0.4 g | Carbohydrates: 5.3 g | Sugar: 0.0 g

Peachy Pork Chops

The mixture of the peach jelly, ketchup, Worcestershire sauce, and lemon juice creates a sweet barbecue sauce of sorts. The air fryer sears all sides of the chops while keeping the inside juicy!

HANDS-ON TIME: 5 minutes
COOK TIME: 12 minutes

INGREDIENTS | SERVES 2

2 tablespoons peach jelly

1 tablespoon ketchup

1 teaspoon Worcestershire sauce

1 tablespoon lemon juice

1 tablespoon olive oil

2 (1"-thick) bone-in pork chops, approximately 1 pound

What Exactly Is Worcestershire Sauce?

Worcestershire sauce, developed back in the 1830s, is a fermented sauce that contains malt vinegar, anchovies, onions, molasses, garlic, cloves, chili pepper extract, and its secret ingredient, tamarind. Whether shaken on steaks or added to the perfect Bloody Mary, Worcestershire sauce lends a smoky, salty, acidic, somewhat peppery flavor to dishes and drinks.

1. In a medium bowl, whisk together peach jelly, ketchup, Worcestershire sauce, lemon juice, and olive oil. Add pork chops and refrigerate covered 30 minutes.

2. Preheat air fryer at 350°F for 3 minutes.

3. Place pork chops in air fryer basket. Cook 4 minutes. Flip. Cook 4 minutes more. Flip. Cook an additional 4 minutes. The internal temperature should be at least 145°F when checked with a meat thermometer.

4. Let pork rest on a cutting board 5 minutes before serving warm.

PER SERVING Calories: 258 | Fat: 13.5 g | Protein: 27.4 g | Sodium: 73 mg | Fiber: 0.0 g | Carbohydrates: 1.2 g | Sugar: 1.1 g

Parmesan-Crusted Pork Chops

The Parmesan cheese coating sets these air-fried pork chops apart from any others. Done in 12 minutes, they can rest while you plate the rest of your food. By the time the plate makes it to the table, they will be ready to eat!

HANDS-ON TIME: 5 minutes
COOK TIME: 12 minutes

INGREDIENTS | SERVES 2

1 large egg
1 tablespoon Dijon mustard
¼ cup grated Parmesan cheese
¼ cup panko bread crumbs
¼ teaspoon freshly ground black pepper
2 (1"-thick) bone-in pork chops, approximately 1 pound

Why Do Chicken Eggs Come in Different Sizes and Colors?

Most grocery stores typically sell chicken eggs ranging from small to jumbo. And white and brown eggs are the colors you generally see, but sometimes eggs are bluish or greenish. These variations all come down to the breed and age of the hen. Where you really get a different flavor is not necessarily from the size of the egg or age of the hen, but from the freshness, the way the chicken was raised, and the quality of its diet.

1. Preheat air fryer at 350°F for 3 minutes.

2. In a small dish, whisk together egg and Dijon mustard. In a shallow dish combine Parmesan cheese, bread crumbs, and black pepper.

3. Dip pork chops in egg mixture. Dredge in bread crumb mixture.

4. Place pork on lightly greased air fryer basket. Cook 4 minutes. Flip. Cook 4 minutes more. Flip. Cook an additional 4 minutes. The internal temperature should be at least 145°F when checked with a meat thermometer.

5. Let pork rest on a cutting board 5 minutes before serving warm.

PER SERVING Calories: 376 | Fat: 17.8 g | Protein: 34.3 g | Sodium: 425 mg | Fiber: 0.1 g | Carbohydrates: 12.3 g | Sugar: 0.6 g

Pork Schnitzel

Pork schnitzel, or Schweineschnitzel, *is pork cutlet that has been pounded thin and breaded. The air fryer cooks all sides to a tasty crispness. Serve this schnitzel with your favorite potato dish for a complete German dining experience.*

HANDS-ON TIME: 15 minutes
COOK TIME: 42 minutes

INGREDIENTS | YIELDS 6 SCHNITZELS

6 boneless center-cut pork loin chops, each approximately ½" thick (about 1 pound total)

½ cup all-purpose flour

1 large egg, whisked

1 cup panko bread crumbs

1 tablespoon ground dry mustard

1 teaspoon freshly ground black pepper

2 tablespoons lemon juice

2 teaspoons salt

1 medium lemon, cut into 6 wedges

The Difference Between Schnitzel and Wiener Schnitzel

Schnitzel is simply the cooking preparation of pounding meat until thin, breading it, and lightly frying it. Wiener schnitzel is still prepared this way, but it is always veal. Other popular versions are *Jägerschnitzel*, which is schnitzel served with a mushroom gravy, and *Rahmschnitzel*, which is served with a cream sauce.

1. Place a loin between two pieces of parchment paper. Using the flat side of a mallet, pound out pork until it is ⅛" thick. Repeat with remaining loins. Set aside.

2. In a small bowl, add flour. In another bowl, add whisked egg. In a shallow dish, combine bread crumbs, ground mustard, and black pepper.

3. Preheat air fryer at 350°F for 3 minutes.

4. Sprinkle each loin with lemon juice and salt on both sides.

5. Coat each loin in flour. Shake off excess. Dip in egg and shake off excess. Dredge in bread crumbs.

6. Place pork on lightly greased air fryer basket. Cook 4 minutes. Flip. Cook 3 minutes. Repeat with remaining pork. The internal temperature should be at least 145°F when checked with a meat thermometer.

7. Let pork rest on a cutting board 5 minutes before serving warm with lemon wedges.

PER SERVING Calories: 156 | Fat: 3.4 g | Protein: 19.7 g | Sodium: 852 mg | Fiber: 0.3 g | Carbohydrates: 11.3 g | Sugar: 0.5 g

Stuffed Pork Loin Chops

The apple in the stuffing lends a sweetness to this dish. It also provides moisture to keep the pork from drying out. Serve with a baked sweet potato for a comforting holiday feel to your meal.

HANDS-ON TIME: 5 minutes
COOK TIME: 11 minutes

INGREDIENTS | SERVES 3

3 boneless center-cut pork loin chops, each approximately 1" thick (about 1 pound total)

2 slices hearty wheat bread, diced into ¼" cubes

¼ cup peeled, cored, and grated Granny Smith apple

2 teaspoons finely chopped fresh sage leaves

1 tablespoon butter, melted

½ teaspoon salt

½ teaspoon freshly ground black pepper

1. Cut a pocket in the thickness of each pork loin chop, ensuring that the knife doesn't cut all the way through.

2. In a medium bowl, combine bread cubes, apple, sage, butter, salt, and pepper.

3. Preheat air fryer at 350°F for 3 minutes.

4. Stuff a third of bread mixture into each pork chop.

5. Place pork chops on lightly greased air fryer basket. Cook 11 minutes. The internal temperature should be at least 145°F when checked with a meat thermometer.

6. Let pork rest on a cutting board 5 minutes before serving warm.

PER SERVING Calories: 298 | Fat: 9.4 g | Protein: 38.6 g | Sodium: 622 mg | Fiber: 1.9 g | Carbohydrates: 13.5 g | Sugar: 2.2 g

Why Is the Granny Smith Apple So Often Suggested in Recipes?

Although there seem to be a million varieties of apples available these days, that good old stand-in, the Granny Smith, seems to still be gold when making recipes. Why? A Granny Smith is a firm and sour apple that not only holds its shape when baking, but its tartness works as a great companion to both savory and sweet flavors.

Sweet and Sour Pork

As an added component to this dish, use the pineapple juice from a can of pineapple chunks. Then toss the chunks in the sauce with the pork at the end of this recipe. Serve the mixture over rice to complete the take-out experience...and don't forget to buy those fortune cookies!

HANDS-ON TIME: 15 minutes
COOK TIME: 20 minutes

INGREDIENTS | SERVES 4

3 tablespoons cornstarch, divided

1 tablespoon water

2 tablespoons rice vinegar

2 tablespoons ketchup

⅓ cup pineapple juice

2 tablespoons brown sugar

2 teaspoons soy sauce

1 large egg

2 tablespoons all-purpose flour

1 pound boneless pork loin, cut into 1" cubes

Cornstarch Substitutions

Cornstarch is an ingredient used to thicken such things as sauces and puddings. It is also sometimes used in frying, as it can lend a crispier breading. However, if you have run out of it or have certain diet restrictions, the following can be used— flour, arrowroot flour, tapioca flour, rice flour, and even potato starch.

1. In a small bowl, create a slurry by whisking together 1 tablespoon cornstarch and water. Set aside.

2. In a small saucepan over medium heat, combine rice vinegar, ketchup, pineapple juice, sugar, and soy sauce. Cook 3 minutes, stirring continuously. Add cornstarch slurry and heat 1 more minute. Set pan away from heat and allow to thicken.

3. In a medium bowl, whisk together egg, flour, and 2 tablespoons cornstarch.

4. Preheat air fryer at 350°F for 3 minutes.

5. Dredge pork cubes in egg batter. Shake off any excess.

6. Add pork in two batches to air fryer basket. Cook 4 minutes. Shake gently. Cook an additional 4 minutes. Check the pork using a meat thermometer to ensure the internal temperature is at least 145°F.

7. Transfer to a bowl. Add sauce and toss until coated. Serve warm.

PER SERVING Calories: 227 | Fat: 4.1 g | Protein: 24.5 g | Sodium: 291 mg | Fiber: 0.3 g | Carbohydrates: 20.5 g | Sugar: 10.7 g

Crispy Teriyaki Pork and Rice

By thinly slicing the pork prior to cooking, you allow the air fryer to give those delicious crispy edges to this succulent meat, which adds another dimension of flavor and texture to this simple dish.

HANDS-ON TIME: 10 minutes
COOK TIME: 17 minutes

INGREDIENTS | SERVES 4

1 pound pork shoulder, trimmed and thinly sliced into thin 1"-long strips

½ cup plus 1 tablespoon teriyaki sauce

2 tablespoons water

1 tablespoon honey

2 cups cooked rice

¼ cup chopped fresh cilantro

1. In a medium bowl, add pork and ½ cup teriyaki sauce. Refrigerate covered 30 minutes.

2. Preheat air fryer at 350°F for 3 minutes. Add water to bottom of air fryer.

3. Place pork in air fryer basket. Cook 5 minutes. Toss. Cook 6 minutes more. Toss. Cook an additional 6 minutes.

4. In a small bowl, whisk together 1 tablespoon teriyaki sauce and honey. Toss cooked pork in sauce.

5. Serve pork over cooked rice and garnish with cilantro.

PER SERVING Calories: 350 | Fat: 13.4 g | Protein: 23.4 g | Sodium: 909 mg | Fiber: 0.4 g | Carbohydrates: 30.1 g | Sugar: 7.5 g

BBQ Pork Bowl

Pork, barbecue sauce, fresh corn, and mashed potatoes—if there is a way to someone's heart through their stomach, these four ingredients combined should do the trick!

HANDS-ON TIME: 15 minutes
COOK TIME: 20 minutes

INGREDIENTS | SERVES 4

1 pound pork shoulder, trimmed and thinly sliced into 1"-long strips

½ cup barbecue sauce of your choice

2 tablespoons water

1 cup corn kernels

2 large Russet potatoes, peeled and diced into ¼" cubes

2 tablespoons butter

¼ cup whole milk

1 teaspoon salt

1 teaspoon freshly ground black pepper

¼ cup chopped fresh parsley

Kitchen Hack: Obtaining Fresh Corn Kernels

Using an angel food or Bundt pan, place corn on its end in the center of the pan. Using a sharp knife, gently cut down the sides of the corn. The kernels will catch in the pan. Afterward, take a butter knife and run it down the cob to get that fresh "milk." That juice adds flavor you don't want to miss.

1. In a medium bowl, add pork and barbecue sauce. Refrigerate covered 30 minutes.

2. Preheat air fryer at 350°F for 3 minutes. Add water to bottom of air fryer.

3. Place pork in air fryer basket. Cook 6 minutes. Toss. Cook 6 minutes more. Add corn and toss. Cook an additional 3 minutes.

4. While pork is cooking, add potatoes to a pot of boiling salted water and cook 4–5 minutes until fork-tender. Drain potatoes and transfer to a medium bowl. Add butter, milk, salt, and pepper. Mash until smooth.

5. Serve pork and corn over mashed potatoes and garnish with fresh parsley.

PER SERVING Calories: 407 | Fat: 19.6 g | Protein: 23.4 g | Sodium: 1,026 mg | Fiber: 2.8 g | Carbohydrates: 32.1 g | Sugar: 9.7 g

Asian Pork Meatballs

Serve these tasty meatballs over rice noodles or lo mein for an Asian play on spaghetti and meatballs! To toss with the noodles, mix up 1 tablespoon soy sauce, 3 minced garlic cloves, ¼ teaspoon coriander, and ¼ teaspoon ground ginger plus 1 teaspoon of honey and 1 teaspoon of hot sauce (sriracha, gochujang, or sambal oelek).

HANDS-ON TIME: 15 minutes
COOK TIME: 16 minutes

INGREDIENTS | SERVES 4

1 pound lean ground pork

1 large egg

1 teaspoon ground ginger

½ teaspoon ground coriander

2 cloves garlic, minced

1 teaspoon soy sauce

¼ cup plain bread crumbs

1 scallion, trimmed and divided, white part finely chopped and green part sliced

1. Preheat air fryer at 350°F for 3 minutes.

2. In a medium bowl, combine pork, egg, ginger, coriander, garlic, soy sauce, bread crumbs, and scallion whites. Form into sixteen meatballs, about 2 tablespoons each.

3. Add eight meatballs to fryer basket and cook 6 minutes. Flip meatballs. Cook an additional 2 minutes. Transfer to a plate. Repeat with remaining meatballs.

4. Serve warm garnished with scallion greens.

PER SERVING Calories: 193 | Fat: 5.6 g | Protein: 26.3 g | Sodium: 204 mg | Fiber: 0.5 g | Carbohydrates: 6.1 g | Sugar: 0.5 g

The Difference Between a Scallion and a Green Onion

If your recipe calls for a scallion but your grocery store only has green onions, don't fret. They are the same thing! However, if for some reason neither are available, feel comfortable substituting ramps (wild leeks), spring onions, or shallots for a reasonable swap.

Spaghetti and Meatballs

Cooking the meatballs in the air fryer basket before coating them with the marinara sauce allows them to get a sear on the exterior before bathing in the aromatic marinara! Top with grated Parmesan cheese and fresh parsley, and there will be no confusion why this is a staple on so many family tables.

HANDS-ON TIME: 15 minutes
COOK TIME: 16 minutes

INGREDIENTS | SERVES 4

1 pound dry spaghetti
1 pound ground pork
1 large egg
¼ cup chopped fresh basil
2 cloves garlic, minced
½ teaspoon salt
¼ cup plain bread crumbs
2 cups marinara sauce
4 tablespoons grated Parmesan cheese
¼ cup chopped fresh parsley

Different Kinds of Pork Sausage

This recipe calls for ground pork, which is sold loose in most grocery stores. However, right next to it, you'll usually see mild Italian sausage or hot Italian sausage. These are both seasoned pork sausage, which, for this recipe, would work great. Chorizo, a Mexican-seasoned pork sausage, probably wouldn't be a first choice for this Italian dish, but go for it; it can be your new fusion creation!

1. Cook spaghetti noodles according to box directions.

2. Preheat air fryer at 350°F for 3 minutes.

3. In a medium bowl, combine pork, egg, basil, garlic, salt, and bread crumbs. Form into sixteen meatballs, about 2 tablespoons each.

4. Add eight meatballs to fryer basket and cook 6 minutes. Transfer to cake barrel (accessory). Repeat with remaining eight meatballs. Pour marinara sauce over meatballs. Place cake barrel with all the meatballs in air fryer basket. Cook an additional 4 minutes.

5. Distribute spaghetti evenly among four bowls. Top each with meatballs and sauce. Garnish with Parmesan cheese and fresh parsley. Serve warm.

PER SERVING Calories: 665 | Fat: 8.6 g | Protein: 43.4 g | Sodium: 797 mg | Fiber: 5.3 g | Carbohydrates: 96.1 g | Sugar: 7.2 g

Pork Lettuce Cups

This seems like a long list of ingredients, but once you make this recipe, you'll want to make it over and over again. You'll just have to replenish the fresh ingredients each time. The bottled ingredients will be on hand already!

HANDS-ON TIME: 10 minutes
COOK TIME: 40 minutes

INGREDIENTS | SERVES 6

½ cup rice vinegar

¼ cup sugar

Pinch salt

1 large carrot, peeled and julienned

1 medium English cucumber, peeled and diced

1 scallion, trimmed and diced

1 (2-pound) boneless pork loin roast

1 teaspoon salt

½ teaspoon freshly ground black pepper

¼ cup soy sauce

2 tablespoons honey

1 tablespoon sriracha

2 teaspoons fish sauce

1 teaspoon ground ginger

1 teaspoon ground white pepper

12 Bibb lettuce leaves

½ cup chopped fresh basil

Substitutions for Bibb Lettuce

Bibb lettuce is simply a suggestion for these lettuce cups. Iceberg can be used for added crunch. Butter lettuce and green-leaf lettuce are also popular varieties. And, if you are serving this as an appetizer, consider filling the thick end of endive leaves. They are sturdy and smaller bites for your guests to manage.

1. In a medium bowl, whisk together vinegar, sugar, and salt. Add carrot, cucumber, and scallion. Toss to coat and refrigerate covered until ready to use.

2. Preheat air fryer at 350°F for 3 minutes.

3. Season roast with salt and black pepper.

4. Place pork in air fryer basket. Cook 20 minutes. Flip. Cook 20 minutes more. The internal temperature should be at least 145°F when checked with a meat thermometer.

5. Let pork rest on a cutting board 5 minutes, then shred pork using two forks.

6. In a large bowl, whisk together soy sauce, honey, sriracha, fish sauce, ginger, and white pepper. Add in sliced pork and toss to fully coat.

7. Assemble lettuce cups by adding an equal portions of coated pork to the center of each lettuce leaf. Top with vegetable mixture and garnish with fresh basil.

PER SERVING Calories: 349 | Fat: 17.2 g | Protein: 29.2 g | Sodium: 1,286 mg | Fiber: 1.1 g | Carbohydrates: 14.0 g | Sugar: 11.7 g

Berbere Country Pork Ribs

The beautiful Ethiopian spices of berbere combine so well with the sweet maple syrup and citric orange juice, balancing the flavor of these country pork ribs. And the air fryer does its job in a big way by cooking these to delicious perfection.

HANDS-ON TIME: 10 minutes
COOK TIME: 40 minutes

INGREDIENTS | SERVES 4

1 tablespoon berbere seasoning
1 teaspoon salt
2 pounds country-style pork ribs
2 tablespoons water
½ cup freshly squeezed orange juice
1 tablespoon maple syrup

What Are Country-Style Pork Ribs?

Are you ready to be confused? Here we go. So, country-style pork ribs aren't actually cut from the ribs. They come from the end of the pork shoulder, which, interestingly enough, is also referred to as pork butt! Regardless, these boneless, delicious, fatty "ribs" are so, so very tender and worth a try.

1. Massage berbere seasoning and salt into ribs.

2. Preheat air fryer at 350°F for 3 minutes. Add water to bottom of air fryer.

3. Add pork to air fryer basket. Cook 40 minutes, flipping every 10 minutes.

4. In a large bowl, whisk together orange juice and maple syrup. Add cooked ribs and toss. Serve warm.

PER SERVING Calories: 421 | Fat: 23.5 g | Protein: 38.3 g | Sodium: 977 mg | Fiber: 0.1 g | Carbohydrates: 7.4 g | Sugar: 5.6 g

Hawaiian Spam Tacos with Pineapple Salsa

Your guests will be screaming "Mahalo"—"thank you"—for cooking up this homage to the beautiful islands. Hawaii consumes more Spam than any other US state does, and the Pineapple Salsa is just a tasty nod to the islands' symbol, the pineapple, or hala kahiki.

HANDS-ON TIME: 15 minutes
COOK TIME: 7 minutes

INGREDIENTS | SERVES 2

Pineapple Salsa

1 cup diced pineapple, fresh or canned

½ cup fresh lime juice

1 tablespoon fresh lime zest

2 medium Roma tomatoes, seeded and diced

¼ cup finely diced red onion

1 medium avocado, peeled, pitted, and diced

¼ cup chopped fresh cilantro

¼ cup chopped fresh mint

1 teaspoon sea salt

Other Taco Ingredients

1 (12-ounce) can Spam

1 cup coleslaw mix (shredded cabbage and carrots)

Sriracha Mayonnaise (see Chapter 15)

6 (6") flour tortillas

1. In a medium bowl, combine salsa ingredients and refrigerate covered until ready to use.

2. Preheat air fryer at 375°F for 3 minutes.

3. Slice Spam into ¼" fries. Place in air fryer basket and cook 3 minutes. Flip fries. Cook an additional 4 minutes. Transfer to a plate.

4. Build tacos by adding Spam, coleslaw mix, Pineapple Salsa, and a squeeze of Sriracha Mayonnaise to the flour tortillas. Fold each taco in half to serve.

PER SERVING Calories: 1,202 | Fat: 68.8 g | Protein: 38.3 g | Sodium: 4,520 mg | Fiber: 14.4 g | Carbohydrates: 111.9 g | Sugar: 20.2 g

Beer Bratwurst

This German classic just clamors to be served with your favorite potato dish and a little spicy mustard to drag your bratwurst through. If you are opposed to using beer in this recipe, substitute beef broth and a dash or two of Worcestershire sauce. It will be equally as delicious!

HANDS-ON TIME: 15 minutes
COOK TIME: 21 minutes

INGREDIENTS | SERVES 4

1 pound uncooked pork bratwurst

1 (12-ounce) bottle or can of beer

2 cups water

½ medium yellow onion, peeled and sliced

1. Pierce each bratwurst two times with the tines of a fork. Add to a medium saucepan with beer, water, and onion. Bring to a boil. Reduce heat and simmer 15 minutes. Drain.

2. Preheat air fryer at 400°F for 3 minutes.

3. Place bratwurst and onions in fryer basket. Cook 3 minutes. Flip and cook an additional 3 minutes. Check with a meat thermometer to ensure an internal temperature of 160°F.

4. Transfer bratwurst and onions to a plate and serve warm.

PER SERVING Calories: 309 | Fat: 24.8 g | Protein: 12.6 g | Sodium: 767 mg | Fiber: 0.2 g | Carbohydrates: 4.0 g | Sugar: 0.6 g

Italian Sausage–Stuffed Large Portabellas

Don't skip the marinating stage; it tenderizes the mushrooms and also lends flavor and moisture. Also, choose your heat preference on the Italian sausage; it is sold both as mild and spicy hot.

HANDS-ON TIME: 15 minutes
COOK TIME: 17 minutes

INGREDIENTS | SERVES 2

½ cup balsamic vinaigrette

2 large portabella mushroom caps, stems removed and black gills scraped out

⅓ pound Italian sausage, loose or removed from casings

2 tablespoons minced yellow onion

2 tablespoons marinara sauce

Pinch salt

⅓ cup ricotta cheese

⅓ cup shredded mozzarella cheese

2 tablespoons panko bread crumbs

2 teaspoons melted butter

Why Do You Scrape the Black Gills from Large Portabella Caps?

Although edible, the black gills tend to hide dirt or sand, which can lend a gritty texture to your meal. Also, they can turn your sauce or filling into a murky brown, which can appear unappetizing.

1. In a large plastic resealable bag, add balsamic vinaigrette and cleaned mushroom caps. Seal and refrigerate 30 minutes.

2. While mushrooms are marinating, cook sausage and onions in a medium skillet over medium-high heat 4–5 minutes until sausage is no longer pink. Remove from heat and drain excess grease.

3. Transfer sausage mixture to a medium bowl. Add marinara sauce, salt, ricotta cheese, and mozzarella cheese.

4. Preheat air fryer at 350°F for 3 minutes.

5. Place mushrooms in a strainer to remove excess vinaigrette. Divide sausage mixture between the mushroom caps. Top with panko bread crumbs and drizzle melted butter over bread crumbs.

6. Place stuffed mushrooms (one at a time) in air fryer and cook 6 minutes each.

7. Transfer to a plate and serve warm.

PER SERVING Calories: 454 | Fat: 29.3 g | Protein: 26.1 g | Sodium: 1,588 mg | Fiber: 3.7 g | Carbohydrates: 26.7 g | Sugar: 11.9 g

Greek Lamb Burgers

These are a fun twist on the classic American burger. The ground lamb is mixed with traditional Greek flavors, such as red onion, garlic, mint, dill, and olives.

HANDS-ON TIME: 10 minutes
COOK TIME: 24 minutes

INGREDIENTS | SERVES 4

1 pound ground lamb
2 tablespoons minced red onion
1 tablespoon minced Kalamata olives
2 cloves garlic, minced
1 large egg white
¼ cup panko bread crumbs
2 teaspoons dried mint
2 teaspoons dried dill
Pinch salt
4 thick slices large tomato

1. Preheat air fryer at 350°F for 3 minutes.

2. In a medium bowl, combine lamb, onion, olives, garlic, egg white, bread crumbs, mint, dill, and salt. Form into four patties, making a slight indentation in the middle of each patty.

3. Add two patties to lightly greased fryer basket and cook 6 minutes. Flip burgers and cook an additional 6 minutes or until desired doneness when checked with a meat thermometer. Repeat with remaining burgers.

4. Transfer to a plate and serve warm with a thick slice of tomato on each burger.

PER SERVING Calories: 294 | Fat: 16.9 g | Protein: 23.6 g | Sodium: 167 mg | Fiber: 0.6 g | Carbohydrates: 7.5 g | Sugar: 1.2 g

Moroccan Lamb Pizza

Talk about a twist! The tahini on this unique pizza acts as the sauce. Topped with Moroccan-spiced lamb, pine nuts, and fresh herbs, your taste buds will be working overtime. The creamy goat cheese is mild enough to let all of those flavors shine.

HANDS-ON TIME: 15 minutes
COOK TIME: 39 minutes

INGREDIENTS | YIELDS 2 PERSONAL PIZZAS

¼ pound ground lamb
½ medium red onion, peeled and diced
2 cloves garlic, minced
½ teaspoon ground cardamom
½ teaspoon ground ginger
¼ teaspoon ground cinnamon
4 tablespoons tahini
1 tablespoon lemon juice
½ teaspoon salt
½ pound fresh pizza dough (about the size of a tennis ball)
½ cup crumbled goat cheese
2 tablespoons chopped fresh mint
2 tablespoons chopped fresh parsley
2 teaspoons pine nuts

1. In a medium skillet over medium-high heat, stir-fry lamb, onion, garlic, cardamom, ginger, and cinnamon. Cook 4–5 minutes until lamb is browned. Set aside.

2. In a small bowl, combine tahini, lemon juice, and salt. Set aside.

3. Preheat air fryer at 200°F for 6 minutes.

4. Press out half of dough to fit pizza pan (accessory). Cook 7 minutes.

5. Turn up heat to 275°F.

6. Remove basket and spread half of tahini mixture over dough, leaving a ¼" outer crust uncovered. Add half of lamb mixture. Cook an additional 10 minutes.

7. Gently transfer pizza to a cutting board. Add half of goat cheese, mint, parsley, and pine nuts.

8. Repeat making pizza with remaining ingredients. Serve warm.

PER SERVING Calories: 824 | Fat: 44.1 g | Protein: 37.8 g | Sodium: 1,550 mg | Fiber: 5.8 g | Carbohydrates: 66.4 g | Sugar: 8.7 g

Garlic-Rosemary Lamb Loin Chops

There is no need to overcomplicate these little lamb chops, as they are so flavorful.

HANDS-ON TIME: 5 minutes
COOK TIME: 9 minutes

INGREDIENTS | SERVES 3

¼ cup olive oil

2 teaspoons lemon juice

4 cloves garlic, minced

1 teaspoon salt

¼ teaspoon freshly ground black pepper

4 sprigs fresh rosemary

3 lamb loin chops, each approximately 1" thick (about 1 pound total)

Fresh Lemon Juice versus Lemon Juice in Plastic Lemons

So let's say it all together: fresh is *always* the best choice. As with anything on a shelf, bottled lemon juice is going to have preservatives. Case in point, here are the ingredients in one of those plastic lemon bottles: lemon juice from concentrate (water, concentrated lemon juice), sodium benzoate, sodium metabisulfite, sodium sulfite (preservatives), and lemon oil. The other drawback of plastic lemons is that they don't have any zest.

1. In a shallow dish, whisk together oil, lemon juice, garlic, salt, and pepper. Add rosemary sprigs and lamb. Refrigerate covered 30 minutes.

2. Preheat air fryer at 375°F for 3 minutes.

3. Add lamb chops to fryer basket and cook 5 minutes. Flip chops and cook an additional 4 minutes. Use a meat thermometer to ensure that the meat is at least 130°F.

4. Transfer to a cutting board and let rest 5 minutes. Serve warm.

PER SERVING Calories: 417 | Fat: 24.6 g | Protein: 41.0 g | Sodium: 695 mg | Fiber: 0.1 g | Carbohydrates: 1.3 g | Sugar: 0.1 g

Rack of Lamb with Mint Pesto

Fresh pesto can make anything taste good. And this minty variation on the classic basil pesto pairs naturally with a fancy rack of lamb. This dish is guest-worthy if you are trying to impress and sexy enough for a dinner for two.

HANDS-ON TIME: 10 minutes
COOK TIME: 25 minutes

INGREDIENTS | SERVES 2

1½ cups fresh parsley

1½ cups fresh mint leaves

⅓ cup pine nuts

4 cloves garlic, halved

¾ cup freshly grated Parmesan cheese

3–4 tablespoons olive oil

Pinch salt

1 (8-rib) Frenched rack of lamb (about 1½ pounds)

½ teaspoon salt

½ teaspoon freshly ground black pepper

What Is a Frenched Rack of Lamb?

Frenching a rack of lamb is simply removing that fat and cartilage from the small end of the rib bones. It creates a more visually appealing look to your final product. It is pretty easy to do on your own, especially with the assistance of a *YouTube* video, but just ask your butcher. He or she would be happy to clean up your lamb.

1. In a food processor, pulse parsley, mint, and pine nuts. Add garlic, Parmesan cheese, and 1 tablespoon olive oil. Pulse again. Slowly add remaining oil until desired consistency. Add a pinch salt. Transfer to a jar and refrigerate. Pesto can be made the night before.

2. Season lamb with salt and pepper.

3. Preheat air fryer at 250°F for 3 minutes.

4. Add lamb to fryer basket and cook 20 minutes. Increase temperature to 400°F and cook an additional 5 minutes. Use a meat thermometer to ensure that the meat is at least 120°F.

5. Transfer lamb to a cutting board, wrap in aluminum foil, and let rest 10 minutes, which will increase the temperature to 125°F–130°F, yielding a medium-rare cook.

6. Slice between the ribs and serve warm with mint pesto.

PER SERVING Calories: 1,310 | Fat: 99.7 g | Protein: 67.4 g | Sodium: 1,532 mg | Fiber: 4.1 g | Carbohydrates: 16.2 g | Sugar: 1.3 g

CHAPTER 9

Fish and Seafood Main Dishes

Buffalo-Style Fried Oysters

If you didn't think anything else could be coated in buffalo sauce, then you thought wrong. Choose your heat level with your favorite bottled buffalo sauce and then sit back and enjoy!

HANDS-ON TIME: 10 minutes
COOK TIME: 16 minutes

INGREDIENTS | SERVES 2

½ pound raw oysters, excluding shells
½ cup all-purpose flour
½ cup bottled buffalo sauce
1 cup panko bread crumbs, crushed fine
½ teaspoon salt, divided

Freshly Shucked Oysters

If you want fresh oysters but don't want the hassle of shucking them yourself, ask your fishmonger to do it for you. It is usually a free service that they will do for you while you finish shopping.

1. Rinse and drain oysters. Pat dry with a paper towel. Set aside.

2. Add flour to a small bowl. Add buffalo sauce to another small bowl. Add bread crumbs to a shallow dish.

3. Preheat air fryer at 400°F for 3 minutes.

4. Roll oysters in flour. Shake off excess flour. Dredge oysters in buffalo sauce. Shake off excess sauce. Roll in bread crumbs. Remove to a plate.

5. Add half of oysters to fryer basket. Cook 4 minutes. Carefully flip oysters. Cook an additional 4 minutes.

6. Transfer oysters from basket to a serving plate. Sprinkle with half of the salt. Cook remaining oysters.

7. Transfer to the serving plate and sprinkle with remaining salt. Serve warm.

PER SERVING Calories: 291 | Fat: 4.7 g | Protein: 24.6 g | Sodium: 1,332 mg | Fiber: 0.4 g | Carbohydrates: 33.2 g | Sugar: 0.5 g

Parmesan Fish Sticks

Cod and pollack are the typical fishes used in traditional fish sticks. But when making this recipe, feel free to try salmon, sea bass, or other firm, flaky fish that is fresh at your seafood counter. Serve these fish sticks with your favorite dipping sauce.

HANDS-ON TIME: 10 minutes
COOK TIME: 20 minutes

INGREDIENTS | SERVES 4

½ cup all-purpose flour
1 large egg, whisked
½ cup panko bread crumbs, crushed fine
½ cup grated Parmesan cheese
1 pound cod, cut into 1" sticks

Parmesan Cheese—Fresh or Grated?

There really isn't a huge taste difference between the cheese found in the green shakers and the hunks of cheese you grate yourself. The big difference is in how you use it. With the fresh chunk of cheese, you are able to either grate it on some meals or use a vegetable slicer to peel slices for other meals. Pasta and salads are lovely places to showcase those beautiful Parmesan cheese curls.

1. Add flour to a small bowl. Add egg to another small bowl. Add bread crumbs and Parmesan cheese to a shallow dish.

2. Preheat air fryer at 350°F for 3 minutes.

3. Roll fish sticks in flour. Shake off excess flour. Dip in whisked egg. Shake off excess egg. Roll in bread crumb mixture. Remove to a plate.

4. Add half of fish sticks to fryer basket. Cook 5 minutes. Carefully flip fish sticks. Cook an additional 5 minutes. Repeat with remaining fish.

5. Transfer fish sticks to a serving plate and serve warm.

PER SERVING Calories: 160 | Fat: 2.4 g | Protein: 20.7 g | Sodium: 468 mg | Fiber: 0.2 g | Carbohydrates: 11.9 g | Sugar: 0.3 g

Crab-Stuffed Mushrooms

As a full meal, side dish, or appetizer, these scrumptious and creamy Crab-Stuffed Mushrooms have a nice crunch from the bread crumb topping made crisp in the air fryer.

HANDS-ON TIME: 10 minutes
COOK TIME: 20 minutes

INGREDIENTS | SERVES 6

2 ounces cream cheese, at room temperature

½ cup lump crabmeat, picked over and any shells discarded

1 teaspoon prepared horseradish

1 teaspoon lemon juice

½ teaspoon salt

½ teaspoon freshly ground black pepper

16 ounces baby bella (cremini) mushrooms, stems removed

2 tablespoons panko bread crumbs

2 tablespoons butter, melted

¼ cup chopped fresh parsley

1. In a medium bowl, combine cream cheese, crabmeat, horseradish, lemon juice, salt, and pepper.

2. Preheat air fryer at 350°F for 5 minutes.

3. Evenly stuff cream cheese mixture into mushroom caps. Distribute bread crumbs over stuffed mushrooms. Drizzle melted butter over bread crumbs.

4. Place half of mushrooms in fryer basket. Cook 10 minutes. Transfer to serving plate. Repeat with remaining mushrooms.

5. Garnish with chopped parsley. Serve warm.

PER SERVING Calories: 101 | Fat: 6.6 g | Protein: 4.9 g | Sodium: 305 mg | Fiber: 0.6 g | Carbohydrates: 5.7 g | Sugar: 1.8 g

Should You Discard the Mushroom Stems?

Don't throw away those mushroom stems! Clean and dice them and place in a lidded container and refrigerate. These healthy stems, which are usually discarded, are ideal additions to soups, broths, frittatas, sauces, and even to nutritious green smoothies in the morning.

Crab Cakes

For a fancy brunch, top these crab delicacies with a poached egg and silky hollandaise sauce and delight in your eggs Benedict upgrade! Or serve with your preferred dipping sauce.

HANDS-ON TIME: 15 minutes
COOK TIME: 10 minutes

INGREDIENTS | SERVES 4

1 pound lump crabmeat, picked over and any shells discarded

⅓ cup mayonnaise

1 teaspoon Dijon mustard

1 teaspoon lemon juice

1 tablespoon minced yellow onion

½ cup crushed Ritz crackers

2 tablespoons chopped fresh parsley

1 large egg

1 teaspoon Old Bay Seasoning

Pinch salt

1. In a medium bowl, carefully combine crabmeat, mayonnaise, mustard, lemon juice, onion, cracker crumbs, parsley, egg, Old Bay Seasoning, and salt. Form mixture into eight patties.

2. Preheat air fryer at 400°F for 3 minutes.

3. Place patties in lightly greased air fryer basket. Cook 5 minutes. Flip crab cakes. Cook an additional 5 minutes.

4. Transfer to a serving dish and let rest 5 minutes before serving warm.

PER SERVING Calories: 289 | Fat: 17.5 g | Protein: 22.9 g | Sodium: 1,068 mg | Fiber: 0.3 g | Carbohydrates: 7.0 g | Sugar: 1.1 g

Choosing Crabmeat

Fresh lump crabmeat is the best option for this recipe—but it can be pricey. Fortunately, there are many different varieties and sections of the crab that can be purchased at a lower price point. Crab is even sold in cans like the more familiar tuna. Although there is imitation "krab" available, draw the line at that. It is stringy and packed with starch and chemicals.

Curried Shrimp Cakes

When choosing shrimp for these cakes don't worry about the size of the shrimp, because they will be finely chopped. So choose based on freshness and make sure they weigh out to a pound. Thawed frozen shrimp is also an option.

HANDS-ON TIME: 15 minutes
COOK TIME: 20 minutes

INGREDIENTS | SERVES 4

1 pound raw shrimp, peeled, deveined, and finely chopped

¼ cup seeded and finely diced red bell pepper

1 tablespoon red curry paste

3 cloves garlic, minced

1 teaspoon lime juice

1 tablespoon minced shallot

½ cup panko bread crumbs

1 large egg

2 tablespoons mayonnaise

1 teaspoon grated fresh ginger

Pinch salt

1 cup diced fresh mango, peeled

¼ cup chopped fresh Thai basil (or regular basil)

1 large lime, cut into 8 wedges

1. In a medium bowl, combine shrimp, bell pepper, curry, garlic, lime juice, shallot, bread crumbs, egg, mayonnaise, ginger, and salt. Form into eight shrimp cakes.

2. Preheat air fryer at 400°F for 3 minutes.

3. Place four shrimp cakes in lightly greased air fryer basket. Cook 5 minutes. Flip shrimp cakes. Cook an additional 5 minutes. Repeat with remaining cakes.

4. Transfer to a serving plate. Garnish with diced mango and chopped basil. Serve warm with lime wedges.

PER SERVING Calories: 233 | Fat: 7.7 g | Protein: 19.5 g | Sodium: 870 mg | Fiber: 1.1 g | Carbohydrates: 20.1 g | Sugar: 7.0 g

What Is Thai Basil?

Thai basil has a purple stem and is stronger in flavor than the traditional Italian basil found in most grocery stores simply labeled "basil." Although some stores carry Thai basil, you can definitely find it at your local Asian market. The varieties have different taste and aroma profiles, and some chefs say they are interchangeable in a recipe. Some chefs actually advise to substitute with mint. To clear up that argument, a mix of both is also a great option.

Salmon Patties with Apple Salsa

This recipe calls for canned salmon for ease; however, leftover cooked salmon or freshly cooked salmon flaked into pieces are perfectly viable options.

HANDS-ON TIME: 20 minutes
COOK TIME: 10 minutes

INGREDIENTS | SERVES 4

Apple Salsa

½ cup diced red onion

½ cup seeded and diced red bell pepper

1 small Granny Smith apple, peeled, cored, and diced

1 tablespoon chopped fresh dill

Juice of 1 small lime

Pinch salt

Salmon Patties

1 (14.75-ounce) can wild-caught salmon

½ cup mayonnaise

1 large egg

2 tablespoons seeded and finely minced red bell pepper

½ cup panko bread crumbs

Pinch salt

1. In a small bowl, combine Apple Salsa ingredients. Refrigerate covered until ready to use.

2. In a medium bowl, combine salmon, mayonnaise, egg, bell pepper, bread crumbs, and salt. Form mixture into eight salmon patties.

3. Preheat air fryer at 400°F for 3 minutes.

4. Place in lightly greased air fryer basket. Cook 5 minutes. Flip salmon patties. Cook an additional 5 minutes.

5. Transfer to a serving dish and let rest 5 minutes before serving warm with Apple Salsa.

PER SERVING Calories: 483 | Fat: 27.6 g | Protein: 36.6 g | Sodium: 771 mg | Fiber: 1.4 g | Carbohydrates: 18.5 g | Sugar: 5.9 g

There Are Bones in My Canned Salmon!

Although you have to spend time picking shells out of canned crabmeat, the bones in canned salmon are a different thing altogether. The cooking and canning process makes these bones soft and edible, and they are an excellent source of calcium. This same theory goes for sardines. You eat the whole fish, right? You can also eat the bones in canned salmon.

Fried Sardines

There's no need for an egg dip with this breading, as the olive oil gives enough slickness for the bread crumbs to adhere. For a flavor boost, purchase sardines already marinated in mustard or marinara sauce, then follow this recipe per usual!

HANDS-ON TIME: 5 minutes
COOK TIME: 6 minutes

INGREDIENTS | SERVES 2

½ cup panko bread crumbs

2 (3.75-ounce) cans skinless, boneless sardines in pure olive oil, drained

2 lemon wedges

Why You Should Give Sardines a Try

You either love sardines or you are like most of America and don't. To some, they just seem weird. But, seriously, sardines are amazing and are packed with nutrition. Plus, breading them and giving them a whirl in the air fryer takes some of the visual scary away. Sardines are not only tasty but also loaded with omega-3 fatty acids, vitamin D, protein, and selenium. And as a bonus they are economical and low in mercury and other metals.

1. Preheat air fryer at 350°F for 3 minutes.

2. Place bread crumbs in a shallow dish. Roll sardines to coat with bread crumbs.

3. Place in lightly greased air fryer basket. Cook 3 minutes. Gently flip sardines and cook an additional 3 minutes.

4. Serve warm with lemon wedges.

PER SERVING Calories: 244 | Fat: 12.3 g | Protein: 18.5 g | Sodium: 354 mg | Fiber: 0.0 g | Carbohydrates: 15.0 g | Sugar: 0.8 g

Seared Sea Scallops

The convection oven–style of cooking in the air fryer sears these scallops beautifully on all sides. Serve the scallops with steamed asparagus, mashed potatoes, and a drizzle of fresh hollandaise sauce over everything for decadent bites of yummy!

HANDS-ON TIME: 5 minutes
COOK TIME: 8 minutes

INGREDIENTS | SERVES 2

2 tablespoons butter, melted
1 tablespoon fresh lemon juice
1 pound jumbo sea scallops (about 10)

1. Preheat air fryer at 400°F for 3 minutes.

2. In a small bowl, combine butter and lemon juice. Roll scallops in mixture to coat all sides.

3. Place scallops in air fryer basket. Cook 2 minutes. Flip scallops. Cook 2 minutes more. Brush the tops of each scallop with butter mixture. Cook 2 minutes. Flip scallops. Cook an additional 2 minutes.

4. Transfer scallops to a serving plate and serve warm.

PER SERVING Calories: 254 | Fat: 11.4 g | Protein: 28.1 g | Sodium: 909 mg | Fiber: 0.0 g | Carbohydrates: 7.9 g | Sugar: 0.2 g

Breaded Sea Scallops

The crispy coating on your sea scallops will give you a crunchy texture that complements the buttery and soft insides of the scallop. Make sure you choose the larger sea scallops. Bay scallops are small and wouldn't work with this recipe.

HANDS-ON TIME: 5 minutes
COOK TIME: 8 minutes

INGREDIENTS | SERVES 2

1 large egg
2 tablespoons whole milk
¼ cup plain bread crumbs
¼ cup cornmeal
1 tablespoon Old Bay Seasoning
1 pound jumbo sea scallops (about 10)
2 tablespoons butter, melted

1. Preheat air fryer at 400°F for 3 minutes.

2. In a small bowl, whisk together egg and milk.

3. In a shallow dish, combine bread crumbs, cornmeal, and Old Bay Seasoning.

4. Coat scallops in egg mixture and dredge in bread crumb mixture.

5. Place scallops in air fryer basket. Cook 4 minutes. Flip scallops. Brush with melted butter. Cook an additional 4 minutes.

6. Transfer scallops to a plate and serve warm.

PER SERVING Calories: 422 | Fat: 14.9 g | Protein: 34.9 g | Sodium: 1,890 mg | Fiber: 1.4 g | Carbohydrates: 33.6 g | Sugar: 2.0 g

Lobster Tails

If those big lobster tanks at the grocery store give you the heebie-jeebies and prevent you from cooking lobster at home, you're probably not alone. But most grocers sell little tails of 5–6 ounces in the seafood section, which makes handling this elegant meat much easier.

HANDS-ON TIME: 10 minutes
COOK TIME: 8 minutes

INGREDIENTS | SERVES 2

2 (5–6 ounce) small uncooked lobster tails
1 tablespoon butter, melted
½ teaspoon Old Bay Seasoning
1 tablespoon chopped fresh parsley
2 lemon wedges

Making Broth with Lobster Tail Shells

Don't discard those empty lobster tail shells. You can make a beautiful broth for lobster bisque, crab soup, or even a seafood gumbo. Place the shells in a Dutch oven or heavy-bottomed pot with 4 cups water, 1 peeled and diced yellow onion, 1 peeled and diced carrot, 1 diced celery stalk, and 2 peeled, halved garlic cloves. Bring to boil. Reduce heat and simmer covered 30 minutes. Use a slotted spoon to remove and discard the solids from the broth. Strain the remaining liquid through a fine-mesh sieve or cheesecloth. Cover broth and refrigerate up to 4 days or freeze up to 6 months.

1. Using kitchen shears, cut down the middle of each lobster tail on the softer side. Carefully run your finger between the lobster meat and the soft underside of the shell to loosen meat.

2. Preheat air fryer at 400°F for 3 minutes.

3. Place tails in air fryer basket, cut side up. Cook 4 minutes. Brush with butter and sprinkle with Old Bay Seasoning. Cook an additional 3–4 minutes, depending on the size of the lobster tail.

4. Serve warm garnished with parsley and lemon wedges.

PER SERVING Calories: 171 | Fat: 6.4 g | Protein: 25.9 g | Sodium: 800 mg | Fiber: 0.1 g | Carbohydrates: 0.1 g | Sugar: 0.1 g

Cornflake-Crusted Cod

The cornflakes give this fish an unconventional breading, and the horseradish mustard gives it a delightful contrasting sharpness. Serving this dish with a creamy sauce brings it home!

HANDS-ON TIME: 10 minutes
COOK TIME: 10 minutes

INGREDIENTS | SERVES 2

½ cup crushed cornflakes
1 teaspoon dried dill
⅛ teaspoon salt
1 tablespoon horseradish mustard
1 teaspoon lemon juice
1 tablespoon butter, melted
2 (6-ounce) cod fillets

1. In a small bowl, combine cornflakes, dill, salt, mustard, lemon juice, and butter.

2. Preheat air fryer at 350°F for 3 minutes.

3. Press the cornflake mixture evenly across the top of the cod fillets. Place fish in lightly greased air fryer basket.

4. Cook 10 minutes or until fish is opaque and flakes easily with a fork. Cooking times may vary due to size and thickness of fillets.

5. Transfer to serving plates and serve warm.

PER SERVING Calories: 277 | Fat: 6.9 g | Protein: 32.6 g | Sodium: 571 mg | Fiber: 0.7 g | Carbohydrates: 17.9 g | Sugar: 2.0 g

Berbere Salmon Fillets

Berbere is an Ethiopian spice and herb blend that is a little fiery and a lot aromatic, which makes this dish a perfect romantic meal for two. The spice blend can be found in specialty spice shops or online and is great on almost any protein.

HANDS-ON TIME: 5 minutes
COOK TIME: 7 minutes

INGREDIENTS | SERVES 2

1 teaspoon olive oil
2 (6-ounce) salmon fillets, about 1" thick
½ teaspoon berbere seasoning
2 lemon quarters

1. Preheat air fryer at 375°F for 3 minutes.

2. Rub oil over salmon fillets. Sprinkle fillets with berbere seasoning.

3. Place salmon skin side up in air fryer basket. Cook 7 minutes.

4. Transfer to plates and let rest 5 minutes. Garnish with lemon quarters to squeeze over fillets. Serve warm.

PER SERVING Calories: 263 | Fat: 11.7 g | Protein: 33.7 g | Sodium: 132 mg | Fiber: 0.0 g | Carbohydrates: 0.3 g | Sugar: 0.0 g

Baked Halibut with Blood Orange Aioli

Although the more readily available navel orange can be used as a substitute in this recipe, the gorgeous red-fleshed blood orange not only lends color but flavor with its berry undertones.

HANDS-ON TIME: 10 minutes
COOK TIME: 10 minutes

INGREDIENTS | SERVES 2

¼ cup mayonnaise
1 teaspoon Dijon mustard
1 teaspoon fresh blood orange zest
4 teaspoons fresh blood orange juice
¾ teaspoon salt, divided
2 (6-ounce) halibut fillets
½ teaspoon freshly ground black pepper
1 tablespoon chopped fresh chives

1. In a small bowl, whisk together mayonnaise, Dijon mustard, orange zest, orange juice, and ¼ teaspoon salt. Refrigerate covered until ready to use.

2. Preheat air fryer at 350°F for 3 minutes.

3. Season halibut fillets with ½ teaspoon salt and pepper.

4. Place halibut in lightly greased air fryer basket. Cook 10 minutes or until fish is opaque and flakes easily with a fork. Cooking times may vary due to size and thickness of fillets.

5. Transfer to serving plates and serve warm with blood orange aioli. Garnish with chives.

PER SERVING Calories: 352 | Fat: 22.2 g | Protein: 32.2 g | Sodium: 1,224 mg | Fiber: 0.3 g | Carbohydrates: 2.0 g | Sugar: 1.1 g

Macadamia-Crusted Sea Bass
with Horseradish-Lemon Aioli

The buttery and decadent sea bass coupled with the buttery and creamy nature of macadamia nuts makes this a double threat. Served with tangy Horseradish-Lemon Aioli, this dish makes a five-star meal meant for a queen.

HANDS-ON TIME: 10 minutes
COOK TIME: 12 minutes

INGREDIENTS | SERVES 2

2 tablespoons crushed salted macadamia nuts

2 tablespoons panko bread crumbs

1 teaspoon horseradish mustard

1 teaspoon lime juice

1 tablespoon butter, melted

2 (6-ounce) sea bass fillets

2 tablespoons Horseradish-Lemon Aioli (see Chapter 15)

1. In a small bowl, combine macadamia nuts, bread crumbs, mustard, lime juice, and butter.

2. Preheat air fryer at 350°F for 3 minutes.

3. Press the nut mixture evenly across the tops of the sea bass. Place fish in lightly greased air fryer basket.

4. Cook 12 minutes, ensuring that the sea bass is opaque and flakes easily with a fork.

5. Transfer to serving plates and serve warm with Horseradish-Lemon Aioli on the side.

PER SERVING Calories: 367 | Fat: 21.4 g | Protein: 33.1 g | Sodium: 257 mg | Fiber: 0.8 g | Carbohydrates: 6.8 g | Sugar: 0.8 g

Bacon-Wrapped Stuffed Shrimp

Shrimp stuffed with cheese and wrapped in bacon is an irresistible combination.
Make sure you buy the large shrimp for this recipe. The bacon takes longer to
cook than small shrimp, so the end result is better with larger shrimp.

HANDS-ON TIME: 10 minutes
COOK TIME: 18 minutes

INGREDIENTS | SERVES 4

1 pound (about 20) large raw shrimp, deveined and shelled

3 tablespoons crumbled goat cheese

2 tablespoons panko bread crumbs

2 dashes Worcestershire sauce

½ teaspoon prepared horseradish

¼ teaspoon garlic powder

2 teaspoons mayonnaise

¼ teaspoon freshly ground black pepper

2 tablespoons water

5 slices bacon, quartered

¼ cup chopped fresh parsley

1. Butterfly shrimp by cutting down the spine of each shrimp without going all the way through.

2. In a medium bowl, combine goat cheese, bread crumbs, Worcestershire sauce, horseradish, garlic powder, mayonnaise, and pepper.

3. Preheat air fryer at 400°F for 3 minutes. Pour 2 tablespoons water into bottom of air fryer.

4. Evenly press goat cheese mixture into shrimp. Wrap a piece of bacon around each piece of shrimp to hold in cheese mixture.

5. Place half of shrimp in fryer basket. Cook 5 minutes. Flip shrimp. Cook an additional 4 minutes. Transfer to serving plate. Repeat with remaining shrimp.

6. Garnish with chopped parsley. Serve warm.

PER SERVING Calories: 150 | Fat: 8.6 g | Protein: 12.9 g | Sodium: 568 mg | Fiber: 0.4 g | Carbohydrates: 3.7 g | Sugar: 0.3 g

Coconut Shrimp

The simple approach to this recipe highlights the sweetness of the coconut breading and allows the shrimp to shine. Choose a fun dipping sauce to enjoy with this dish.

HANDS-ON TIME: 10 minutes
COOK TIME: 8 minutes

INGREDIENTS | SERVES 2

⅓ cup all-purpose flour
2 tablespoons cornstarch
1 teaspoon salt
¼ cup whole milk
1 large egg
¼ cup panko bread crumbs
½ cup sweetened shredded coconut
½ pound (about 40) medium raw shrimp, tail on, deveined and shelled

1. In a medium bowl, combine flour, cornstarch, and salt.

2. In another medium bowl, whisk together milk and egg.

3. In a shallow dish, combine bread crumbs and coconut.

4. Preheat air fryer at 375°F for 3 minutes.

5. Toss shrimp in flour mixture. Dredge in egg mixture and then dip in bread crumb mixture. Shake off excess at each step.

6. Place shrimp in lightly oiled air fryer basket. Cook 4 minutes. Gently flip shrimp. Cook an additional 4 minutes.

7. Transfer shrimp to a plate and serve warm.

PER SERVING Calories: 410 | Fat: 12.3 g | Protein: 24.8 g | Sodium: 1,978 mg | Fiber: 1.7 g | Carbohydrates: 47.0 g | Sugar: 12.2 g

Tuna Croquettes

When you don't have salmon on hand, open a few cans of tuna for an old-fashioned meal with a modern twist using your air fryer. Creamy and crunchy and filled with nutrition, these Tuna Croquettes are a great lunch or an addition atop a light salad.

HANDS-ON TIME: 15 minutes
COOK TIME: 12 minutes

INGREDIENTS | SERVES 4

3 (5-ounce) cans tuna in water, drained
⅓ cup mayonnaise
1 teaspoon lemon juice
¼ teaspoon Worcestershire sauce
1 tablespoon minced red onion
½ cup crushed panko bread crumbs
2 tablespoons chopped fresh parsley
1 large egg
½ teaspoon ground mustard
Pinch salt
¼ teaspoon freshly ground black pepper
1 medium lime, cut into 6 wedges

1. In a medium bowl, combine tuna, mayonnaise, lemon juice, Worcestershire sauce, onion, bread crumbs, parsley, egg, mustard, salt, and pepper. Form mixture into sixteen croquettes approximately 2 tablespoons each, which are similar to a large potato tot with rounded ends.

2. Preheat air fryer at 400°F for 3 minutes.

3. Place eight croquettes in lightly greased air fryer basket. Cook 3 minutes. Flip croquettes. Cook an additional 3 minutes. Transfer to a serving plate. Repeat with remaining croquettes.

4. Squeeze lime over croquettes. Enjoy warm with preferred sauce.

PER SERVING Calories: 353 | Fat: 21.5 g | Protein: 26.0 g | Sodium: 539 mg | Fiber: 0.2 g | Carbohydrates: 10.9 g | Sugar: 0.9 g

Beer-Battered Calamari Rings

Calamari can be found in the frozen section of your store, sometimes cut into circles; however, fresh squid tubes can usually be purchased at the fish counter and are easy to slice. The flavor of this recipe can be changed simply by swapping out the kind of beer you use. Serve them with your favorite dipping sauce.

HANDS-ON TIME: 15 minutes
COOK TIME: 8 minutes

INGREDIENTS | SERVES 4

½ cup beer
¼ cup all-purpose flour
1 cup panko bread crumbs
1 teaspoon salt
½ teaspoon freshly ground black pepper
⅓ pound (about 6) calamari tubes, cut into 6 rings per tube
¼ cup chopped fresh parsley
1 medium lime, quartered

1. In a small bowl, whisk together beer and flour.

2. In a shallow dish, combine bread crumbs, salt, and pepper.

3. Preheat air fryer at 400°F for 3 minutes.

4. Dredge the calamari rings in beer mixture. Shake off excess. Roll all of the rings through bread crumb mixture.

5. Place half of the calamari rings in lightly greased air fryer basket. Cook 2 minutes. Flip calamari. Cook an additional 2 minutes. Transfer to a serving dish and repeat with remaining calamari.

6. Garnish with parsley and lime quarters.

PER SERVING Calories: 101 | Fat: 0.9 g | Protein: 7.9 g | Sodium: 336 mg | Fiber: 0.3 g | Carbohydrates: 14.6 g | Sugar: 0.5 g

Pesto Tilapia Roulade

Tilapia is a very mild whitefish that is the perfect vessel to showcase the fresh and bright flavors of herbaceous pesto. Topping the roulade with crushed cornflakes adds a layer of texture, making these simple ingredients shine.

HANDS-ON TIME: 15 minutes
COOK TIME: 6 minutes

INGREDIENTS | SERVES 4

4 (5-ounce) tilapia fillets
1 large egg
2 tablespoons water
1 cup crushed cornflakes
1 teaspoon salt
½ teaspoon freshly ground black pepper
4 teaspoons Traditional Pesto (see Chapter 15)
2 tablespoons butter, melted
4 lime wedges

1. Between two pieces of parchment paper, gently pound tilapia fillets until "rollable," about ¼" thickness.

2. In a small bowl, whisk together egg and water.

3. In a shallow dish, combine cornflakes, salt, and pepper.

4. Preheat air fryer at 350°F for 3 minutes.

5. Spread 1 teaspoon pesto on each fish fillet. Tightly and gently roll a fillet from one short end to the other. Secure with a toothpick. Repeat with each fillet.

6. Roll each fillet in egg mixture and dredge in cornflake mixture.

7. Place fish in lightly greased air fryer basket. Drizzle tops with melted butter. Cook 6 minutes.

8. Transfer to a serving dish and let rest 5 minutes. Remove toothpicks. Serve warm with lime wedges.

PER SERVING Calories: 226 | Fat: 10.1 g | Protein: 31.2 g | Sodium: 499 mg | Fiber: 0.5 g | Carbohydrates: 8.4 g | Sugar: 0.9 g

Crab-Stuffed Sole Roulade

This mouthwatering and succulent Crab-Stuffed Sole Roulade is a beautiful dish to serve when entertaining. Plus, let's be honest, crab is dreamy in anything you serve!

HANDS-ON TIME: 15 minutes
COOK TIME: 6 minutes

INGREDIENTS | SERVES 4

4 (5-ounce) sole fillets
½ cup lump crabmeat, picked over and any shells discarded
2 teaspoons mayonnaise
1 teaspoon horseradish mustard
½ teaspoon chopped fresh dill
1 large egg
2 tablespoons water
1 cup panko bread crumbs
1 teaspoon salt
½ teaspoon freshly ground black pepper
2 tablespoons butter, melted
4 lime wedges

1. Between two pieces of parchment paper, gently pound sole fillets until "rollable," about ¼" thickness.

2. In a small bowl, combine crab, mayonnaise, horseradish mustard, and dill.

3. In a separate small bowl, whisk together egg and water.

4. In a shallow dish, combine bread crumbs, salt, and pepper.

5. Preheat air fryer at 350°F for 3 minutes.

6. Divide crab mixture among fillets and spread evenly. Tightly and gently roll a fillet from one short end to the other. Secure with a toothpick. Repeat with each fillet.

7. Roll each fillet in egg mixture and dredge in bread crumb mixture.

8. Place fish in lightly greased air fryer basket. Drizzle tops with melted butter. Cook 6 minutes.

9. Transfer to a serving dish and let rest 5 minutes. Remove toothpicks. Serve warm with lime wedges.

PER SERVING Calories: 241 | Fat: 10.2 g | Protein: 23.1 g | Sodium: 888 mg | Fiber: 0.1 g | Carbohydrates: 10.3 g | Sugar: 0.5 g

CHAPTER 10

Vegetarian and Vegan Dishes

Tofu Buddha Bowl

Buddha bowls are all the rage these days. Packed with vegetables, beans, tofu, quinoa, and arugula, this bowl is overflowing with flavors, texture, and nutrition. The heartiness of the ingredients will ensure that you stay full and satisfied for many hours.

HANDS-ON TIME: 15 minutes
COOK TIME: 16 minutes

INGREDIENTS | SERVES 4

½ small yellow onion, peeled and sliced

1 cup peeled, diced sweet potato (¼" cubes)

1 teaspoon avocado oil

8 ounces extra-firm tofu, cut into ¼" cubes

1 cup canned chickpeas, drained and rinsed

½ teaspoon five spice powder

½ teaspoon chili powder

¼ teaspoon salt

2 teaspoons fresh lime zest

1 cup cooked quinoa

2 cups arugula

2 medium carrots, peeled and shredded

1 medium avocado, peeled, pitted, and diced

1. In a medium bowl, combine onion, sweet potato, and avocado oil.

2. In another bowl, combine tofu, chickpeas, five spice powder, chili powder, and salt.

3. Preheat air fryer at 350°F for 3 minutes.

4. Place onion mixture into lightly greased air fryer basket. Cook 8 minutes. Add tofu mixture to onion mixture. Stir. Cook an additional 8 minutes.

5. Stir lime zest into cooked quinoa.

6. Prepare four Buddha bowls by evenly distributing arugula, carrots, avocado, quinoa, and tofu mixture among the bowls. Serve immediately.

PER SERVING Calories: 252 | Fat: 8.3 g | Protein: 10.8 g | Sodium: 308 mg | Fiber: 8.3 g | Carbohydrates: 33.6 g | Sugar: 6.0 g

Why Is It Called a Buddha Bowl?

These nutritious bowls of goodness are described in the *Urban Dictionary* as "a bowl which is packed so full that it has a rounded 'belly' appearance on the top much like the belly of a Buddha." There are many versions but they are usually heavy on vegetables and served with a grain, such as quinoa or rice. Although these bowls are mostly seen in vegan and vegetarian circles, meat doesn't necessarily have to be excluded for those who indulge.

Tofu Tikka Masala over Turmeric Rice

Tikka masala is a gorgeous purée of tomatoes, cream, and spices such as cinnamon, cardamom, nutmeg, coriander, peppercorns, and more. The tofu takes on these flavors and adds protein.

HANDS-ON TIME: 15 minutes
COOK TIME: 24 minutes

INGREDIENTS | SERVES 2

8 ounces extra-firm tofu, cut into ¼" cubes

½ medium yellow onion, peeled and thinly sliced

½ cup jarred tikka masala, divided

1 teaspoon coconut oil

2 cloves garlic, minced

2 teaspoons ground turmeric

½ cup basmati rice

1 cup vegetable broth

¼ cup chopped fresh cilantro

Turmeric 101

Turmeric is the main ingredient in several Indian curry dishes, but it is also what gives that yellow Spanish rice its beautiful golden hue. This aromatic spice filled with notes of ginger and citrus adds a depth of flavor to many dishes. Its original form is a root, which can be handled similarly to ginger-root. Turmeric is said to stimulate digestion, reduce inflammation, and even help boost brain health.

1. In a medium bowl, combine cubed tofu, onion, and ¼ cup tikka masala. Toss to coat.

2. In a medium saucepan, heat coconut oil over medium heat until melted. Add garlic and sauté 1 minute. Add turmeric, rice, and broth. Bring to a boil. Reduce heat and simmer covered 15 minutes.

3. Preheat air fryer at 350°F for 3 minutes.

4. Place tofu mixture into air fryer basket. Cook 4 minutes. Shake. Cook an additional 4 minutes. Transfer to a medium bowl and toss with remaining ¼ cup tikka masala.

5. Spoon rice into two bowls. Top with tofu. Garnish with cilantro and serve warm.

PER SERVING Calories: 346 | Fat: 8.9 g | Protein: 13.5 g | Sodium: 550 mg | Fiber: 3.5 g | Carbohydrates: 51.9 g | Sugar: 5.5 g

Rice Bowl with Cauliflower and Tahini Aioli

This complex bowl of flavor contains rice mixed with wilted spinach leaves and topped with seasoned air-fried cauliflower florets. A drizzle of the Tahini Aioli ties everything together.

HANDS-ON TIME: 15 minutes
COOK TIME: 8 minutes

INGREDIENTS | SERVES 4

Tahini Aioli

¼ cup tahini

2 tablespoons Veganaise

1 teaspoon dried cilantro

1 tablespoon tamari

½ teaspoon honey

2 teaspoons lime juice

Rice Bowl

4 cups cauliflower florets (about 1 small head)

1 tablespoon coconut oil, melted

1 tablespoon ground turmeric

¼ teaspoon salt

¼ teaspoon ground white pepper

Pinch cayenne pepper

Pinch ground cinnamon

2 cloves garlic, minced

4 cups cooked rice

2 cups baby spinach

1. In a medium bowl, whisk together Tahini Aioli ingredients. Refrigerate covered until ready to use.

2. Add cauliflower florets to a large bowl. Toss with coconut oil, turmeric, salt, white pepper, cayenne pepper, ground cinnamon, and garlic until evenly coated.

3. Preheat air fryer at 350°F for 3 minutes.

4. Place cauliflower in air fryer basket. Cook 4 minutes. Toss cauliflower. Cook an additional 4 minutes.

5. Divide rice among four bowls. Add spinach leaves. Top with cooked cauliflower and toss to wilt spinach. Drizzle with Tahini Aioli. Serve immediately.

PER SERVING Calories: 431 | Fat: 16.1 g | Protein: 10.1 g | Sodium: 502 mg | Fiber: 5.2 g | Carbohydrates: 57.0 g | Sugar: 3.2 g

Shepherdless Pie

Loaded with vegetables and Beefless Ground, this Shepherdless Pie delivers all the punch that meat eaters get from their version. The rich filling is topped with creamy and cheesy mashed potatoes. For a different decorative effect, pipe those mashed potatoes in dollops on top before cooking.

HANDS-ON TIME: 15 minutes
COOK TIME: 21 minutes

INGREDIENTS | SERVES 4

Potato Topping

1 large Russet potato, scrubbed and diced

1 tablespoon avocado oil

¼ cup nondairy Cheddar shreds

2 tablespoons unsweetened almond milk

½ teaspoon salt

½ teaspoon freshly ground black pepper

Meatless Filling

2 teaspoons avocado oil

1 cup Beefless Ground

½ small yellow onion, peeled and diced

1 medium carrot, peeled and diced

¼ cup seeded and diced green bell pepper

1 small celery stalk, diced

⅔ cup tomato sauce

1 teaspoon chopped fresh rosemary

1 teaspoon fresh thyme leaves

½ teaspoon salt

½ teaspoon freshly ground black pepper

1. Add diced potatoes to a medium pot of boiling salted water and cook until fork-tender 4–5 minutes.

2. While potatoes are cooking, add 2 teaspoons avocado oil, Beefless Ground, onion, carrot, bell pepper, and celery to a large skillet. Cook over medium-high heat 3–4 minutes until vegetables are tender. Stir in tomato sauce, rosemary, thyme, ½ teaspoon salt, and ½ teaspoon black pepper.

3. Drain potatoes and transfer to a medium bowl. Add 1 tablespoon avocado oil, Cheddar shreds, almond milk, ½ teaspoon salt, and ½ teaspoon pepper. Mash until smooth.

4. Preheat air fryer at 350°F for 3 minutes.

5. Spoon meatless filling into lightly greased round cake barrel (accessory). Top with mashed potatoes. Using the tines of a fork, run shallow lines in the top of the potatoes for a decorative touch.

6. Cook 12 minutes. Remove barrel from air fryer and let rest 10 minutes. Serve warm.

PER SERVING Calories: 163 | Fat: 8.7 g | Protein: 6.5 g | Sodium: 1,065 mg | Fiber: 4.0 g | Carbohydrates: 16.3 g | Sugar: 3.5 g

Romesco Vegetable–Orzo Casserole

Romesco sauce is a roasted red pepper–based sauce rich in flavor that was traditionally created in Spain as a sauce for fish dishes. It is dynamic tossed in with the mushrooms, Kalamata olives, orzo, and feta cheese. Topped with fresh basil, this casserole is a flavor explosion!

HANDS-ON TIME: 14 minutes
COOK TIME: 14 minutes

INGREDIENTS | SERVES 4

2 teaspoons avocado oil

½ medium red onion, peeled and diced

1 medium red bell pepper, seeded and diced

1 cup sliced baby bella (cremini) mushrooms

1 cup pitted and halved Kalamata olives

2 cups Super Easy Romesco Sauce (see Chapter 15)

2 cups cooked orzo

¼ cup feta cheese

¼ cup chopped fresh basil

Difference Between Kalamata and Black Olives

Although you can certainly substitute the more common black olives in this recipe, each olive variety possesses a different taste, texture, and even method of brining. With its meaty texture and medium size, the wine vinegar–brined Kalamata olive is no exception. The taste is head and shoulders above the humble black olive.

1. In a medium skillet over medium-high heat, warm avocado oil 1 minute. Add onion, bell pepper, and mushrooms. Stir-fry 3–4 minutes until vegetables are tender. Add olives and Super Easy Romesco Sauce. Stir in orzo.

2. Preheat air fryer at 350°F for 3 minutes.

3. Transfer mixture into lightly greased round cake barrel (accessory) and place in air fryer basket. Cook 7 minutes. Add feta cheese in an even layer on top of casserole. Cook an additional 2 minutes.

4. Remove barrel from air fryer and let rest 10 minutes. Serve warm and garnish with fresh basil leaves.

PER SERVING Calories: 436 | Fat: 27.6 g | Protein: 10.6 g | Sodium: 1,880 mg | Fiber: 5.1 g | Carbohydrates: 38.1 g | Sugar: 4.9 g

Neapolitan Pizza Tarts

Puff pastry has been deemed vegan, but stay away from the "butter puff" variety. And vegan cheese has come a long way since its inception. It not only tastes like "real" cheese, but it does in fact melt, lending that ooey-gooey mouthfeel you are used to with traditional mozzarella cheese.

HANDS-ON TIME: 15 minutes
COOK TIME: 18 minutes

INGREDIENTS | SERVES 3

¼ cup all-purpose flour

1 sheet puff pastry, thawed to room temperature

½ cup Marinara Sauce (see Chapter 15)

1 (3-ounce) meatless Italian sausage, cut into 30 slices

¼ cup nondairy mozzarella shreds

2 medium Roma tomatoes, cut into 12 slices

½ cup julienned fresh basil leaves

2 teaspoons olive oil

2 teaspoons balsamic vinegar

1. Scatter flour over a flat, clean surface. Unfold puff pastry sheet on the floured surface. Cut into six equal rectangles.

2. Top each rectangle with Marinara Sauce, sausage, and mozzarella shreds.

3. Preheat air fryer at 350°F for 3 minutes.

4. Place two tarts at a time in lightly greased air fryer basket. Cook 6 minutes. Repeat with remaining tarts.

5. Top tarts with 2 slices tomato each and equal portions of basil. Lightly drizzle with oil and balsamic vinegar. Serve warm.

PER SERVING Calories: 204 | Fat: 12.8 g | Protein: 7.6 g | Sodium: 468 mg | Fiber: 2.8 g | Carbohydrates: 15.6 g | Sugar: 3.1 g

Taco Tuesday Tarts

*Make sure you place your thawed puff pastry on the cutting board about
30 minutes before using. It will handle easier when room temperature. Feel free
to add other favorite taco toppings, like black olives or diced avocado!*

HANDS-ON TIME: 15 minutes
COOK TIME: 21 minutes

INGREDIENTS | SERVES 3

¼ cup all-purpose flour

1 sheet puff pastry, thawed to room temperature

3 teaspoons avocado oil, divided

1½ cups Beefless Ground

½ teaspoon ground cumin

½ teaspoon chili powder

¼ teaspoon salt

¼ cup nondairy Cheddar shreds

2 medium Roma tomatoes, seeded and diced

1 medium avocado, peeled, pitted, and sliced

1. Scatter flour over a flat, clean surface. Unfold puff pastry sheet on the floured surface. Cut into six equal rectangles. With 1 teaspoon avocado oil, lightly brush the perimeter of each rectangle.

2. In a skillet over medium heat, heat the other 2 teaspoons avocado oil. Add Beefless Ground, cumin, chili powder, and salt. Stir-fry 3 minutes to combine spices. Allow to cool 2–3 minutes.

3. Top each pastry rectangle with beefless mixture. Add Cheddar shreds.

4. Preheat air fryer at 350°F for 3 minutes.

5. Place two tarts at a time in lightly greased air fryer basket. Cook 6 minutes. Repeat with remaining tarts.

6. Top each tart with diced tomatoes and sliced avocado. Serve immediately.

PER SERVING Calories: 399 | Fat: 30.1 g | Protein: 12.3 g | Sodium: 575 mg | Fiber: 6.9 g | Carbohydrates: 19.5 g | Sugar: 2.0 g

Bean and Cheese Taquitos

You would think that all refried beans are vegetarian, but many are not. Some contain animal lard or even dairy. So be aware when you pick up a can of vegetarian refried beans and, as always, give those labels a quick once-over.

HANDS-ON TIME: 10 minutes
COOK TIME: 16 minutes

INGREDIENTS | SERVES 4

1 cup vegetarian refried beans
2 cups nondairy Cheddar shreds
16 (6") corn tortillas
1 cup Pico Guacamole (see Chapter 15)

1. Evenly spread refried beans and Cheddar shreds down the center of each corn tortilla. Roll each tortilla tightly and place them all seam side down on a platter.

2. Preheat air fryer at 350°F for 3 minutes.

3. Place four rolled tortillas seam side down in air fryer basket. Cook 4 minutes. Repeat with remaining tortillas.

4. Transfer to a serving tray and serve warm with Pico Guacamole.

PER SERVING Calories: 545 | Fat: 26.3 g | Protein: 10.5 g | Sodium: 1,265 mg | Fiber: 16.1 g | Carbohydrates: 72.0 g | Sugar: 2.6 g

Baked Spaghetti Squash

Once this squash is cooked, take a fork and pull out the long strands resembling spaghetti noodles. In addition, you can dress it up as you would pasta with Spicy Marinara Sauce or our homemade Super Easy Romesco Sauce (both in Chapter 15).

HANDS-ON TIME: 5 minutes
COOK TIME: 25 minutes

INGREDIENTS | SERVES 2

2 teaspoons olive oil
1 (1½-pound) spaghetti squash, halved and seeded
½ teaspoon salt, divided

1. Preheat air fryer at 375°F for 3 minutes.

2. Rub olive oil over both halves of spaghetti squash. Sprinkle squash with ¼ teaspoon salt. Place flat side down in air fryer basket. Cook 25 minutes.

3. Transfer to a cutting board and let cool until easy to handle. Using a fork, gently pull strands out of squash into a medium bowl. Season with remaining salt. Serve warm.

PER SERVING Calories: 70 | Fat: 4.6 g | Protein: 0.8 g | Sodium: 601 mg | Fiber: 1.6 g | Carbohydrates: 7.5 g | Sugar: 2.9 g

Fried Avocado Tacos

The breaded avocado fries are amazingly crisp on the outside and divinely smooth on the inside. Topped with the crunchy slaw, the fresh salsa, and the creamy kick from the Sriracha Mayonnaise, these Fried Avocado Tacos will quickly become a household favorite.

HANDS-ON TIME: 10 minutes
COOK TIME: 10 minutes

INGREDIENTS | SERVES 2

Sriracha Mayonnaise

½ cup Veganaise
2 teaspoons sriracha
1 teaspoon lime juice
Pinch salt

Salsa

2 medium Roma tomatoes, seeded and diced
¼ cup finely diced red onion
1 tablespoon fresh lime juice
1 teaspoon fresh lime zest
¼ cup chopped fresh cilantro
1 teaspoon salt

Avocado Fries

1 medium avocado
Egg substitute equaling 1 large egg
2 tablespoons unsweetened almond milk
1 cup plain bread crumbs

Remaining Taco Ingredients

6 (6") flour tortillas
1 cup coleslaw mix (shredded cabbage and carrots)

Making Your Own Coleslaw Mix

Although you can find coleslaw mix already combined to make life easier, if you'd like to make your own, just use 1 cup peeled, grated carrot per 4 cups shredded cabbage. Depending on the recipe, other vegetables can be used to tailor your slaw. Heck, trade out the carrot for a parsnip if you'd like!

1. In a small bowl, combine Sriracha Mayonnaise ingredients and refrigerate covered until ready to use.

2. In a medium bowl, combine salsa ingredients and refrigerate covered until ready to use.

3. Cut avocado in half. Remove pit. Use a soup spoon to gently scrape the avocado away from the skin. Gently slice each half into six "fries."

4. Whisk together egg substitute and almond milk in a small bowl. Put bread crumbs in a shallow dish.

5. Preheat air fryer at 375°F.

6. Dip avocado slices in egg mixture. Dredge in bread crumbs to coat. Place half of avocado slices into air fryer basket. Cook 5 minutes. Transfer to serving plate. Repeat with remaining avocado slices.

7. Add two fried avocado slices to each tortilla. Top with coleslaw mix, salsa, and a squeeze of Sriracha Mayonnaise.

PER SERVING Calories: 885 | Fat: 51.7 g | Protein: 14.9 g | Sodium: 2,560 mg | Fiber: 10.3 g | Carbohydrates: 80.1 g | Sugar: 10.0 g

Black Bean and Couscous Burgers

Whether you are vegan or a meat lover, you'll agree that these black bean burgers are just good! Both the couscous and black beans are full of nutrients. The creamy treenut cheese not only lends flavor but also acts as a binder in these patties. Serve as is or on a bun with your favorite toppings!

HANDS-ON TIME: 10 minutes
COOK TIME: 6 minutes

INGREDIENTS | SERVES 4

⅓ cup water

1 tablespoon plus ½ teaspoon olive oil, divided

1 teaspoon salt, divided

⅓ cup whole-wheat couscous

1 cup canned black beans, drained and rinsed

2 tablespoons finely chopped onion

2 tablespoons chopped fresh parsley

¼ teaspoon chipotle chili powder

2 tablespoons creamy treenut cheese

What Is Treenut Cheese?

Treenut cheese is a nondairy, gluten-free, and non-GMO cheese that is an excellent choice for vegans and those affected by gluten and/or dairy. Made from cashews, acidophilus cultures, and seasonings, this creamy cheese is great as a binder in these burgers and as a spread on crackers.

1. In a small saucepan, bring water, ½ teaspoon olive oil, and ½ teaspoon salt, and bring to a boil. Remove from heat and stir in couscous. Cover and let rest 5 minutes.

2. In a medium bowl, mash black beans. Add cooked couscous, onion, parsley, chili powder, remaining salt, and treenut cheese. Form into four patties.

3. Preheat air fryer at 350°F for 3 minutes.

4. Place patties in lightly greased air fryer basket. Cook 3 minutes. Flip. Brush patties with remaining tablespoon olive oil. Cook an additional 3 minutes.

5. Transfer to a plate and serve warm.

PER SERVING Calories: 182 | Fat: 52.5 g | Protein: 7.0 g | Sodium: 754 mg | Fiber: 5.4 g | Carbohydrates: 22.1 g | Sugar: 0.6 g

Beet Falafel

Falafel is traditionally a fried ball of ground chickpeas and spices. Almost like a Middle Eastern fritter, if you will. The addition of beets in this variation lends an earthiness and sweetness that makes these falafels irresistible! Try dipping them in Tzatziki Sauce (see Chapter 15).

HANDS-ON TIME: 10 minutes
COOK TIME: 40 minutes

INGREDIENTS | SERVES 4

1 (15-ounce) can chickpeas, rinsed and drained
1 cup sliced cooked beets
2 cloves garlic, minced
¼ cup spelt flour
1 tablespoon dried cilantro
½ teaspoon ground ginger
½ teaspoon salt
¼ teaspoon ground white pepper
¼ cup chopped fresh parsley

1. In a medium bowl, mash chickpeas and beets. Stir in garlic, flour, cilantro, ginger, salt, and pepper. Form into twenty balls.

2. Preheat air fryer at 350°F for 3 minutes.

3. Place six balls in lightly greased pizza pan (accessory) and place in air fryer basket. Cook 5 minutes. Flip. Cook an additional 5 minutes. Repeat with remaining balls.

4. If they flattened in the cooking process, re-form into ball shapes when cool enough to handle. Continue to cool another 2–3 minutes and garnish with parsley before serving.

PER SERVING Calories: 136 | Fat: 1.4 g | Protein: 6.3 g | Sodium: 454 mg | Fiber: 6.2 g | Carbohydrates: 24.3 g | Sugar: 4.9 g

Corn Fritters

Served as a snack or side dish, these Corn Fritters are amazing. The cornmeal in the breading lends a little rustic flair and adds to the corn theme in these crispy little nuggets. Serve with your favorite dipping sauce for even more flavor!

HANDS-ON TIME: 10 minutes
COOK TIME: 10 minutes

INGREDIENTS | SERVES 3

½ cup corn kernels

¼ cup seeded and finely diced red bell pepper

½ cup shredded zucchini

2 cloves garlic, minced

¼ cup cornmeal

¼ cup plain bread crumbs

1 tablespoon all-purpose flour

½ teaspoon salt

½ teaspoon freshly ground black pepper

1½ tablespoons vegetable oil

1½ tablespoons water

1. In a medium bowl, combine corn, bell pepper, zucchini, garlic, cornmeal, bread crumbs, flour, salt, black pepper, vegetable oil, and water. Form into nine balls.

2. Preheat air fryer at 350°F for 3 minutes.

3. Place the balls in lightly greased pizza pan (accessory) and place in air fryer basket. Cook 5 minutes. Flip. Cook an additional 5 minutes.

4. Let cool 2–3 minutes before serving.

PER SERVING Calories: 184 | Fat: 7.4 g | Protein: 3.7 g | Sodium: 459 mg | Fiber: 2.1 g | Carbohydrates: 25.6 g | Sugar: 3.3 g

Vegetable Egg Rolls

Stuffed with cabbage, carrots, mushrooms, scallions, and bamboo shoots and flavored with sesame oil, garlic, soy sauce, sriracha, and ginger, these Vegetable Egg Rolls will rival the ones on any take-out menu, minus the deep-frying grease!

HANDS-ON TIME: 20 minutes
COOK TIME: 33 minutes

INGREDIENTS | SERVES 6

1 tablespoon sesame oil
1 (16-ounce) bag coleslaw mix
½ cup diced mushrooms
2 scallions, trimmed and diced
2 cloves garlic, minced
1 (8-ounce) can sliced bamboo shoots, drained
2 tablespoons soy sauce
1 tablespoon sriracha
½ teaspoon ground ginger
¼ teaspoon salt
¼ teaspoon ground white pepper
18 egg-roll wrappers
2 tablespoons avocado oil

1. In a large skillet over medium-high heat, drizzle sesame oil. Add coleslaw mix, mushrooms, scallions, garlic, bamboo shoots, soy sauce, sriracha, ginger, salt, and pepper. Stir-fry 5–6 minutes until cabbage is wilted and tender.

2. Drape a damp towel over the stack of egg-roll wrappers. Place one egg-roll wrapper on a cutting board. Place approximately ¼ cup vegetable mixture in a line in the middle of the wrapper. Fold ½" of two opposite sides of the egg roll toward the middle. Roll ends to form an egg roll and place seam side down on a plate. Repeat with remaining wrappers.

3. Preheat air fryer at 325°F for 3 minutes.

4. Place a third of the egg rolls in the air fryer basket. Cook 3 minutes. Lightly brush the tops of egg rolls with avocado oil. Cook an additional 6 minutes. Repeat with remaining egg rolls.

5. Transfer to a serving plate. Serve warm.

PER SERVING Calories: 166 | Fat: 7.1 g | Protein: 4.8 g | Sodium: 593 mg | Fiber: 3.2 g | Carbohydrates: 21.3 g | Sugar: 3.9 g

Bean Chili–Stuffed Baked Potatoes

This is a perfect solution for any leftover chili in your refrigerator. However, if you are just craving some chili-stuffed baked potatoes and you're tight on time, grab a can of bean chili to use in a pinch.

HANDS-ON TIME: 10 minutes
COOK TIME: 48 minutes

INGREDIENTS | SERVES 2

2 large Russet potatoes (about 1 pound), scrubbed
2 teaspoons olive oil
½ teaspoon salt
¼ teaspoon freshly ground black pepper
1 cup canned bean chili
1 cup vegan Cheddar cheese shreds

1. Preheat air fryer at 400°F for 3 minutes.

2. Pierce potatoes 3–4 times with the tines of a fork. Rub olive oil over both potatoes. Season with salt and pepper. Place in air fryer basket.

3. Cook 30 minutes. Flip potatoes. Cook an additional 15 minutes.

4. Once cooled, slice each potato lengthwise about 1" deep without going all the way through. Pinch ends together to open up the slice. Add chili and cheese shreds to inside of potatoes.

5. Place stuffed potatoes back in air fryer basket and cook an additional 3 minutes.

6. Transfer to plates and serve warm.

PER SERVING Calories: 621 | Fat: 25.1 g | Protein: 14.8 g | Sodium: 1,818 mg | Fiber: 14.3 g | Carbohydrates: 90.7 g | Sugar: 5.1 g

Stuffed Bell Peppers

Bell peppers are just one of those vegetables that take on a different flavor once cooked. Tender and flavorful, these peppers are stuffed with a blend of rice, tomatoes, and seasonings with the addition of mushrooms, lending a "meaty" touch to this recipe.

HANDS-ON TIME: 15 minutes
COOK TIME: 20 minutes

INGREDIENTS | SERVES 4

2 medium bell peppers, color of choice
2 teaspoons olive oil
½ cup cooked whole-grain rice
½ cup canned fire-roasted diced tomatoes, including juice
½ cup tomato sauce
1 tablespoon finely diced onion
¼ cup chopped baby bella (cremini) mushrooms
2 teaspoons Italian seasoning
¼ teaspoon smoked paprika
½ teaspoon salt
¼ teaspoon freshly ground black pepper

1. Cut bell peppers in half from top to bottom and seed them. For decorative flair, choose bell peppers with a stem so that each half has a sliced stem. Brush inside and tops of bell pepper with olive oil. Set aside.

2. In a medium bowl, combine rice, tomatoes, tomato sauce, onion, mushrooms, Italian seasoning, smoked paprika, salt, and pepper.

3. Preheat air fryer at 350°F for 3 minutes.

4. Evenly distribute rice mixture among the bell pepper halves.

5. Place two halves in the air fryer basket. Cook 10 minutes.

6. Transfer to a serving plate. Continue with remaining halves. Serve warm.

PER SERVING Calories: 82 | Fat: 2.5 g | Protein: 2.0 g | Sodium: 499 mg | Fiber: 2.8 g | Carbohydrates: 12.9 g | Sugar: 4.6 g

Roasted Garlic

It is amazing how, after cooking garlic bulbs, you can squeeze it out like butter. Great mixed in with mashed potatoes, hummus, and even just spread on bread, roasted garlic is magic, turning whatever it touches into gold!

HANDS-ON TIME: 10 minutes
COOK TIME: 45 minutes

INGREDIENTS | SERVES 8

3 teaspoons olive oil
2 garlic bulbs, unpeeled, with top ¼" cut off
Pinch salt

1. Preheat air fryer at 400°F for 3 minutes.

2. Drizzle olive oil over garlic bulbs and rub it in with your finger. Season with a pinch of salt on each. Roll each bulb up in a square of aluminum foil.

3. Place wrapped garlic bulbs in air fryer basket. Cook 45 minutes.

4. Unwrap each bulb. When cooled, squeeze roasted garlic from each clove and use as desired.

PER SERVING Calories: 28 | Fat: 1.7 g | Protein: 0.6 g | Sodium: 19 mg | Fiber: 0.2 g | Carbohydrates: 3.0 g | Sugar: 0.1 g

Crunchy Tortilla Strips

If you want to avoid the greasy, deep-fried version of chips, the air fryer helps achieve these crisp little tortilla strips. Fantastic on fresh salads and homemade soups, these chips pack a crunch that is a welcome addition to healthy meals.

HANDS-ON TIME: 5 minutes
COOK TIME: 4 minutes

INGREDIENTS | SERVES 4

2 (6") corn tortillas
1 tablespoon avocado oil
2 teaspoons lime juice
½ teaspoon salt
¼ teaspoon freshly ground black pepper

1. Cut each tortilla in half. Slice into ½" strips.

2. Preheat air fryer at 400°F for 3 minutes.

3. In a small bowl, whisk together avocado oil and lime juice. Brush mixture over both sides of tortilla strips. Toss with salt and pepper.

4. Place strips in air fryer basket. Cook 2 minutes. Shake strips. Cook an additional 2 minutes.

5. Transfer chips to a bowl to cool.

PER SERVING Calories: 57 | Fat: 3.7 g | Protein: 0.7 g | Sodium: 295 mg | Fiber: 0.8 g | Carbohydrates: 5.7 g | Sugar: 0.2 g

Tex-Mex Bowl

Everything you like in a taco can be found in this filling and nutritious bowl. It's quick and easy to make on a busy weeknight, and the air fryer gives the beans and corn a little crispy texture, complementing the flavor of the dish. And don't forget to make the Crunchy Tortilla Strips!

HANDS-ON TIME: 5 minutes
COOK TIME: 5 minutes

INGREDIENTS | SERVES 4

1 cup vegan or nondairy sour cream

2 tablespoons unsweetened almond milk

1 teaspoon ground cumin

1 teaspoon chili powder

Pinch cayenne pepper

½ teaspoon salt

1 cup canned black beans, drained and rinsed

1 cup canned corn, drained

4 cups mixed greens

3 medium Roma tomatoes, seeded and diced

1 medium avocado, peeled, pitted, and diced

Crunchy Tortilla Strips (see recipe in this chapter)

1. In a medium bowl, combine sour cream, almond milk, cumin, chili powder, cayenne pepper, and salt. Refrigerate covered until ready to use.

2. Preheat air fryer at 350°F for 3 minutes.

3. Place black beans and corn in air fryer basket and cook 5 minutes.

4. Distribute mixed greens among four bowls. Top with black beans, corn, tomatoes, avocado, and whole Crunchy Tortilla Strips. Drizzle sour cream mixture over salad bowls and serve immediately.

PER SERVING Calories: 313 | Fat: 19.3 g | Protein: 6.8 g | Sodium: 980 mg | Fiber: 12.8 g | Carbohydrates: 32.9 g | Sugar: 1.9 g

Making Homemade Almond Milk Is Easier Than You Think

Soak unsalted raw almonds covered in water for at least 24 hours. Rinse and drain. In a blender or food processor, pulse 1¾ cups water and 1 cup soaked almonds. Strain liquid through a fine-mesh sieve or cheesecloth. Refrigerate covered up to 3 days.

CHAPTER 11

Side Dishes

Sesame Shishito Peppers

Although these mild peppers can be eaten raw, when you air-fry them to get a little char, they are even better. Coupled with just a touch of sesame oil, these make a great side dish or snack!

HANDS-ON TIME: 5 minutes
COOK TIME: 8 minutes

INGREDIENTS | SERVES 2

6 ounces shishito peppers (about 3½ cups)
1 teaspoon sesame oil
1 teaspoon salt, divided
1 teaspoon sesame seeds

What Are Shishito Peppers?

Move over edamame, these shishito peppers are the next best thing in super easy appetizers and are amazing to enjoy with friends over drinks. They're showing up more and more in common grocery stores, and the natural flavor of these mild and sweet chili peppers is enhanced and taken to the next level with a little oil, salt, and char.

1. In a medium bowl, toss peppers with sesame oil and ½ teaspoon salt.

2. Preheat air fryer at 375°F for 3 minutes.

3. Add peppers to fryer basket and cook 4 minutes. Shake peppers. Cook an additional 4 minutes until peppers are blistered.

4. Transfer peppers to a serving dish and garnish with remaining salt and sesame seeds.

PER SERVING Calories: 21 | Fat: 2.2 g | Protein: 2.0 g | Sodium: 1,163 mg | Fiber: 2.8 g | Carbohydrates: 6.1 g | Sugar: 2.8 g

Cooked Carrots

The combination of cinnamon and honey brings out the natural sweetness of these cooked carrots. The air fryer adds a little char to the outside, creating another layer of flavor.

HANDS-ON TIME: 5 minutes
COOK TIME: 10 minutes

INGREDIENTS | SERVES 4

3 large carrots, peeled
1 teaspoon olive oil
1 tablespoon honey
¼ teaspoon ground cinnamon
⅛ teaspoon cayenne pepper
½ teaspoon salt

1. Cut carrots in half lengthwise. Then cut halves into 1" sections.

2. In a medium bowl, whisk together oil, honey, cinnamon, cayenne pepper, and salt. Add carrots and toss.

3. Preheat air fryer at 375°F for 3 minutes.

4. Add carrots to fryer basket and cook 5 minutes. Toss. Cook an additional 5 minutes.

5. Transfer to a bowl and serve warm.

PER SERVING Calories: 47 | Fat: 1.2. g | Protein: 0.5 g | Sodium: 327 mg | Fiber: 1.6 g | Carbohydrates: 9.7 g | Sugar: 6.7 g

Fried Okra

Okra gets a bad rap for its slimy nature when cooked. This slime, or mucilage, is actually edible, but the mouthfeel can turn some people away. Luckily air frying makes these taste incredible and become a great side dish with chicken, steak, or fish!

HANDS-ON TIME: 10 minutes
COOK TIME: 7 minutes

INGREDIENTS | SERVES 2

2 large eggs
¼ cup whole milk
¼ cup plain bread crumbs
¼ cup cornmeal
1 teaspoon salt
½ pound fresh okra, sliced into ½" pieces
1 tablespoon butter, melted

1. In a small bowl, whisk together eggs and milk. In a shallow dish, combine bread crumbs, cornmeal, and salt.

2. Preheat air fryer at 400°F for 3 minutes.

3. Dip okra in egg mixture. Dredge in bread crumb mixture. Place okra in air fryer basket. Cook 4 minutes. Shake. Brush okra with melted butter. Cook an additional 3 minutes.

4. Transfer to a dish and serve warm.

PER SERVING Calories: 187 | Fat: 8.4 g | Protein: 7.0 g | Sodium: 970 mg | Fiber: 3.6 g | Carbohydrates: 20.3 g | Sugar: 2.8 g

Fried Green Beans

These green beans are quick and crispy and perfect for snacking on while enjoying a cold brew. Also, if you have some picky eaters, these may be the trick to get them to try something green!

HANDS-ON TIME: 10 minutes
COOK TIME: 14 minutes

INGREDIENTS | SERVES 2

1 large egg
1 tablespoon whole milk
1 tablespoon honey
2 tablespoons cornmeal
2 tablespoons cornstarch
2 tablespoons finely grated Parmesan cheese
½ teaspoon salt, plus an extra pinch for garnish
10 ounces green beans, trimmed (about 3 cups)

1. In a medium bowl, whisk together egg, milk, and honey.

2. In a shallow dish, combine cornmeal, cornstarch, cheese, and salt.

3. Preheat air fryer at 375°F for 3 minutes.

4. Coat green beans with egg mixture and shake off any excess. Dredge in the cornmeal mixture.

5. Place green beans in air fryer basket. Cook 7 minutes. Gently toss green beans. Cook an additional 7 minutes.

6. Transfer green beans to a serving dish and garnish with a pinch of salt. Serve warm.

PER SERVING Calories: 171 | Fat: 2.9 g | Protein: 6.7 g | Sodium: 774 mg | Fiber: 4.5 g | Carbohydrates: 31.0 g | Sugar: 9.8 g

How Do You "Trim" Green Beans?

You may say "trimming" green beans, but a cooking term that means the same thing is to "top and tail" the beans. If the beans are young and fresh, you only need to line up a handful of the stem end of the beans and give one uniform chop, then repeat with the remaining beans. However, if the beans are more mature, after you slice off the stem ends you'll have to cut the opposite end off one at a time and then gently pull the string off and discard it.

Asian Brussels Sprouts

The saltiness of the soy sauce and the sweetness of the maple syrup help counter the bitter flavor that some may detect in Brussels sprouts. Rounded out even more with the small kick of heat from the sriracha, this side dish will have your family asking for seconds!

HANDS-ON TIME: 5 minutes
COOK TIME: 14 minutes

INGREDIENTS | SERVES 2

¼ cup freshly squeezed orange juice
1 tablespoon pure maple syrup
1 tablespoon soy sauce
¼ teaspoon sriracha
1 tablespoon olive oil
1 pound Brussels sprouts, halved
Pinch salt

Brussels Sprouts—Love 'Em or Hate 'Em?

There are a couple of reasons why some folks love Brussels sprouts and others run quickly in the opposite direction. For one, we eat first with our sense of smell, and the Brussels sprout, a cruciferous vegetable, has a bitterness that turns some away immediately. Also, some people are born with more sensitive bitter receptors on the tongue, so their reaction is going to be different from that of someone with less sensitive bitter receptors. By adding flavoring to this vegetable, instead of a simple salt-and-pepper steam job, minds can be changed and we can all come together and love these itty-bitty cabbages!

1. In a large bowl, whisk together orange juice, maple syrup, soy sauce, sriracha, and olive oil. Toss in Brussels sprouts. Refrigerate 30 minutes.

2. Preheat air fryer at 350°F for 3 minutes.

3. Add Brussels sprouts to air fryer. Cook 7 minutes. Toss. Cook an additional 7 minutes.

4. Transfer Brussels sprouts to a serving dish, season with salt, and serve warm.

PER SERVING Calories: 123 | Fat: 3.7 g | Protein: 6.1 g | Sodium: 304 mg | Fiber: 6.4 g | Carbohydrates: 20.2 g | Sugar: 8.1 g

Baby Bacon Hasselbacks

If a baked potato and home fries had a baby, it'd be this dish. The slices of potatoes allow the melted butter to cook down in the nooks and crannies, creating multiple crisp edges, and the bacon between slices yields a salty pork flavor that only bacon can give.

HANDS-ON TIME: 15 minutes
COOK TIME: 20 minutes

INGREDIENTS | SERVES 3

6 baby red potatoes, scrubbed
1 slice uncooked bacon, diced
1 tablespoon olive oil
2 tablespoons butter, melted
Pinch salt
6 teaspoons sour cream
¼ cup chopped fresh parsley

1. Make slices in the width of potatoes about ¼" apart without cutting all the way through. Press a small dice of bacon between each slice. Brush potatoes with olive oil.

2. Preheat air fryer at 350°F for 3 minutes.

3. Add potatoes to air fryer basket. Cook 10 minutes. Brush with melted butter, ensuring the butter gets between slices. Cook an additional 10 minutes.

4. Transfer potatoes to a serving dish. Season with salt. Add a dollop of sour cream to the top of each potato. Garnish with chopped parsley. Serve warm.

PER SERVING Calories: 383 | Fat: 14.8 g | Protein: 8.2 g | Sodium: 181 mg | Fiber: 6.0 g | Carbohydrates: 54.7 g | Sugar: 4.7 g

Baked Gnocchi

Gnocchi are pillowy little potato dumplings that are traditionally served with a rich sauce. In this recipe, the pillows are still fluffy, but the air fryer gives them a crispy exterior.

HANDS-ON TIME: 5 minutes
COOK TIME: 27 minutes

INGREDIENTS | SERVES 4

2 medium Russet potatoes, peeled and diced
½ teaspoon onion powder
½ teaspoon salt
½ teaspoon freshly ground black pepper
1 large egg
¼ cup all-purpose flour
1 tablespoon butter, melted
½ teaspoon garlic salt

1. Add potatoes to a large pot with enough water to cover potatoes. Bring to boil. Reduce heat and simmer 4–5 minutes until potatoes are fork-tender.

2. Drain potatoes and transfer to a medium bowl. Add onion powder, salt, and pepper to the bowl. Mash seasoned potatoes until smooth. Add egg and mix until combined.

3. Sprinkle some of the flour on a flat, clean surface. With floured hands, knead dough to incorporate some of the flour and reduce stickiness.

4. Break off a small ball of dough. Work into a rope ½" wide. Using a knife cut into ½" sections. If you'd like the classic lines on the gnocchi, roll each gnocchi under the tines of a fork. Repeat with the rest of the dough.

5. Bring a pot of salted water to a boil. Add gnocchi in two batches to water. Using a slotted spoon, remove once they rise to the top, after about 2 minutes.

6. Preheat air fryer at 350°F for 3 minutes.

7. Add gnocchi to air fryer basket. Cook 5 minutes. Gently toss. Cook another 5 minutes. Toss and brush gnocchi with butter. Cook 4 minutes. Toss again and cook an additional 4 minutes.

8. Transfer gnocchi to a bowl and toss with garlic salt. Serve warm.

PER SERVING Calories: 116 | Fat: 3.8 g | Protein: 3.1 g | Sodium: 754 mg | Fiber: 1.8 g | Carbohydrates: 17.2 g | Sugar: 0.8 g

Walnut-Crusted Goat Cheese Bombs

Whether serving these beside a juicy steak, adding a fresh twist to a summer salad, or just popping them in your mouth, these Walnut-Crusted Goat Cheese Bombs will add smiles to the faces of all those around you.

HANDS-ON TIME: 10 minutes
COOK TIME: 16 minutes

INGREDIENTS | SERVES 4

5 ounces goat cheese, at room temperature

5 ounces mascarpone cheese, at room temperature

¼ teaspoon salt

¼ teaspoon freshly ground black pepper

1 teaspoon fresh thyme leaves

¼ cup all-purpose flour

1 large egg, whisked

⅓ cup finely crushed walnuts

⅓ cup panko bread crumbs

What Is Mascarpone Cheese?

Mascarpone (pronounced mahs-kar-POH-nay) is just an Italian version of cream cheese. Cream cheese is slightly tangier, and mascarpone cheese has a higher fat content, so if splitting hairs, I'm sure some chefs will argue the difference; however, for most home chefs, consider that these unripened cheeses are pretty much inter-changeable in recipes.

1. In a medium bowl, combine goat cheese, mascarpone cheese, salt, pepper, and thyme. Form into sixteen balls of equal size.

2. Add flour to a small bowl. Add whisked egg to another small bowl. Mix walnut crumbs and bread crumbs in a shallow dish.

3. Roll cheese bombs in flour. Shake off any excess. Dip cheese bombs in egg. Shake off any excess. Dredge cheese bombs in bread crumb mixture. Place coated cheese bombs in freezer 30 minutes.

4. Preheat air fryer at 375°F for 3 minutes.

5. Add eight cheese bombs to lightly greased air fryer basket. Cook 8 minutes. Repeat with remaining cheese bombs.

6. Transfer to a serving plate and serve warm.

PER SERVING Calories: 338 | Fat: 24.7 g | Protein: 13.5 g | Sodium: 338 mg | Fiber: 0.6 g | Carbohydrates: 14.0 g | Sugar: 1.9 g

Nutty Roasted Acorn Squash

The sweet orange flesh of this autumnal side dish is highlighted with a bit of butter, sugar, cinnamon, and nutmeg. Adding the pecans lends texture and earthiness, which helps make acorn squash a seasonal favorite!

HANDS-ON TIME: 10 minutes
COOK TIME: 35 minutes

INGREDIENTS | SERVES 2

½ large acorn squash, seeds removed

1 teaspoon butter, melted

1 teaspoon brown sugar

1 teaspoon honey

Pinch ground cinnamon

Pinch ground nutmeg

Pinch salt

1 tablespoon pecan pieces

Can You Eat the Seeds of an Acorn Squash?

Yes! A lot of us scoop out the innards of those big orange pumpkins at Halloween and then roast those beautiful seeds. But why do we overlook the other winter squash? Butternut and acorn squash have very tasty seeds as well. Whether a snack or a crunchy topping on autumnal soups, these little nutritious roasted, crunchy gems should not be discarded!

1. Turn the acorn squash cut side up and slice off about ¼" of the bottom so it can sit flat.

2. In a small bowl, combine butter, sugar, honey, cinnamon, nutmeg, and salt. Brush over top of squash and pour any extra in the hole.

3. Preheat air fryer at 400°F for 3 minutes.

4. Add acorn squash to air fryer. Cook 30 minutes. Add pecans. Cook an additional 5 minutes.

5. Cut in half and transfer to two plates. Serve warm.

PER SERVING Calories: 102 | Fat: 4.2 g | Protein: 1.2 g | Sodium: 76 mg | Fiber: 2.0 g | Carbohydrates: 17.0 g | Sugar: 5.3 g

Prosciutto-Wrapped Asparagus

The air fryer knows how to crisp up prosciutto, and wrapped asparagus is a such a bonus. There is no need for seasoning. The salty nature of prosciutto lends just enough flavor for these tasty spears. Enjoy as a side dish, snack, or appetizer, either alone or with a homemade dipping sauce!

HANDS-ON TIME: 10 minutes
COOK TIME: 12 minutes

INGREDIENTS | SERVES 4

3 ounces prosciutto
18 thick spears of asparagus, trimmed of woody ends

Why Is Some Asparagus White?

First brought to America by German immigrants, white asparagus is given special care prior to harvesting so sunlight does not touch it. The plants are grown below mounds of dirt and the result is tender white stalks of asparagus. If you are a true fan, visit Schwetzingen, Germany, which is the *spargel*, or asparagus, capital of the world!

1. Slice prosciutto lengthwise into eighteen even slices. Spiral wrap the prosciutto strips from the bottom of the asparagus to the top, stopping before covering the tip.

2. Preheat air fryer at 400°F for 3 minutes.

3. Place wrapped asparagus in air fryer basket. Cook 6 minutes. Shake. Cook an additional 6 minutes until prosciutto is crisp.

4. Transfer to a plate and serve.

PER SERVING Calories: 80 | Fat: 4.8 g | Protein: 6.5 g | Sodium: 86 mg | Fiber: 1.9 g | Carbohydrates: 4.0 g | Sugar: 1.7 g

Sweet Chili Baby Bok Choy

Air frying these baby clusters of bok choy yields tender cabbage with crispy edges. The homemade Sweet Chili Sauce balances out the slight bitterness of the bok choy. Serve alongside a piece of cod for a light and healthy meal.

HANDS-ON TIME: 10 minutes
COOK TIME: 12 minutes

INGREDIENTS | SERVES 4

2 medium clusters baby bok choy, quartered lengthwise

¼ cup Sweet Chili Sauce (see Chapter 15)

Pinch salt

What Is Bok Choy?

Native to China, bok choy is most closely related to cabbage. Traditionally found in stir-fries and kimchi (Korean fermented veggies), bok choy is also a crunchy alternative in coleslaw and is beautiful brushed with oil and grilled next to your steak. High in vitamins and nutrients, this vegetable is a powerhouse that will be welcomed by all in the family!

1. Clean quartered baby bok choy and let drain on paper towels. Pat dry.

2. Preheat air fryer at 350°F for 3 minutes.

3. Brush bok choy with Sweet Chili Sauce. Place half in air fryer basket and cook 3 minutes. Flip bok choy. Cook an additional 3 minutes. Repeat with remaining bok choy.

4. Transfer to a serving plate, season with a pinch of salt, and serve warm.

PER SERVING Calories: 134 | Fat: 0.3 g | Protein: 3.3 g | Sodium: 255 mg | Fiber: 2.1 g | Carbohydrates: 31.0 g | Sugar: 27.7 g

Squash Fritters

Basically, these are individual bites of a squash casserole. The only difference? You get a crunch with every bite.

HANDS-ON TIME: 10 minutes
COOK TIME: 22 minutes

INGREDIENTS | YIELDS 12 FRITTERS

2 cups grated summer squash (approximately 1 large squash)

½ cup shredded Cheddar cheese

2 tablespoons minced yellow onion

1 tablespoon all-purpose flour

1 tablespoon cornmeal

1 tablespoon unsalted butter, melted

1 large egg

¼ teaspoon salt

½ teaspoon freshly ground black pepper

1 cup plain bread crumbs

What Are Fritters?

Either savory or sweet, fritters are loosely defined as fried balls consisting of dough, filling ingredients, and a breading. And then there is the debate over hush puppies and beignets. Some consider these fritters, but there is no filling, so others will disagree. Similar to the question of whether a hot dog is a sandwich, we can split hairs about the silly details, but we can all agree that they are just good to eat!

1. Squeeze grated squash between paper towels to remove excess moisture and transfer to a large bowl. Add cheese, onion, flour, cornmeal, butter, egg, salt, and pepper and combine.

2. Add bread crumbs to a shallow dish.

3. Preheat air fryer at 350°F for 3 minutes.

4. Form squash mixture into twelve balls, approximately 2 tablespoons each. Roll each ball in bread crumbs to cover all sides.

5. Place half of the fritters on a pizza pan (accessory). Cook 6 minutes. Flip fritters and cook an additional 5 minutes. Transfer to a plate.

6. Repeat with remaining fritters and serve warm.

PER SERVING Calories: 60 | Fat: 2.9 g | Protein: 2.7 g | Sodium: 117 mg | Fiber: 0.5 g | Carbohydrates: 5.3 g | Sugar: 0.8 g

Fried Corn on the Cob

If you've ever been to a state fair, then you know that everything gets fried unless it's nailed down. This includes perfect cobs of sweet, golden corn.

HANDS-ON TIME: 5 minutes
COOK TIME: 20 minutes

INGREDIENTS | SERVES 4

1 large egg
1 cup buttermilk
1 cup all-purpose flour
2 teaspoons salt
½ teaspoon sugar
1 teaspoon dried thyme
¼ cup grated Parmesan cheese
4 ears corn, shucked and halved, silk removed
3 tablespoons butter, melted

Buttermilk Substitutes

If you don't have buttermilk on hand, simply mix together 1 cup whole milk and 1 tablespoon lemon juice. Let stand 5 minutes. This will give enough time to allow the milk to curdle. Another option is to whisk together ¼ cup whole milk and ¾ cup plain yogurt.

1. In a medium bowl, whisk together egg and buttermilk.

2. In a shallow dish, combine flour, salt, sugar, thyme, and Parmesan cheese.

3. Preheat air fryer at 400°F for 3 minutes.

4. Roll corn in egg mixture and dredge in flour mixture. Shake off excess.

5. Add 4 half ears of corn to fryer basket and cook 7 minutes. Flip corn and brush with melted butter. Cook an additional 3 minutes. Repeat with remaining corn.

6. Transfer fried corn to a plate and serve warm.

PER SERVING Calories: 260 | Fat: 11.3 g | Protein: 8.0 g | Sodium: 694 mg | Fiber: 2.5 g | Carbohydrates: 33.5 g | Sugar: 8.4 g

Roasted Corn Salad

By air frying the corn, you add a little char, which in turn adds a lot of flavor. Refrigerate this salad covered overnight to really allow the flavors to marry together for an even better experience.

HANDS-ON TIME: 5 minutes
COOK TIME: 7 minutes

INGREDIENTS | SERVES 4

3 ears corn, shucked and halved, silk removed

2 medium Roma tomatoes, seeded and diced

1 cup canned black beans, drained and rinsed

1 medium avocado, peeled, pitted, and diced

½ cup chopped fresh cilantro

½ cup diced red onion

¼ cup balsamic vinegar

2 tablespoons olive oil

½ teaspoon salt

¼ teaspoon freshly ground black pepper

1. Preheat air fryer at 400°F for 3 minutes.

2. Add corn to fryer basket and cook 5 minutes. Shake basket. Cook an additional 2 minutes.

3. Transfer corn to a plate and allow to cool until easy to handle. Cut kernels from cob and add to a medium bowl.

4. Add remaining ingredients, combine, and serve.

PER SERVING Calories: 264 | Fat: 12.4 g | Protein: 7.4 g | Sodium: 450 mg | Fiber: 8.8 g | Carbohydrates: 33.1 g | Sugar: 9.1 g

Cilantro—Yuck?

Back off cilantro; half of us hate you. Ohhh, but half of us love you so much! Why, you ask? Well, some people have a gene that actually makes cilantro taste like soap. Who wants that? So, when you see recipes that call for cilantro, don't just discard the recipe altogether. Depending on the recipe, use your best judgment and substitute fresh parsley or mint. It won't taste the same as cilantro, but it will add that fresh herb flavor that your dish is screaming for!

Blistered Grape Tomatoes

Adding heat to tomatoes brings out their natural sugars. Tossed with tangy balsamic vinegar, this side dish is an excellent accompaniment to a steak fresh off the grill.

HANDS-ON TIME: 5 minutes
COOK TIME: 15 minutes

INGREDIENTS | SERVES 4

8 ounces (approximately 30) grape tomatoes
2 teaspoons olive oil
¼ teaspoon salt
1 tablespoon balsamic vinegar
1 tablespoon chopped fresh basil

Can I Use Other Tomato Varieties to Blister?

Of course! Grape tomatoes are small, oval tomatoes with a sweet flavor, but there are other varieties of baby tomatoes that bene-fit from the char flavor. Cherry tomatoes, pear tomatoes (both red and yellow), and Super Sweet 100s are all terrific choices for blistering.

1. Preheat air fryer at 350°F for 3 minutes.

2. In a small bowl, toss tomatoes, olive oil, and salt.

3. Transfer tomatoes to air fryer basket and cook 5 minutes. Shake basket. Cook 5 minutes. Shake basket. Cook 5 minutes.

4. Transfer tomatoes to a bowl. Toss with balsamic vinegar and garnish with chopped basil.

PER SERVING Calories: 33 | Fat: 2.3 g | Protein: 0.5 g | Sodium: 148 mg | Fiber: 0.7 g | Carbohydrates: 2.9 g | Sugar: 2.1 g

Fried Deviled Eggs

Fried Deviled Eggs have all the traditional flavors of the originals with the added texture of breading and air frying the white of the egg. Then spoon or pipe on the creamy yolk mixture for something unique that your guests will be talking about for a while.

HANDS-ON TIME: 15 minutes
COOK TIME: 10 minutes

INGREDIENTS | SERVES 5

5 hard-boiled large eggs
1 large egg
¼ cup whole milk
1 cup panko bread crumbs
¼ cup all-purpose flour
1 teaspoon salt
¼ cup mayonnaise
1 teaspoon yellow mustard
½ teaspoon dill pickle juice
1 tablespoon finely diced dill pickles
⅛ teaspoon salt
⅛ teaspoon freshly ground black pepper
⅛ teaspoon smoked paprika

1. Peel eggs and discard shells. Slice each egg in half lengthwise. Place yolks in a small bowl.

2. In a separate small bowl, whisk together egg and milk.

3. In a shallow dish, combine bread crumbs, flour, and salt.

4. Preheat air fryer at 400°F for 3 minutes.

5. Coat egg white halves in egg mixture and then dredge in bread crumb mixture. Shake off excess.

6. Add half of egg white halves to fryer basket and cook 5 minutes. Repeat with remaining egg whites.

7. While eggs are cooking, combine egg yolks with mayonnaise, mustard, pickle juice, pickles, salt, and pepper.

8. Transfer fried egg halves to a plate. Spoon the yolk filling into the egg white halves. Lightly sprinkle with paprika. Keep refrigerated and covered until ready to serve.

PER SERVING Calories: 230 | Fat: 13.7 g | Protein: 9.3 g | Sodium: 488 mg | Fiber: 0.3 g | Carbohydrates: 14.2 g | Sugar: 1.7 g

Baked Potatoes

The air fryer can cook the potatoes much faster than your oven. Although a microwave can achieve this cook in an even shorter time, the air fryer crisps up the outer skin while cooking the center to perfection!

HANDS-ON TIME: 5 minutes
COOK TIME: 45 minutes

INGREDIENTS | SERVES 2

2 large Russet potatoes (about 1 pound), scrubbed

2 teaspoons olive oil

2 tablespoons butter, cut into 2 pats

½ teaspoon salt

¼ teaspoon freshly ground black pepper

1. Preheat air fryer at 400°F for 3 minutes.

2. Rub olive oil over both potatoes. Place in air fryer basket.

3. Cook 30 minutes. Flip potatoes. Cook an additional 15 minutes.

4. Once cooled, slice each potato lengthwise about ½" deep. Pinch ends to open up slice. Add a pat of butter and season with salt and pepper. Serve warm.

PER SERVING Calories: 419 | Fat: 15.3 g | Protein: 7.6 g | Sodium: 1,606 mg | Fiber: 6.7 g | Carbohydrates: 63.4 g | Sugar: 3.5 g

Butter-Thyme Baby Reds

Naturally buttery and firm, baby red potatoes are enhanced with a bit of added butter, thyme, garlic salt, and black pepper. Cook these while the chicken or steak is on the outdoor grill or anytime you need a tasty side!

HANDS-ON TIME: 5 minutes
COOK TIME: 19 minutes

INGREDIENTS | SERVES 6

1 pound baby red potatoes, scrubbed and halved

2 tablespoons unsalted butter, melted

½ teaspoon dried thyme

¼ teaspoon garlic salt

⅛ teaspoon freshly ground black pepper

1. Preheat air fryer at 350°F for 3 minutes.

2. In a large bowl, combine potatoes, butter, thyme, garlic salt, and pepper.

3. Place potatoes in air fryer basket. Cook 10 minutes. Toss potatoes. Cook an additional 9 minutes.

4. Transfer to a serving bowl.

PER SERVING Calories: 82 | Fat: 3.6 g | Protein: 1.4 g | Sodium: 94 mg | Fiber: 1.2 g | Carbohydrates: 11.0 g | Sugar: 0.9 g

Twice-Baked Potatoes

*You may not want to make these for your family, because once you do,
you will have to make this recipe over and over again!*

HANDS-ON TIME: 10 minutes
COOK TIME: 47 minutes

INGREDIENTS | SERVES 4

2 teaspoons olive oil

2 large Russet potatoes (about 1 pound), scrubbed

½ teaspoon garlic salt

¼ teaspoon freshly ground black pepper

1 tablespoon unsalted butter

½ cup shredded Cheddar cheese

¼ cup sour cream

3 slices bacon, cooked and crumbled

¼ cup chopped fresh parsley

Alternative Fillings

Bacon, cheese, and sour cream are the trinity when it comes to this humble little tuber, but think outside of the potato. Don't be afraid to change up the meat or cheese or use vegetables or herbs. Feta and chopped Kalamata olives…pimiento cheese and ham cubes…horseradish, Swiss cheese, and chopped pastrami—what combinations can you and your family come up with?

1. Preheat air fryer at 400°F for 3 minutes.

2. Rub olive oil over both potatoes. Place in air fryer basket.

3. Cook 30 minutes. Flip potatoes. Cook an additional 15 minutes.

4. Once cooled, slice each potato lengthwise. Scoop out potato to form four boats with the skins, leaving a ¼" layer of potato flesh in each. Place scooped-out potato in a medium bowl.

5. To scooped-out potato, mash in garlic salt, pepper, butter, Cheddar cheese, sour cream, and bacon. Spoon mixture into potato boats.

6. Place boats back into air fryer basket and cook an additional 2 minutes. Garnish with parsley and serve warm.

PER SERVING Calories: 310 | Fat: 14.5 g | Protein: 10.5 g | Sodium: 504 mg | Fiber: 3.5 g | Carbohydrates: 32.7 g | Sugar: 2.3 g

Ranch Purple Potatoes

Toss these gorgeous spuds with some ranch dressing for creamy flavor. If you don't prefer cilantro, simply swap it out for some chopped fresh parsley!

HANDS-ON TIME: 5 minutes
COOK TIME: 19 minutes

INGREDIENTS | SERVES 6

1 pound small purple potatoes, scrubbed and halved

2 tablespoons butter, melted

¼ teaspoon salt

⅛ teaspoon freshly ground black pepper

¼ cup ranch dressing

¼ cup chopped fresh cilantro

1. Preheat air fryer at 350°F for 3 minutes.

2. In a large bowl, combine potatoes, butter, salt, and pepper.

3. Place potatoes in air fryer basket. Cook 10 minutes. Toss potatoes. Cook an additional 9 minutes.

4. Transfer to a serving bowl and toss with ranch dressing. Garnish with cilantro and serve warm.

PER SERVING Calories: 84 | Fat: 3.9 g | Protein: 1.4 g | Sodium: 115 mg | Fiber: 1.2 g | Carbohydrates: 11.0 g | Sugar: 0.9 g

Roasted Garlic Mashed Potatoes

The skins of the potatoes not only add nutrition to your mashed potatoes, but also contribute to the texture and rustic flavor of the dish.

HANDS-ON TIME: 10 minutes
COOK TIME: 14 minutes

INGREDIENTS | SERVES 4

1 pound Yukon Gold potatoes (2 medium), scrubbed and diced into 1" cubes

3 cloves garlic, halved

2 tablespoons butter, melted

½ teaspoon salt

½ teaspoon freshly ground black pepper

¼ cup heavy cream

1 tablespoon butter (not melted)

¼ cup chopped fresh parsley

Alternatives to Heavy Cream

Ahhhh…heavy cream. It's heavy and it's creamy! Sometimes we only use this when guests come over and we want to put our best foodie foot forward. But for our every-day consumption, a lower caloric punch is welcomed. Use skim, 2 percent, or whole milk. Or, if you are a vegan or dairy upsets your gut health, unsweetened almond milk can work just as well!

1. Preheat air fryer at 350°F for 3 minutes.

2. In a large bowl, combine potatoes, garlic, and melted butter.

3. Place potato mixture in air fryer basket. Cook 7 minutes. Toss. Cook an additional 7 minutes. Transfer to a large bowl.

4. Add salt, pepper, half the cream, and 1 tablespoon butter and mash. Slowly add remaining cream until desired consistency.

5. Garnish with parsley and serve warm.

PER SERVING Calories: 203 | Fat: 13.4 g | Protein: 2.4 g | Sodium: 315 mg | Fiber: 2.7 g | Carbohydrates: 17.8 g | Sugar: 1.7 g

CHAPTER 12

Sandwiches

Fried Spam and Scrambled Egg Breakfast Sandwich

The air fryer not only crisps up the Spam, but it evenly toasts the bread, making this a perfect sandwich for dorm room late nights.

HANDS-ON TIME: 10 minutes
COOK TIME: 9 minutes

INGREDIENTS | SERVES 4

1 (12-ounce) can Spam
8 slices bread
4 large eggs, whisked
8 teaspoons mayonnaise

What Is Spam?

Spam is a canned meat of ham, spices, gelatin, fillers, and all sorts of other things. It obviously isn't on the powerhouse foods list, but it has a unique following dating back to World War II, when fresh meat was a luxury and food needed to be nonperishable and portable. Apparently, only a small group of people actually knows what Spam stands for, but the rumors lie heavily with "spiced ham" being the inspiration.

1. Preheat air fryer at 375°F for 3 minutes.

2. Slice Spam into ¼" fries. Place in air fryer basket and cook 3 minutes. Flip fries. Cook 3 minutes more. Flip fries. Cook an additional 3 minutes. Transfer to a plate.

3. While the fries are cooking, toast the bread and scramble the eggs.

4. Spread 1 teaspoon mayonnaise on each piece of toast. Layer with eggs and Spam fries. Serve warm.

PER SERVING Calories: 556 | Fat: 35.4 g | Protein: 22.9 g | Sodium: 1,587 mg | Fiber: 1.6 g | Carbohydrates: 32.6 g | Sugar: 3.6 g

Oyster Po'boys

Do you love po'boys but don't want the fried-food aspect of this Louisiana staple? Well, the air fryer is your new friend. And don't forget to make air-fried French fries to go along with this meal!

HANDS-ON TIME: 10 minutes
COOK TIME: 18 minutes

INGREDIENTS | SERVES 2

½ pound raw oysters, excluding shells (approximately 10 medium oysters)
½ cup all-purpose flour
1 large egg
½ cup buttermilk
1 cup panko bread crumbs, crushed fine
¼ cup cornmeal
½ teaspoon salt
1 tablespoon Old Bay Seasoning
2 hoagie rolls, split
3 tablespoons butter, melted
½ cup shredded iceberg lettuce
1 medium tomato, seeded and diced
¼ cup Remoulade Special Sauce (see Chapter 15)

The Origin of the Po'boy

There are several conflicting stories about how the name po'boy got started. The most popular is about two guys, Bennie and Clovis Martin, who had a locally owned restaurant in New Orleans who provided free sandwiches to the "poor boys" on strike from a streetcar company. With the Southern, French dialect, "poor boys" sounded more like "po'boys."

1. Rinse and drain oysters. Pat dry with a paper towel. Set aside.

2. Add flour to a small bowl.

3. In another small bowl, whisk together egg and buttermilk.

4. Combine bread crumbs, cornmeal, salt, and Old Bay Seasoning in a shallow dish.

5. Preheat air fryer at 400°F for 3 minutes.

6. Roll a few oysters in flour. Shake off excess flour. Dip oysters in egg mixture and shake off excess. Roll oysters in bread crumb mixture. Transfer to a plate. Repeat with remaining oysters.

7. Add half of oysters to fryer basket. Cook 4 minutes. Carefully flip oysters. Cook an additional 4 minutes.

8. Transfer oysters from basket to a serving plate. Cook remaining oysters.

9. Brush hoagie rolls with melted butter. One at time, cook 1 minute, butter side down, in air fryer basket.

10. Construct sandwiches by layering oysters, lettuce, and tomatoes, and drizzle 2 tablespoons of Remoulade Special Sauce on each roll.

PER SERVING Calories: 1,000 | Fat: 42.4 g | Protein: 42.7 g | Sodium: 1,639 mg | Fiber: 3.7 g | Carbohydrates: 102.8 g | Sugar: 9.8 g

Fried Fish Sandwich

When choosing your fish fillets, keep in mind to pick a "square" fillet, as it will fit better on a bun. If you don't see what you like, ask your fishmonger to cut a fillet to your liking. They are usually happy to help!

HANDS-ON TIME: 10 minutes
COOK TIME: 9 minutes

INGREDIENTS | SERVES 2

1 large egg

1 tablespoon whole milk

2 teaspoons lemon juice

½ cup plain bread crumbs

¼ teaspoon salt

2 (4-ounce) cod fillets

2 hamburger buns

2 tablespoons Tartar Sauce (see Chapter 15)

8 slices dill pickle

⅓ cup shredded iceberg lettuce

1. In a small bowl, whisk together egg, milk, and lemon juice.

2. In a shallow dish, combine bread crumbs and salt.

3. Dip fillets in egg mixture and then dredge all sides of the fish in bread crumb mixture.

4. Preheat air fryer at 350°F for 3 minutes.

5. Place fillets in lightly greased air fryer basket. Cook 9 minutes, ensuring that the cod is opaque and flakes easily with a fork.

6. Transfer fish to buns and dress with Tartar Sauce, pickles, and lettuce. Serve warm.

PER SERVING Calories: 353 | Fat: 9.1 g | Protein: 26.4 g | Sodium: 1,360 mg | Fiber: 2.3 g | Carbohydrates: 38.3 g | Sugar: 5.0 g

Lobster Rolls

This classic to New Englanders can be yours in minutes. The lobster meat shines with very little seasoning. Traditionally served on a top-slit buttered hot dog bun, the lobster salad is great on its own or even in a lettuce wrap!

HANDS-ON TIME: 15 minutes
COOK TIME: 10 minutes

INGREDIENTS | SERVES 2

2 (5–6 ounce) small uncooked lobster tails
3 tablespoons butter, melted, divided
2 tablespoons mayonnaise
1 small stalk celery, diced
2 teaspoons fresh lemon juice
½ teaspoon fresh lemon zest
¼ teaspoon smoked paprika
¼ teaspoon salt
⅛ teaspoon freshly ground black pepper
2 top-split buns
½ cup shredded lettuce

How to Shred Lettuce

Although shredded lettuce comes conveniently prepackaged, it is easy and more economical to do on your own. Simply take a cleaned head of iceberg lettuce and give it a quick pound, stem-side down, on your counter. This will allow you to easily remove and discard the core. Cut the remaining lettuce in quarters and then grate on the large holes of a box grater.

1. Using kitchen shears, cut down the middle of the lobster tail on the softer side. Carefully run your finger between the lobster meat and the shell to loosen meat.

2. Preheat air fryer at 400°F for 3 minutes.

3. Place tails in air fryer basket, cut side up. Cook 4 minutes. Brush with 1 tablespoon butter. Cook an additional 3–4 minutes, depending on the size of the lobster tail.

4. Roughly chop lobster meat and transfer to a medium bowl. Combine lobster with mayonnaise, celery, lemon juice, lemon zest, paprika, salt, and pepper. Refrigerate covered until ready to use.

5. Brush remaining butter on each inner side of the buns. Cook 1–2 minutes at 400°F in air fryer.

6. Distribute lobster mixture and lettuce between the buns and serve.

PER SERVING Calories: 489 | Fat: 28.8 g | Protein: 30.6 g | Sodium: 1,266 mg | Fiber: 1.6 g | Carbohydrates: 23.0 g | Sugar: 3.6 g

Lamb Meatball Gyros

Gyros are traditionally made with meat cooked on a vertical rotisserie, but most of us don't own one. By using meatballs as an alternative, you still get the flavors of the classic without any of the mess.

HANDS-ON TIME: 5 minutes
COOK TIME: 8 minutes

INGREDIENTS | SERVES 2

½ pound ground lamb

½ cup plain bread crumbs

1 teaspoon chopped fresh mint

¼ teaspoon ground coriander

2 cloves garlic, minced

1 teaspoon salt

2 pita rounds

2 medium Roma tomatoes, seeded and diced

¼ cup diced red onion

¼ cup Tzatziki Sauce (see Chapter 15)

1. Preheat air fryer at 350°F for 3 minutes.

2. In a medium bowl, combine lamb, bread crumbs, mint, coriander, garlic, and salt. Form into eight meatballs, about 2 tablespoons each.

3. Add meatballs to fryer basket and cook 6 minutes. Flip meatballs. Cook an additional 2 minutes. Transfer to a plate.

4. Open pita rounds and add half the meatballs to each. Add half the tomatoes, red onion, and Tzatziki Sauce to each and serve.

PER SERVING Calories: 562 | Fat: 19.4 g | Protein: 34.4 g | Sodium: 1,881 mg | Fiber: 2.8 g | Carbohydrates: 55.3 g | Sugar: 3.6 g

How Do You Pronounce "Gyro"?

Riddle me this: How the heck do you pronounce "gyro"? Many people say JAI-roh, so because you subscribe to a sort of groupthink and don't want to sound snooty, you'll pronounce it that way too. Who cares? But, really, don't you secretly want to know how to say it correctly? One gyro is pronounced YEE-roh, and two or more gyri are pronounced YEE-ree. There you go! Now go forth and teach!

Marinara Meatball Subs

If this sub doesn't scream game day, then what does? Premake the meatballs in the air fryer the night before and then prepare the meatball subs in waves for your hungry sports fans as they build up an appetite for the win!

HANDS-ON TIME: 10 minutes
COOK TIME: 11 minutes

INGREDIENTS | SERVES 2

¼ pound ground beef

¼ pound ground pork

1 teaspoon grated Asiago cheese

½ teaspoon Italian seasoning

¼ teaspoon onion powder

¼ teaspoon salt

1 tablespoon panko bread crumbs

¾ cup plus 1 tablespoon Marinara Sauce (see Chapter 15), divided

2 top-split hoagie rolls

4 (1-ounce) slices fresh mozzarella

¼ cup julienned fresh basil leaves

1. In a medium bowl, combine beef, pork, Asiago cheese, Italian seasoning, onion powder, salt, bread crumbs, and 1 tablespoon marinara sauce. Form into six equal meatballs.

2. Preheat air fryer at 350°F for 3 minutes.

3. Place meatballs in air fryer basket. Cook 5 minutes.

4. Transfer meatballs to cake barrel (accessory). Top with remaining marinara sauce. Cook an additional 5 minutes.

5. Load hoagie rolls with three meatballs each along with half the sauce on each. Top each with 2 mozzarella slices.

6. Place meatball subs back in air fryer basket and cook 1 minute to melt the cheese.

7. Transfer subs to a serving plate, garnish with fresh basil, and serve warm.

PER SERVING Calories: 512 | Fat: 20.8 g | Protein: 42.0 g | Sodium: 1,291 mg | Fiber: 3.0 g | Carbohydrates: 34.3 g | Sugar: 7.3 g

Pork Meatball Banh Mi

A banh mi, a Vietnamese sandwich, is made a hundred different ways, but the basics are a baguette, meat, vegetables, and a sauce. The recipe has a long list of ingredients, but use them all. There is a balance achieved by using every one.

HANDS-ON TIME: 15 minutes
COOK TIME: 9 minutes

INGREDIENTS | SERVES 2

¼ cup rice vinegar
⅛ cup water
⅛ cup honey
1 large carrot, peeled and shredded
6 medium radishes, julienned
2 tablespoons diced white onion
¼ cup julienned cucumbers
½ pound lean ground pork
½ teaspoon ground ginger
½ teaspoon ground cumin
1 teaspoon fish sauce
1 teaspoon soy sauce
½ cup plain bread crumbs
1 (12") French baguette, cut crosswise into 2 (6") sections
½ cup shredded iceberg lettuce
¼ cup Sriracha Mayonnaise (see Chapter 15)

Should I Just Skip the Fish Sauce?

The answer is a resounding no. Fish sauce might sound gross when it is defined as fermented anchovy juice. Most of us have had anchovies mashed up in restaurant sauces and didn't even know it but couldn't put our finger on why the sauce tasted so good. Fish sauce provides the umami (taste sensation) that brings the flavors all together. Use it as a salt substitute in stir-fries and other homemade Asian dishes.

1. In a small saucepan over medium-high heat, heat vinegar, water, and honey 1 minute. Set aside 5 minutes.

2. Place carrot, radishes, onion, and cucumbers in a medium bowl and pour vinegar sauce over them to pickle them. Refrigerate covered 30 minutes or until ready to use. Strain.

3. Preheat air fryer at 350°F for 3 minutes.

4. Combine pork, ginger, cumin, fish sauce, soy sauce, and bread crumbs. Form into eight meatballs, about 2 tablespoons each.

5. Add meatballs to fryer basket and cook 6 minutes. Flip meatballs. Cook an additional 2 minutes. Transfer to a plate.

6. Slice baguettes lengthwise and add four meatballs to each. Top with pickled vegetables and lettuce. Drizzle each sandwich with half the Sriracha Mayonnaise. Serve immediately.

PER SERVING Calories: 560 | Fat: 24.6 g | Protein: 23.3 g | Sodium: 1,248 mg | Fiber: 4.4 g | Carbohydrates: 58.4 g | Sugar: 9.9 g

Grilled Pimiento Cheese and Tomato Sandwiches

There's nothing more sought after in the South than sweet tea and a pimiento cheese sandwich for lunch. Make these sandwiches and make them soon.

HANDS-ON TIME: 10 minutes
COOK TIME: 24 minutes

INGREDIENTS | SERVES 4

8 ounces shredded sharp Cheddar cheese

1 (4-ounce) jar diced pimientos, including juice

½ cup mayonnaise

¼ teaspoon salt

8 slices whole-wheat bread

4 medium Campari tomatoes, sliced

¼ teaspoon freshly ground black pepper

4 tablespoons butter, melted

What Are Campari Tomatoes?

Campari tomatoes have been showing up in grocery stores lately, and you need to give them a try. Larger than cherry tomatoes and smaller than Roma tomatoes, they are grown hydroponically (in water). They are so sweet and always have a beautiful deep-red color, making them gorgeous to use in cooking and garnishes.

1. In a medium bowl, combine cheese, pimientos including juice, mayonnaise, and salt. Refrigerate covered 30 minutes.

2. Spread pimiento cheese evenly over 4 slices of bread. Distribute tomato slices and season tomatoes with ground black pepper. Top with remaining bread slices.

3. Preheat air fryer at 350°F for 3 minutes.

4. Brush the outside top and bottom of a sandwich lightly with melted butter. Place sandwich in air fryer basket and cook 3 minutes. Flip and cook an additional 3 minutes.

5. Repeat for remaining sandwiches. Serve warm.

PER SERVING Calories: 685 | Fat: 48.1 g | Protein: 22.8 g | Sodium: 983 mg | Fiber: 5.2 g | Carbohydrates: 32.2 g | Sugar: 5.5 g

Raisin Bread Monte Cristo

Move over traditional Monte Cristo; this sandwich just got elevated. Dipped in an egg wash and then air-fried, this French classic just got an American upgrade!

HANDS-ON TIME: 10 minutes
COOK TIME: 12 minutes

INGREDIENTS | SERVES 2

½ cup grated Gruyère cheese

2 tablespoons cream cheese, at room temperature

2 teaspoons Dijon mustard

Pinch salt

Pinch freshly ground black pepper

1 large egg

4 slices raisin bread

2 thick slices deli ham

1. In a medium bowl, combine Gruyère cheese, cream cheese, mustard, salt, and pepper.

2. In a small bowl, whisk egg.

3. Spread cheese mixture evenly over 2 slices of bread. Add ham. Top slices with remaining bread.

4. Preheat air fryer at 350°F for 3 minutes.

5. Dip one sandwich in whisked egg on both sides. Place in lightly greased air fryer basket and cook 3 minutes. Flip and cook an additional 3 minutes.

6. Repeat with other sandwich. Serve warm.

PER SERVING Calories: 375 | Fat: 20.0 g | Protein: 20.3 g | Sodium: 875 mg | Fiber: 2.4 g | Carbohydrates: 29.4 g | Sugar: 3.8 g

Fried Peanut Butter and Banana Sandwiches

Peanut butter and banana are a wonderful combination. With the addition of honey and then air frying the sandwich, the extra sweetness and crunchy sandwich bread almost makes this a dessert.

HANDS-ON TIME: 10 minutes
COOK TIME: 12 minutes

INGREDIENTS | SERVES 2

2 tablespoons creamy peanut butter

4 slices white sandwich bread

1 large banana, sliced

2 teaspoons honey

2 tablespoons butter, melted

Why Is Some Honey Runny and Some Thicker?

All honey is actually in a liquid state when jarred; however, raw honey isn't filtered, so the pollen and beeswax are still present. It goes through a natural crystallization state, causing it to harden a bit in the jar. The type of flower from which the bee gets its nectar determines how fast the honey hardens. Runny honey has been filtered and heated, so the hardening quality is diminished but it is easier to use quickly in everyday recipes.

1. Spread peanut butter on one side of 2 slices of bread. Layer each with sliced bananas and drizzle each with honey. Top with remaining bread.

2. Preheat air fryer at 350°F for 3 minutes.

3. Brush the outside top and bottom of a sandwich lightly with melted butter. Place in air fryer basket one at a time and cook 3 minutes. Flip and cook an additional 3 minutes.

4. Repeat with other sandwich. Serve warm.

PER SERVING Calories: 412 | Fat: 17.7 g | Protein: 9.7 g | Sodium: 298 mg | Fiber: 4.2 g | Carbohydrates: 54.6 g | Sugar: 19.2 g

Chicken Parmesan Grilled Cheese Sandwich

What happens when two sought-after foods collide? Chicken Parmesan Grilled Cheese Sandwich! Although the marinara sauce can be used out of a jar, if you take the time to prepare the Spicy Marinara Sauce, the results will be much appreciated.

HANDS-ON TIME: 10 minutes
COOK TIME: 12 minutes

INGREDIENTS | SERVES 2

2 tablespoons Spicy Marinara Sauce (see Chapter 15)

4 (2-ounce) slices sourdough bread

2 tablespoons grated Parmesan cheese

½ cup chopped cooked chicken

4 (1-ounce) slices fresh mozzarella cheese

2 tablespoons butter, melted

1. Spread marinara on one side of 2 slices of bread. Sprinkle with Parmesan cheese. Layer with chicken and mozzarella slices. Top each with remaining slices of bread.

2. Preheat air fryer at 350°F for 3 minutes.

3. Brush the outside top and bottom of a sandwich lightly with melted butter. Place in air fryer basket one at a time and cook 3 minutes. Flip and cook an additional 3 minutes.

4. Repeat with other sandwich. Serve warm.

PER SERVING Calories: 654 | Fat: 25.1 g | Protein: 38.1 g | Sodium: 1,203 mg | Fiber: 2.8 g | Carbohydrates: 62.0 g | Sugar: 6.5 g

Grilled Cheese Croutons

An unexpected pop of cheese is always welcomed. Float these croutons on a bowl of soup or salad. Try complementary cheeses in this recipe for a bumped-up experience each time. Pssst…feta croutons are amazing on a fresh Greek salad!

HANDS-ON TIME: 10 minutes
COOK TIME: 12 minutes

INGREDIENTS | SERVES 2

2 (1-ounce) slices Cheddar cheese
2 (1-ounce) slices provolone cheese
4 (2-ounce) slices sourdough bread
2 tablespoons butter, melted

1. Place 1 slice of Cheddar cheese and 1 slice of provolone cheese between 2 pieces of bread. Repeat.

2. Preheat air fryer at 350°F for 3 minutes.

3. Brush the outside top and bottom of each sandwich lightly with melted butter. Place in air fryer basket one at a time and cook 3 minutes. Transfer sandwich to a clean, flat surface. Gently press sandwich flat with a heavy, flat pan or skillet. Add sandwich back to air fryer basket and cook an additional 3 minutes. Repeat with second sandwich.

4. Cut sandwiches into 1" cubes and serve.

PER SERVING Calories: 598 | Fat: 25.4 g | Protein: 26.3 g | Sodium: 1,114 mg | Fiber: 2.5 g | Carbohydrates: 59.8 g | Sugar: 5.5 g

Gerber Sandwich

This St. Louis classic is just a simple open-faced sandwich. It is traditionally served with Provel cheese, a regional delicacy but hard to find outside of the city. Our version uses a combination of Swiss and provolone cheeses to mimic the taste of the classic.

HANDS-ON TIME: 10 minutes
COOK TIME: 5 minutes

INGREDIENTS | SERVES 2

2 tablespoons butter, melted

2 cloves garlic, minced

1 (6") French baguette, sliced lengthwise in half

¼ pound sliced deli ham

4 slices Swiss cheese

½ cup shredded provolone cheese

¼ teaspoon smoked paprika

1. In a small bowl, whisk together butter and garlic. Spread on each baguette half. Top each with half the ham, Swiss cheese, and provolone cheese. Sprinkle with smoked paprika.

2. Preheat air fryer at 350°F for 3 minutes.

3. Place topped bread in air fryer basket. Cook 5 minutes until cheese is browned and melty. Serve warm.

PER SERVING Calories: 834 | Fat: 40.8 g | Protein: 46.9 g | Sodium: 1,898 mg | Fiber: 2.9 g | Carbohydrates: 70.3 g | Sugar: 6.7 g

Ham and Swiss Sandwiches

When you prepare grilled sandwiches on a stovetop, the heat source is usually round and the sandwiches square. This can create uneven cooking. With the air fryer, the even cooking creates the perfect grilled cheese, or in this case, Ham and Swiss Sandwiches!

HANDS-ON TIME: 10 minutes
COOK TIME: 12 minutes

INGREDIENTS | SERVES 2

1 tablespoon horseradish mustard

4 (2-ounce) slices ciabatta bread (or other crusty artisanal bread)

4 ounces thinly sliced ham

2 ounces thinly sliced Swiss cheese

2 tablespoons butter, melted

1. Spread mustard evenly on 2 slices bread. Top each slice evenly with ham and Swiss cheese. Place bread without mustard on top.

2. Preheat air fryer at 350°F for 3 minutes.

3. Brush the outside top and bottom of a sandwich lightly with melted butter. Place in air fryer basket and cook 3 minutes. Flip and cook an additional 3 minutes.

4. Repeat for other sandwich. Serve warm.

PER SERVING Calories: 597 | Fat: 24.2 g | Protein: 27.7 g | Sodium: 1,550 mg | Fiber: 3.8 g | Carbohydrates: 61.0 g | Sugar: 1.3 g

Brie, Fig, and Prosciutto Open-Faced Sandwiches

Sweet, salty, and creamy, these open-faced sandwiches hit all the yummy buttons. Serve on regular-sized bread for a meal for two or prepare these as appetizers on smaller sliced French bread for some happy partygoers.

HANDS-ON TIME: 5 minutes
COOK TIME: 4 minutes

INGREDIENTS | SERVES 2

¼ cup Brie cheese

¼ cup fig jam

2 (2-ounce) slices ciabatta bread (or other crusty artisanal bread)

½ cup arugula, stems removed

4 slices prosciutto (about 2 ounces), ripped into big, rustic pieces

½ teaspoon olive oil

1. Preheat air fryer at 350°F for 3 minutes.

2. Spread a layer of Brie and then fig jam on each slice of bread.

3. Place topped bread in air fryer basket. Cook 3–4 minutes until cheese is melty and warm.

4. Top each sandwich with arugula and prosciutto pieces. Lightly drizzle ¼ teaspoon olive oil on each sandwich. Serve warm.

PER SERVING Calories: 418 | Fat: 13.2 g | Protein: 16.1 g | Sodium: 580 mg | Fiber: 1.8 g | Carbohydrates: 57.9 g | Sugar: 22.2 g

What Exactly Is Arugula?

Arugula, also known as rocket, is a leafy green that you should be eating. Because of its tangy and natural peppery flavor, it is especially good on sandwiches. A great source of antioxidants and vitamin K, arugula is also high in some B vitamins, which are known to increase your metabolism.

Pesto and Prosciutto Panini

Who said you need an expensive panini maker to create a panini? Halfway through the cooking process, simply transfer your sandwich to a cutting board and give it a press using a heavy skillet or cutting board to achieve that smooshed effect.

HANDS-ON TIME: 10 minutes
COOK TIME: 12 minutes

INGREDIENTS | SERVES 2

1 tablespoon yellow mustard

4 slices ciabatta bread (or other crusty artisanal bread)

6 ounces prosciutto

2 ounces thinly sliced provolone cheese

4 wide slices jarred roasted red peppers, drained

½ cup baby arugula, stems removed

2 tablespoons Traditional Pesto (see Chapter 15)

2 tablespoons butter, melted

1. Spread mustard evenly on 2 slices bread. Top evenly with prosciutto, provolone, red pepper, and arugula. Spread Traditional Pesto on other 2 slices of bread and place on top.

2. Preheat air fryer at 350°F for 3 minutes.

3. Brush the outside top and bottom of a sandwich lightly with melted butter. Place in air fryer basket and cook 3 minutes. Transfer to a cutting board and "smoosh" sandwich down with a skillet or another heavy flat item. Cook an additional 3 minutes.

4. Repeat with other sandwich. Serve warm.

PER SERVING Calories: 743 | Fat: 44.5 g | Protein: 39.8 g | Sodium: 2,037 mg | Fiber: 4.3 g | Carbohydrates: 64.1 g | Sugar: 1.5 g

California Turkey Sandwiches

The avocado, tomato, and sprouts give this sandwich its California name. But the turkey and Rosemary Mayonnaise give a little nod to the holidays, creating a unique combination of tasty! If you don't have Gruyère, substitute Swiss cheese, as it is the closest in taste.

HANDS-ON TIME: 10 minutes
COOK TIME: 12 minutes

INGREDIENTS | SERVES 2

2 tablespoons Rosemary Mayonnaise (see Chapter 15)

4 slices ciabatta bread (or other crusty artisanal bread)

4 ounces thinly sliced deli turkey

4 ounces thinly sliced Gruyère cheese

1 small avocado, peeled, pitted, and sliced

1 medium Roma tomato, thinly sliced

½ cup alfalfa sprouts

2 tablespoons butter, melted

Types of Sprouts

Sprouts are the germinating shoots of seeds. They are not only edible but are incredibly nutritious. In recent years, grocery stores have been offering more than alfalfa and bean sprouts. Broccoli sprouts, radish sprouts, and lentil sprouts are also showing up. Because of the pricey tag, many folks grow their own!

1. Spread Rosemary Mayonnaise on inside of each piece of bread.

2. Build sandwiches between bread slices by evenly distributing turkey, Gruyère cheese, avocado, tomato, and sprouts.

3. Preheat air fryer at 350°F for 3 minutes.

4. Brush the outside top and bottom of a sandwich lightly with melted butter. Place in air fryer basket and cook 3 minutes. Flip and cook an additional 3 minutes.

5. Repeat with other sandwich. Serve warm.

PER SERVING Calories: 894 | Fat: 49.0 g | Protein: 36.7 g | Sodium: 1,923 mg | Fiber: 8.5 g | Carbohydrates: 68.7 g | Sugar: 4.6 g

Caprese Sandwiches

This sandwich is a take on the classic insalata caprese, or caprese salad. You can use cow's milk mozzarella or mozzarella made from buffalo milk.

HANDS-ON TIME: 10 minutes
COOK TIME: 10 minutes

INGREDIENTS | SERVES 2

2 tablespoons balsamic vinegar

4 (2-ounce) slices ciabatta bread (or other crusty artisanal bread)

2 ounces fresh mozzarella, sliced

2 medium Roma tomatoes, sliced

8 fresh basil leaves

2 tablespoons olive oil

Differences in Balsamic Vinegar

Balsamic vinegars are amazing either added to vinaigrettes or reduced for a thick glaze. Although vinegars have some wonderful health benefits, they are not all created equally. Some of the cheaper versions are laced with added sugars and caramel coloring. So heed caution and read your labels.

1. Preheat air fryer at 350°F for 3 minutes.

2. Drizzle balsamic vinegar on bottom slices bread. Layer on mozzarella, tomatoes, and basil leaves. Top with remaining slices bread.

3. Brush the outside top and bottom of a sandwich lightly with olive oil. Place in air fryer basket and cook 3 minutes. Flip and cook an additional 2 minutes.

4. Repeat with other sandwich. Serve warm.

PER SERVING Calories: 502 | Fat: 19.9 g | Protein: 16.9 g | Sodium: 1,059 mg | Fiber: 3.9 g | Carbohydrates: 62.6 g | Sugar: 3.7 g

Roast Beef Sandwiches with Horseradish Sauce

This is a hearty sandwich that is perfect eaten in the outdoors. Prepare the sandwiches and then tightly wrap in aluminum foil. Throw them in your backpack, enjoy the outdoors, and then enjoy this incredible sandwich.

HANDS-ON TIME: 5 minutes
COOK TIME: 10 minutes

INGREDIENTS | SERVES 2

2 tablespoons Horseradish Sauce (see Chapter 15)
2 (6") sections French baguette, sliced lengthwise in half
6 ounces sliced roast beef
4 ounces thinly sliced provolone cheese
1 large tomato, sliced
Pinch salt
Pinch freshly ground black pepper
½ cup arugula

1. Spread Horseradish Sauce on bottom halves of baguettes. Top evenly with roast beef and provolone cheese. Place other halves of baguette on top.

2. Preheat air fryer at 350°F for 3 minutes.

3. Place one sandwich in air fryer basket and cook 5 minutes. Open sandwich and add tomatoes. Season with salt and pepper. Add arugula. Repeat with second sandwich.

4. Close sandwiches and serve warm.

PER SERVING Calories: 569 | Fat: 26.7 g | Protein: 46.3 g | Sodium: 1,048 mg | Fiber: 2.3 g | Carbohydrates: 34.7 g | Sugar: 5.2 g

Reuben Sandwiches

The classic Reuben sandwich is arguably the finest sandwich ever created. Air-fried French fries are the best companion to these sandwiches!

HANDS-ON TIME: 10 minutes
COOK TIME: 12 minutes

INGREDIENTS | SERVES 2

2 tablespoons Thousand Island dressing
4 slices rye bread
6 ounces sliced corned beef
4 ounces thinly sliced Swiss cheese
½ cup sauerkraut, drained
2 tablespoons butter, melted

1. Preheat air fryer at 350°F for 3 minutes.

2. Prepare sandwiches by spreading Thousand Island dressing on 2 slices rye bread. Distribute corned beef, cheese, and sauerkraut between the sandwiches. Top with remaining bread.

3. Brush the outside top and bottom of a sandwich lightly with melted butter. Place in air fryer basket and cook 3 minutes. Flip and cook an additional 3 minutes.

4. Repeat with other sandwich. Serve warm.

PER SERVING Calories: 1,040 | Fat: 65.3 g | Protein: 59.0 g | Sodium: 1,656 mg | Fiber: 4.5 g | Carbohydrates: 39.3 g | Sugar: 7.1 g

Open-Faced Tuna Melts

For someone who likes bread but not too much of it, an open-faced sandwich is the way to go. These tuna melts are creamy and cheesy, with a delectable crunch from the air fryer's toasted bread.

HANDS-ON TIME: 10 minutes
COOK TIME: 4 minutes

INGREDIENTS | SERVES 2

1 (5-ounce) can tuna in water, drained
¼ cup mayonnaise
2 teaspoons Dijon mustard
1 tablespoon small-diced celery
1 tablespoon dill pickle relish
Pinch salt
Pinch freshly ground black pepper
2 English muffins, split
4 slices large tomato
½ medium avocado, peeled, pitted, and cut into 4 slices
½ cup shredded sharp Cheddar cheese

1. In a small bowl, combine tuna, mayonnaise, mustard, celery, relish, salt, and pepper.

2. Preheat air fryer at 350°F for 3 minutes.

3. Distribute tuna salad among the 4 English muffin halves and spread it. Add a tomato slice to each sandwich. Add avocado slices and top each with cheese.

4. Place open-faced sandwiches in air fryer basket and cook 4 minutes or until cheese starts to brown. Serve warm.

PER SERVING Calories: 586 | Fat: 30.1 g | Protein: 27.2 g | Sodium: 1,098 mg | Fiber: 5.1 g | Carbohydrates: 33.0 g | Sugar: 3.8 g

What Kind of Canned Tuna Is Best?

Sustainability is a huge concern for some tuna eaters. Do some research on tuna suppliers, as there are vast differences among the brands. Although albacore is high in omega-3 fatty acids, it is a larger fish, so it contains a higher mercury level. Also, tuna packed in water is preferred because it has fewer calories. Water-packed tuna allows users more control, letting them add their own healthy fats when preparing a meal with tuna.

CHAPTER 13

One-Pot Wonders

Tuna Noodle Casserole

As American as apple pie, Tuna Noodle Casserole has been made for generations.
The soft egg noodles are great with tuna, peas, celery, and other fillings.

HANDS-ON TIME: 15 minutes
COOK TIME: 15 minutes

INGREDIENTS | SERVES 4

½ pound egg noodles, cooked

½ cup canned sweet peas, drained

1 (10.75-ounce) can condensed cream
of mushroom soup

¼ cup sour cream

¼ cup grated Parmesan cheese

2 tablespoons whole milk

1 tablespoon soy sauce

1 (5-ounce) can tuna packed in water,
drained

2 tablespoons minced onion

1 stalk celery, diced

¼ cup panko bread crumbs

2 tablespoons butter, melted

1. Preheat air fryer at 375°F for 3 minutes.

2. In a medium bowl, combine egg noodles, peas,
   mushroom soup, sour cream, Parmesan cheese, milk,
   soy sauce, tuna, onion, and celery.

3. Lightly spray or brush oil on a round cake barrel
   (accessory). Add noodle mixture. Scatter bread
   crumbs across the top and drizzle evenly with butter.
   Cook 15 minutes.

4. Remove barrel from air fryer and let rest 10 minutes.
   Serve warm.

PER SERVING Calories: 442 | Fat: 16.1 g | Protein: 19.5 g |
Sodium: 995 mg | Fiber: 3.6 g | Carbohydrates: 50.9 g |
Sugar: 3.4 g

Chicken Potpie

There is just something magical about a chicken potpie. Is it the creamy filling loaded with chicken and vegetables, or is it the fluffy and crunchy biscuit topping? Maybe all of these contribute to the goodness, mixed in with a little dose of nostalgia.

HANDS-ON TIME: 15 minutes
COOK TIME: 15 minutes

INGREDIENTS | SERVES 4

Chicken Filling
¾ cup chicken broth
¼ cup whole milk
2 tablespoons all-purpose flour
2 cups diced cooked chicken
1 (14.5-ounce) can mixed vegetables
2 tablespoons finely diced yellow onion
1 tablespoon fresh thyme leaves
½ teaspoon salt
¼ teaspoon freshly ground black pepper

Biscuit Topping
1 cup all-purpose flour
1½ teaspoons baking powder
¾ teaspoon salt
¼ teaspoon freshly ground black pepper
4 tablespoons whole milk
1 tablespoon butter, melted

1. In a large bowl, whisk together broth, milk, and flour. Toss in chicken, mixed vegetables, onion, thyme, salt, and pepper.

2. Preheat air fryer at 375°F for 3 minutes.

3. Lightly spray or brush oil on a round cake barrel (accessory). Add chicken mixture. Place barrel in air fryer basket and cook 5 minutes.

4. While chicken is cooking, mix Biscuit Topping ingredients in a small bowl. When chicken mixture is ready, drop sticky spoonfuls over it. Cook an additional 10 minutes.

5. Remove barrel from air fryer and let rest 10 minutes. Serve warm.

PER SERVING Calories: 363 | Fat: 8.6 g | Protein: 29.9 g | Sodium: 1,297 mg | Fiber: 5.1 g | Carbohydrates: 37.1 g | Sugar: 1.9 g

Can You Use Frozen Mixed Vegetables?

Yes, as a matter of fact, some people prefer their vegetables frozen over canned due to freshness. Companies will freeze the vegetables straight from picking. And some canned foods can be high in sugar or sodium and can have fewer nutrients than the frozen variety, as nutrients are often destroyed during the canning process. If you want to use frozen vegetables for this recipe, thaw the frozen bag of vegetables in the refrigerator the night before preparation of the potpie for optimum results.

Ham and Potatoes au Gratin

Rich and creamy, salty and cheesy—these Ham and Potatoes au Gratin are layered to indulgent perfection. Make sure you get those potatoes paper-thin to ensure their tenderness. A mandoline is a great tool for this job.

HANDS-ON TIME: 15 minutes
COOK TIME: 20 minutes

INGREDIENTS | SERVES 4

½ cup half-and-half

2 large eggs

1 tablespoon all-purpose flour

1 teaspoon salt

1 teaspoon freshly ground black pepper

1 teaspoon smoked paprika

2 medium Russet potatoes, scrubbed and sliced paper-thin

1 cup diced cooked ham

½ cup grated Gruyère cheese

1 tablespoon butter, melted

1 tablespoon grated Parmesan cheese

1 tablespoon panko bread crumbs

1 tablespoon fresh thyme leaves

The Differences Between Smoked, Sweet, and Hot Paprika

For purposes of this recipe and most cooking situations, paprika is interchangeable depending on your taste. All three spices are powders made from dried red peppers; however, each one comes from a pepper with different heat, as noted by their names: smoky, sweet, or hot. For smoked paprika, as long as it does not have a "hot" designation on the jar, then it has a sweet and smoky flavor.

1. In a medium bowl, whisk half-and-half, eggs, flour, salt, pepper, and paprika. Add potatoes. Using your hands, ensure that all sides of potato slices are coated.

2. Preheat air fryer at 375°F for 3 minutes.

3. Lightly spray or brush oil on a round cake barrel (accessory). Evenly distribute half of potato slices. Pour half of the egg mixture over potatoes. Layer half of the ham and then half of the Gruyère cheese. Repeat layering.

4. In a small bowl, combine butter, Parmesan cheese, bread crumbs, and thyme. Distribute over casserole. Cover barrel with aluminum foil.

5. Place barrel in air fryer basket. Cook 15 minutes. Remove foil and cook an additional 5 minutes.

6. Remove barrel from air fryer and let rest 10 minutes. Serve warm.

PER SERVING Calories: 386 | Fat: 16.4 g | Protein: 21.3 g | Sodium: 1,272 mg | Fiber: 3.8 g | Carbohydrates: 37.1 g | Sugar: 3.4 g

Pork and Cheesy Mac

The tasty ground pork is a welcome addition to this three-cheese macaroni and cheese. The bread crumb topping is crisped to perfection by the air fryer in this compact casserole.

HANDS-ON TIME: 15 minutes
COOK TIME: 20 minutes

INGREDIENTS | SERVES 4

½ pound uncooked elbow macaroni
½ pound ground pork
1 medium carrot, peeled and diced
1 celery stalk, diced
4 ounces cream cheese, at room temperature
¼ cup feta cheese crumbles
¼ cup shredded Cheddar cheese
¼ cup whole milk
¼ cup plain bread crumbs
1 tablespoon butter, melted

1. Add elbow macaroni to a pot of boiling salted water and cook according to package directions.

2. In a large skillet over medium-high heat, cook pork, carrot, and celery 4–5 minutes until pork is no longer pink. Set aside.

3. Drain pasta and put in a large bowl. Add cream cheese, feta cheese, Cheddar cheese, and milk. Stir until the warm pasta melts the cheeses. Add pork mixture and stir.

4. Preheat air fryer at 375°F for 3 minutes.

5. Mix bread crumbs and butter together in a small bowl.

6. Spoon pasta mixture into lightly greased round cake barrel (accessory). Top with buttered bread crumbs. Cook 15 minutes.

7. Remove barrel from air fryer and let rest 10 minutes. Serve warm.

PER SERVING Calories: 510 | Fat: 18.7 g | Protein: 26.2 g | Sodium: 524 mg | Fiber: 3.4 g | Carbohydrates: 51.8 g | Sugar: 4.1 g

Chili Casserole

This mild beef and bean Chili Casserole is simply spiced with cumin and chili powder. If you like a little heat in your chili, feel free to add your favorite hot sauce or cayenne powder.

HANDS-ON TIME: 15 minutes
COOK TIME: 11 minutes

INGREDIENTS | SERVES 4

½ pound ground beef

½ small yellow onion, peeled and diced

1 celery stalk, diced

1 (16-ounce) can kidney beans in chili sauce

½ cup canned fire-roasted diced tomatoes, including juice

½ teaspoon ground cumin

½ teaspoon chili powder

¼ teaspoon salt

1 cup corn chips, lightly crushed

½ cup Mexican-blend grated cheese

1. In a large skillet over medium-high heat, cook beef, onion, and celery 4–5 minutes until beef is no longer pink. Drain fat. Add beans including sauce, tomatoes including juice, cumin, chili powder, and salt.

2. Preheat air fryer at 350°F for 3 minutes.

3. Spoon beef mixture into a round cake barrel (accessory). Evenly distribute corn chips and top with cheese. Cook 6 minutes.

4. Remove barrel from air fryer and let rest 10 minutes. Serve warm.

PER SERVING Calories: 223 | Fat: 10.7 g | Protein: 22.7 g | Sodium: 750 mg | Fiber: 9.2 g | Carbohydrates: 31.9 g | Sugar: 3.4 g

Smoked Sausage and Wild Rice Casserole

This creamy rice mixture mixed with smoked sausage is a hearty dish that is quick to make for those busy weeknights. Filled with vegetables, protein, starch, and dairy, this delicious one-pot wonder cooks in only 15 minutes!

HANDS-ON TIME: 10 minutes
COOK TIME: 15 minutes

INGREDIENTS | SERVES 4

3 cups cooked wild rice

¼ cup finely diced yellow onion

1 medium carrot, peeled and shredded

1 cup baby spinach

¼ cup mayonnaise

¼ cup crumbled goat cheese

2 tablespoons sour cream

1 teaspoon salt

1 teaspoon freshly ground black pepper

7 ounces smoked sausage, cut into 1" pieces

Baby Spinach versus Regular Spinach

Baby spinach has been harvested earlier than the more mature leaves. Research is divided on which stage of the harvested spinach yields the most nutrition. From a chef's perspective, baby spinach is a bit more tender, sweeter, and easier to work with, as the stems are less tough.

1. In a large bowl, combine wild rice, onion, carrot, spinach, mayonnaise, goat cheese, sour cream, salt, and pepper. Mix together. Add smoked sausage and mix again. Transfer mixture to lightly greased cake barrel (accessory).

2. Preheat air fryer at 350°F for 3 minutes.

3. Place cake barrel into air fryer basket and cook casserole 15 minutes.

4. Remove barrel from air fryer and let rest 10 minutes. Serve warm.

PER SERVING Calories: 426 | Fat: 26.4 g | Protein: 13.2 g | Sodium: 1,172 mg | Fiber: 3.1 g | Carbohydrates: 30.7 g | Sugar: 2.3 g

Broccoli Casserole

People who don't really care for broccoli will find themselves scooping up a second helping of this creamy casserole. Add it as a side dish to most any meat dish and watch it disappear!

HANDS-ON TIME: 15 minutes
COOK TIME: 14 minutes

INGREDIENTS | SERVES 4

4 cups steamed broccoli florets (about 1 medium-large head), chopped
¼ cup diced yellow onion
½ cup diced white mushrooms
1 large egg
2 tablespoons sour cream
¼ cup mayonnaise
1 teaspoon salt
½ teaspoon freshly ground black pepper
1 cup crushed Ritz crackers
1 tablespoon butter, melted

1. In a large bowl, combine broccoli, onion, mushrooms, egg, sour cream, mayonnaise, salt, and pepper. Spoon mixture into a round cake barrel (accessory). Evenly distribute cracker crumbs over the top of broccoli. Drizzle evenly with butter.

2. Preheat air fryer at 350°F for 3 minutes.

3. Cook casserole 14 minutes.

4. Remove barrel from air fryer and let rest 10 minutes. Serve warm.

PER SERVING Calories: 322 | Fat: 20.0 g | Protein: 8.1 g | Sodium: 493 mg | Fiber: 7.6 g | Carbohydrates: 29.8 g | Sugar: 4.7 g

Squash Casserole

This Southern classic is a staple at any get-together below the Mason-Dixon Line. Add a small, drained jar of pimientos for a pleasant surprise!

HANDS-ON TIME: 15 minutes
COOK TIME: 18 minutes

INGREDIENTS | SERVES 4

3 cups summer squash, sliced into ¼" rounds

1 slice white sandwich bread, torn into small pieces

2 tablespoons whole milk

2 tablespoons butter, melted

½ cup diced yellow sweet onion

1 large egg

1 teaspoon salt

½ teaspoon freshly ground black pepper

1 cup shredded Cheddar cheese, divided

1. In a medium pot of boiling water, cook squash 4–5 minutes until tender. Drain well.

2. Transfer squash to a medium bowl. Use the back of a fork to somewhat mash the squash. Add bread, milk, butter, onion, egg, salt, pepper, and ½ cup cheese. Stir until combined and bread is wet. Transfer mixture to a cake barrel (accessory).

3. Preheat air fryer at 350°F for 3 minutes.

4. Cook 10 minutes. Sprinkle remaining cheese in a layer over squash casserole. Cook an additional 3 minutes.

5. Remove casserole from air fryer and let rest 10 minutes. Serve warm.

PER SERVING Calories: 229 | Fat: 15.3 g | Protein: 10.6 g | Sodium: 823 mg | Fiber: 1.6 g | Carbohydrates: 9.4 g | Sugar: 3.7 g

Shepherd's Pie

The term Shepherd's Pie is incorrectly used on many menus. It should only be called this if it contains ground lamb, because a shepherd tended sheep. Mixed with vegetables and fresh herbs and topped with homemade mashed potatoes, this "pie" is hearty, healthy, and comforting.

HANDS-ON TIME: 15 minutes
COOK TIME: 22 minutes

INGREDIENTS | SERVES 4

Potato Topping
1 large Russet potato, peeled and diced
2 tablespoons butter
2 tablespoons whole milk
½ teaspoon salt
½ teaspoon freshly ground black pepper

Meat Filling
½ pound ground lamb
1 medium carrot, peeled and diced
¼ cup peas
¼ cup corn kernels
½ small yellow onion, peeled and diced
1 tablespoon all-purpose flour
⅔ cup tomato sauce
1 teaspoon chopped fresh rosemary
1 teaspoon fresh thyme leaves
½ teaspoon salt
½ teaspoon freshly ground black pepper

1. Add diced potatoes to a medium pot of boiling salted water and cook 4–5 minutes until fork-tender.

2. While potatoes are cooking, add lamb, carrot, peas, corn, and onion to a large skillet. Cook over medium-high heat 4–5 minutes until lamb is no longer pink. Add flour, tomato sauce, rosemary, thyme, salt, and pepper and combine.

3. Drain potatoes and transfer to a medium bowl. Add butter, milk, salt, and pepper. Mash until smooth.

4. Preheat air fryer at 350°F for 3 minutes.

5. Spoon meat filling into lightly greased round cake barrel (accessory). Top with mashed potatoes. Using the tines of a fork, run shallow lines in the top of the potatoes for a decorative touch. Cook 12 minutes.

6. Remove barrel from air fryer and let rest 10 minutes. Serve warm.

PER SERVING Calories: 282 | Fat: 13.5 g | Protein: 13.9 g | Sodium: 1,005 mg | Fiber: 3.6 g | Carbohydrates: 24.7 g | Sugar: 4.7 g

Cottage Pie

Our Cottage Pie uses ground beef, different than its cousin, Shepherd's Pie, which contains ground lamb. Both have a mashed potato topping, but this recipe has Cheddar cheese mixed into the potatoes for an extra boost of flavor.

HANDS-ON TIME: 15 minutes
COOK TIME: 22 minutes

INGREDIENTS | SERVES 4

Potato Topping

1 large Russet potato, peeled and diced
2 tablespoons butter
2 tablespoons whole milk
¼ cup shredded sharp Cheddar cheese
½ teaspoon salt
½ teaspoon freshly ground black pepper

Meat Filling

½ pound ground beef
1 medium carrot, peeled and diced
½ cup sliced white mushrooms
½ small yellow onion, peeled and diced
1 stalk celery, diced
1 tablespoon all-purpose flour
⅔ cup tomato sauce
2 teaspoons Italian seasoning
½ teaspoon salt
½ teaspoon freshly ground black pepper

1. Add diced potatoes to a pot of boiling salted water and cook 4–5 minutes until fork-tender.

2. While potatoes are cooking, add beef, carrot, mushrooms, onion, and celery to a large skillet. Cook over medium-high heat 4–5 minutes until beef is no longer pink. Add flour, tomato sauce, Italian seasoning, salt, and pepper and combine.

3. Drain potatoes and transfer to a medium bowl. Add butter, milk, cheese, salt, and pepper. Mash until smooth.

4. Preheat air fryer at 350°F for 3 minutes.

5. Spoon meat filling into lightly greased round cake barrel (accessory). Top with mashed potatoes. Using the tines of a fork, run shallow lines in the top of the potatoes for a decorative touch. Cook 12 minutes.

6. Remove barrel from air fryer and let rest 10 minutes. Serve warm.

PER SERVING Calories: 268 | Fat: 12.0 g | Protein: 15.4 g | Sodium: 1,051 mg | Fiber: 3.1 g | Carbohydrates: 22.4 g | Sugar: 3.9 g

Green Chili Chicken Casserole

This is just a big ol' casserole of goodness, and it takes no time to put together. Serve with a salad to add more vegetables to the meal.

HANDS-ON TIME: 10 minutes
COOK TIME: 35 minutes

INGREDIENTS | SERVES 4

1 cup corn kernels

1 (10.5-ounce) can condensed cream of potato soup

1 (7-ounce) can diced green chili peppers

1 pound chicken breast tenders (or chicken breasts cut into strips)

¼ cup panko bread crumbs

1 tablespoon butter, melted

¼ cup shredded Monterey jack cheese

What Are Chicken Tenders?

Chicken tenders aren't just those deep-fried pieces of yuck found in kids' meals. They're actually part of the chicken breast. Each chicken has two of them. They are on the side of each breast, sometimes referred to as a "hanging tender." They are sold as chicken tenders; however, if you can't find any, no worries. There is zero taste difference between them and the breast, so just slice your own "tenders" if necessary.

1. In a small bowl, combine corn, potato soup, and chili peppers.

2. Preheat air fryer at 350°F for 3 minutes.

3. Add chicken tenders to lightly greased square cake barrel (accessory). Spoon corn mixture evenly over tenders. Cook 25 minutes.

4. While chicken is cooking, combine bread crumbs and butter. When chicken is ready, sprinkle crumbs over chicken mixture and cook an additional 5 minutes. Sprinkle cheese over casserole. Cook an additional 5 minutes. Using a meat thermometer, ensure that chicken has an internal temperature of at least 165°F.

5. Remove barrel and let rest 5 minutes. Serve warm.

PER SERVING Calories: 241 | Fat: 6.7 g | Protein: 19.8 g | Sodium: 750 mg | Fiber: 3.3 g | Carbohydrates: 25.0 g | Sugar: 5.3 g

Mama's Little Lasagna

When you don't want a giant tray of lasagna to eat off of for a week, make this little lasagna in your air fryer. Use oven-ready lasagna noodles and break them to fit each small layer.

HANDS-ON TIME: 15 minutes
COOK TIME: 24 minutes

INGREDIENTS | SERVES 4

½ pound Italian sausage, loose or removed from casings

¼ cup diced yellow onion

1 cup Marinara Sauce (see Chapter 15)

1 cup ricotta cheese

⅓ cup grated Parmesan cheese

1 large egg

2 teaspoons Italian seasoning

½ teaspoon salt

5 oven-ready lasagna noodles

1 cup grated mozzarella cheese

What Are Oven-Ready Lasagna Noodles?

Found in the same aisle as the rest of the pasta, these noodles will have "oven-ready" or "no-boil" on the packaging. There is no need to boil these prior to layering your lasagna, saving your fingertips from dealing with those hot noodles. The heated sauce softens the noodles while your dish cooks, yielding a beautiful lasagna. No one will ever know!

1. In a medium skillet over medium heat, cook sausage and onion 5–6 minutes until sausage is no longer pink. Drain fat. Stir in Marinara Sauce. Simmer 3 minutes.

2. In a small bowl, combine ricotta cheese, Parmesan cheese, egg, Italian seasoning, and salt.

3. Lightly spray or brush oil on the square cake barrel (accessory).

4. Spoon a quarter of the meat mixture into barrel. Snap lasagna noodles to fit pan until you have a layer. Layer on a third of the ricotta mixture. Sprinkle a quarter of the mozzarella. Repeat two more times. Finish with the remaining meat sauce and then the mozzarella.

5. Preheat air fryer at 375°F for 3 minutes.

6. Cover lasagna with aluminum foil. Cook 12 minutes. Remove foil and cook uncovered an additional 3 minutes.

7. Remove lasagna from air fryer and let rest 10 minutes. Slice and serve warm.

PER SERVING Calories: 544 | Fat: 34.0 g | Protein: 29.3 g | Sodium: 1,325 mg | Fiber: 2.3 g | Carbohydrates: 25.2 g | Sugar: 3.9 g

Simple Ravioli Lasagna

This is the easiest lasagna you'll ever make. The cheese and noodles are already present in ravioli, so why not take advantage of that and just layer the ravioli with meat sauce?

HANDS-ON TIME: 10 minutes
COOK TIME: 20 minutes

INGREDIENTS | SERVES 4

½ pound Italian sausage, loose or removed from casings

½ small yellow onion, peeled and diced

2 teaspoons Italian seasoning

1½ cups Spicy Marinara Sauce (see Chapter 15)

1 (9-ounce) package refrigerated four-cheese ravioli

½ cup mozzarella cheese

Other Varieties of Ravioli

For variety, layer different kinds of ravioli. Whether you enjoy mushrooms, butternut squash, or even the very decadent lobster ravioli, give them all a whirl to find your favorite.

1. In a medium skillet over medium-high heat, cook sausage and onion 5–6 minutes until pork is no longer pink. Drain fat. Stir in Italian seasoning and Spicy Marinara Sauce. Simmer 3 minutes.

2. Lightly spray or brush oil on the square cake barrel (accessory).

3. Add a third of the meat sauce. Layer half of the ravioli. Add another third of meat sauce. Top with half mozzarella cheese. Add a layer of remaining ravioli and then remaining meat sauce. Top with remaining mozzarella.

4. Preheat air fryer at 375°F for 3 minutes.

5. Cover lasagna with aluminum foil. Cook 8 minutes. Remove foil and cook uncovered an additional 3 minutes.

6. Remove lasagna from air fryer and let rest 10 minutes. Spoon and serve warm.

PER SERVING Calories: 474 | Fat: 27.2 g | Protein: 21.4 g | Sodium: 1,215 mg | Fiber: 3.7 g | Carbohydrates: 34.2 g | Sugar: 4.6 g

Cheesy Meatless Spaghetti Pie

For those who don't like a lot of fuss or muss, try this simple Cheesy Meatless Spaghetti Pie. If you want to jazz it up, feel free to add onions or peppers or mushrooms.

HANDS-ON TIME: 10 minutes
COOK TIME: 16 minutes

INGREDIENTS | SERVES 4

½ pound spaghetti, cooked
2 cups Marinara Sauce (see Chapter 15)
1 tablespoon dried basil
½ cup ricotta cheese
¼ cup shredded Parmesan cheese
¼ teaspoon salt
2 large eggs, whisked
½ cup shredded mozzarella cheese

1. Preheat air fryer at 375°F for 3 minutes.

2. In a medium bowl, combine cooked spaghetti, Marinara Sauce, basil, ricotta cheese, Parmesan cheese, and salt.

3. Add spaghetti mixture to lightly greased round cake barrel (accessory). Pour whisked eggs over spaghetti mixture.

4. Cook 12 minutes. Add mozzarella cheese. Cook an additional 4 minutes.

5. Remove spaghetti pie from air fryer and let rest 10 minutes. Slice and serve warm.

PER SERVING Calories: 411 | Fat: 11.2 g | Protein: 21.2 g | Sodium: 855 mg | Fiber: 4.5 g | Carbohydrates: 54.4 g | Sugar: 7.0 g

Cheeseburger Casserole

Skip the drive-through and enjoy this easy-cheesy delight. To complete the meal, serve with shredded lettuce, sliced tomatoes, and diced pickles on the side. Oh, and don't forget those air-fried French fries!

HANDS-ON TIME: 10 minutes
COOK TIME: 13 minutes
INGREDIENTS | SERVES 2

½ pound ground beef
½ small yellow onion, peeled and diced
1 teaspoon dried basil
1 tablespoon ketchup
1 tablespoon Dijon mustard
¼ teaspoon salt
4 (6") flour tortillas
1 cup shredded Cheddar cheese

1. In a large skillet over medium-high heat, cook beef and onions, stir-frying 5–6 minutes until beef is no longer pink. Drain fat. Stir in basil, ketchup, mustard, and salt.

2. Preheat air fryer at 350°F for 3 minutes.

3. Place a tortilla in the bottom of the round cake barrel (accessory). Layer a third of the meat and a quarter of the cheese. Repeat two times. Place final tortilla on top. Scatter with remaining cheese. Cook 7 minutes.

4. Let cool 5 minutes. Serve warm.

PER SERVING Calories: 602 | Fat: 28.0 g | Protein: 39.9 g | Sodium: 1,405 mg | Fiber: 2.0 g | Carbohydrates: 36.2 g | Sugar: 4.7 g

South-of-the-Border Tortilla Pie

The Mexican-inspired flavors in this tortilla pie are layered to create one delicious meal! Although canned corn is certainly permissible, if you have the time, cut the corn straight off the cob. The freshness elevates the flavor of this tasty pie!

HANDS-ON TIME: 10 minutes
COOK TIME: 13 minutes
INGREDIENTS | SERVES 2

½ pound ground beef
½ small yellow onion, peeled and diced
¼ cup black beans, drained and rinsed
¼ cup corn kernels
1 teaspoon ground cumin
½ teaspoon chili powder
¼ teaspoon salt
4 (6") flour tortillas
1 cup shredded Monterey jack cheese
1 cup salsa
¼ cup sour cream

1. In a skillet over medium-high heat, cook beef and onions, stir-frying 5–6 minutes until beef is no longer pink. Drain fat. Stir in beans, corn, cumin, chili powder, and salt.

2. Preheat air fryer at 350°F for 3 minutes.

3. Place a tortilla in the bottom of the round cake barrel (accessory). Layer a third of the meat mixture and a quarter of the cheese. Repeat two times. Place final tortilla on top. Scatter with remaining cheese. Cook 7 minutes.

4. Let cool 5 minutes. Serve with salsa and sour cream.

PER SERVING Calories: 527 | Fat: 29.3 g | Protein: 39.6 g | Sodium: 857 mg | Fiber: 4.7 g | Carbohydrates: 20.1 g | Sugar: 3.1 g

Quick Chicken Enchiladas

This recipe can use that leftover cooked chicken from last night's rotisserie chicken. Sometimes that day-after chicken can become a little dry, but these enchiladas will breathe new life into those leftovers for a fresh new meal!

HANDS-ON TIME: 10 minutes
COOK TIME: 6 minutes

INGREDIENTS | SERVES 2

1 cup shredded or chopped cooked chicken
1 (4.5-ounce) can chopped green chilies
½ teaspoon salt
¼ teaspoon ground coriander
2 cups enchilada sauce, divided
1 cup refried beans
4 (6") flour tortillas
1 cup shredded Monterey jack cheese
1 scallion, trimmed and sliced
2 tablespoons sour cream

1. In a small bowl, combine chicken, chilies, salt, coriander, and ¼ cup enchilada sauce.

2. Add ½ cup enchilada sauce to bottom of the square cake barrel (accessory).

3. Spread ¼ cup refried beans in a line down the middle of each tortilla. Add a quarter of the chicken mixture to each. Top with 1 tablespoon shredded cheese on each tortilla. Roll tortillas and place seam side down in cake barrel. Top with remaining sauce. Sprinkle with remaining cheese.

4. Preheat air fryer at 350°F for 3 minutes.

5. Place enchiladas in air fryer basket. Cook 6 minutes.

6. Transfer to a dish and allow to cool 10 minutes. Serve warm garnished with sliced scallions and a dollop of sour cream.

PER SERVING Calories: 779 | Fat: 28.4 g | Protein: 52.0 g | Sodium: 4,123 mg | Fiber: 12.3 g | Carbohydrates: 72.1 g | Sugar: 21.5 g

Mexican Penne Bake

Two of the most popular cuisines are Mexican and Italian. So doesn't it just make sense to fuse the two together? The Italian penne tubes are the perfect vessels to transport all that Mexican goodness straight to your tummy.

HANDS-ON TIME: 10 minutes
COOK TIME: 16 minutes

INGREDIENTS | SERVES 4

½ pound penne pasta, cooked

1 (14.5-ounce) can diced tomatoes, including juice

1 (4.25-ounce) can chopped black olives, drained

1 cup refried beans

½ teaspoon chili powder

½ teaspoon ground cumin

½ teaspoon salt

¼ teaspoon cayenne pepper

1 tablespoon dried cilantro

1 large egg

½ cup shredded Cheddar cheese

1 cup sour cream

1 cup shredded iceberg lettuce

1. In a medium bowl, combine cooked penne, tomatoes including juice, olives, beans, chili powder, cumin, salt, cayenne pepper, dried cilantro, and egg.

2. Preheat air fryer at 375°F for 3 minutes.

3. Add pasta mixture to lightly greased round cake barrel (accessory). Cook 12 minutes.

4. Add Cheddar cheese. Cook an additional 4 minutes.

5. Remove barrel from air fryer and let rest 10 minutes. Transfer to bowls and serve warm with sour cream and lettuce.

PER SERVING Calories: 518 | Fat: 20.9 g | Protein: 17.6 g | Sodium: 1,078 mg | Fiber: 6.1 g | Carbohydrates: 60.2 g | Sugar: 6.5 g

Tuscan Beans and Sausage

By using sausage that has already been smoked and beans that are canned, you can cut down on the cooking time, making this simple bowl a perfect after-work meal.

HANDS-ON TIME: 10 minutes
COOK TIME: 12 minutes

INGREDIENTS | SERVES 4

14 ounces smoked sausage, cut into 1" sections
1 (14.5-ounce) can fire-roasted diced tomatoes, drained
1 (15.5-ounce) can cannellini beans, rinsed and drained
¼ cup chopped baby spinach
¼ cup chopped fresh basil
¼ cup finely diced yellow onion

1. Preheat air fryer at 375°F for 3 minutes.

2. In a medium bowl, combine all the ingredients.

3. Add sausage mixture to lightly greased round cake barrel (accessory). Cook 12 minutes.

4. Remove barrel from air fryer and let rest 10 minutes. Serve warm.

PER SERVING Calories: 477 | Fat: 26.0 g | Protein: 21.3 g | Sodium: 1,018 mg | Fiber: 7.4 g | Carbohydrates: 32.8 g | Sugar: 3.3 g

Chicken, Mushrooms, and Potatoes

This dish is proof that a full-bodied, tasty meal doesn't have to break the bank. This is also a good recipe to make on a prep day and divide into individual containers for ready-made lunches.

HANDS-ON TIME: 10 minutes
COOK TIME: 20 minutes

INGREDIENTS | SERVES 2

2 chicken thighs (about ½ pound)
½ teaspoon salt
½ teaspoon freshly ground black pepper
4 ounces white mushrooms, quartered
¼ pound fingerling potatoes, scrubbed and thinly sliced
2 teaspoons cooking sherry
1 (14.5-ounce) can fire-roasted diced tomatoes, including juice

1. Preheat air fryer at 350°F for 3 minutes.

2. Place chicken thighs in a round cake barrel (accessory). Season with salt and pepper. Add mushrooms and potatoes. Pour sherry and diced tomatoes including juice over chicken, mushrooms, and potatoes.

3. Cook 20 minutes. Using a meat thermometer, ensure that the internal temperature is at least 165°F.

4. Remove barrel from air fryer and let rest 10 minutes. Serve warm.

PER SERVING Calories: 289 | Fat: 10.6 g | Protein: 22.9 g | Sodium: 1,073 mg | Fiber: 4.8 g | Carbohydrates: 22.6 g | Sugar: 6.5 g

Quick Beefy Hand Pies

These beefy hand pies are so delicious and contain everyday ingredients. Even though the refrigerated biscuits are rolled out a bit, they still puff up around the seasoned beef mixture, making these fun to eat.

HANDS-ON TIME: 5 minutes
COOK TIME: 29 minutes

INGREDIENTS | SERVES 4

½ pound lean ground beef

¼ cup minced onion

3 cloves garlic, minced

1 tablespoon dried cilantro

2 tablespoons peeled, shredded carrots

⅓ cup canned diced tomatoes, including 2 tablespoons juice

1 teaspoon chili powder

½ teaspoon smoked paprika

¼ teaspoon ground cumin

¼ teaspoon salt

¼ cup all-purpose flour

1 (8-count) can refrigerated biscuits

1. In a large skillet over medium-high heat, stir-fry beef and onions 5–6 minutes until beef is no longer pink. Add garlic, cilantro, carrots, tomatoes with juice, chili powder, paprika, cumin, and salt. Stir ingredients while simmering 2–3 minutes. Set aside to cool.

2. Sprinkle a cutting board with 1 tablespoon flour. Use the remaining flour as needed when dough is sticky. Roll out each biscuit to a 6" circle.

3. Using a slotted spoon, transfer 2 overflowing tablespoons of meat mixture to the center of each biscuit circle. Fold dough to form a half-moon shape, crimping the edges tightly with the tines of a fork.

4. Preheat air fryer at 350°F for 3 minutes.

5. Place two hand pies in the air fryer basket. Cook 5 minutes. Transfer to a plate. Repeat with remaining hand pies and serve warm.

PER SERVING Calories: 276 | Fat: 9.9 g | Protein: 14.8 g | Sodium: 772 mg | Fiber: 2.5 g | Carbohydrates: 29.3 g | Sugar: 5.6 g

CHAPTER 14

Desserts

Glazed Cinnamon-Apple Doughnut Bites

These luscious little cinnamon-apple bites are complemented with a simple glaze. They're easy to make and nice for a quick, sweet breakfast or served warm with a dish of creamy cinnamon ice cream after a nice meal.

HANDS-ON TIME: 10 minutes
COOK TIME: 11 minutes

INGREDIENTS | SERVES 5

Doughnut Holes

⅔ cup all-purpose flour

⅛ teaspoon salt

½ teaspoon baking powder

1 teaspoon ground cinnamon

2 tablespoons light brown sugar

½ cup peeled, cored, and shredded Granny Smith apple (approximately 1 medium apple)

3 tablespoons whole milk

1 tablespoon butter, melted

Glaze

2 tablespoons powdered sugar

1–2 teaspoons whole milk

DIY Apple Candles

After a day of apple picking with the family and making these doughnut bites and maybe a batch of applesauce, what should you do with those remaining apples? From the top end where the stem is, core the apple leaving about ½" at the base. Insert a long candle and use it as a beautiful centerpiece.

1. In a medium bowl, combine flour, salt, baking powder, cinnamon, and sugar.

2. Using paper towels, squeeze the moisture out of the shredded apple. Add to flour mixture. Add milk and butter. Stir until combined.

3. Preheat air fryer at 325°F for 5 minutes.

4. Form mixture into ten (1") balls and add to lightly greased pizza pan (accessory). It's all right if they are touching. Cook 11 minutes.

5. Transfer doughnut bites to a cooling rack.

6. When cooled, whisk together glaze ingredients in small bowl, 1 teaspoon milk at a time, until desired consistency, and then gently drizzle over doughnut bites.

PER SERVING Calories: 134 | Fat: 2.6 g | Protein: 2.2 g | Sodium: 112 mg | Fiber: 1.1 g | Carbohydrates: 25.8 g | Sugar: 11.7 g

Strawberry Shortcake

A few ordinary ingredients come together to create extraordinary buttery, flaky biscuits—the perfect foundation for your berry mixture; spoon it on and top with creamy fresh whipped cream.

HANDS-ON TIME: 15 minutes
COOK TIME: 20 minutes

INGREDIENTS | SERVES 4

1 pound fresh strawberries, stemmed and sliced

¼ cup sugar

1 teaspoon fresh lemon zest

1 cup heavy cream

2 tablespoons powdered sugar

2 cups all-purpose flour

2 teaspoons baking powder

1 teaspoon salt

2 tablespoons butter, melted

1 cup buttermilk

Use a Stainless-Steel Bowl When Making Whipped Cream

A stainless-steel bowl, preferably chilled, will yield the beautiful peaks and fluffiness when making fresh whipped cream. The whipping process actually generates heat, and the chilled metal bowl helps the cream stay cold longer while whipping.

1. In a small bowl, combine strawberries, sugar, and lemon zest. Refrigerate covered until ready to use.

2. In a metal bowl, beat together heavy cream and powdered sugar 1–2 minutes until medium peaks form. Refrigerate covered until ready to use.

3. In a medium bowl, combine flour, baking powder, and salt. Add butter and buttermilk until a sticky dough forms.

4. Preheat air fryer at 350°F for 3 minutes.

5. Flour your hands and form mixture into four balls. Add to lightly greased pizza pan (accessory) and gently pat down to flatten the tops. The biscuits will be touching. Cook 20 minutes.

6. Transfer biscuits to plates and cut each one in half. Add strawberry mixture and whipped cream to each biscuit bottom. Place the top part of the biscuit on whipped cream and serve.

PER SERVING Calories: 614 | Fat: 28.0 g | Protein: 10.9 g | Sodium: 914 mg | Fiber: 3.8 g | Carbohydrates: 77.6 g | Sugar: 26.4 g

Dark Chocolate Custard

It is so amazing how simple ingredients like eggs, sugar, and milk can create such pure delight. Drop a dollop of fresh whipped cream on top of this custard with some chocolate curls for a fancy dessert fit for guests!

HANDS-ON TIME: 15 minutes
COOK TIME: 24 minutes

INGREDIENTS | SERVES 4

4 large egg yolks

2 tablespoons sugar

Pinch salt

¼ teaspoon vanilla extract

1½ cups half-and-half

¾ cup dark chocolate chips

The Easiest Decorative Chocolate Curls

So there are many more complicated ways to make chocolate curls, but in a pinch, this does the trick every time. You need two things—a bar of chocolate and a vegetable peeler. Hold chocolate on its side. Using medium pressure and going slowly, peel the side of the chocolate bar into curls. If your chocolate begins to soften, freeze it for a minute or two and continue.

1. In a small bowl, whisk together egg yolks, sugar, salt, and vanilla. Set aside.

2. In a medium saucepan over medium-low heat, heat half-and-half to a low simmer. Whisk a tablespoon of half-and-half into the egg mixture to temper the eggs, then slowly whisk egg mixture back into the saucepan with remaining half-and-half. Add chocolate chips and continually stir 10 minutes on simmer until chocolate is melted. Remove from heat and evenly distribute chocolate mixture among four custard-sized ramekins.

3. Preheat air fryer at 350°F for 3 minutes.

4. Place two ramekins in air fryer. Cook 7 minutes. Transfer ramekins to a cooling rack. Repeat with remaining two ramekins. Allow to cool about 15 minutes. Then refrigerate covered at least 2 hours before serving.

PER SERVING Calories: 365 | Fat: 22.7 g | Protein: 7.8 g | Sodium: 106 mg | Fiber: 1.1 g | Carbohydrates: 29.5 g | Sugar: 26.5 g

Lemon Curd Palmiers

From the end result, these look impossible to make for a home chef, but in actuality, they are quite simple, with layers of phyllo rolled up with "tart-tastic" lemon curd. Try orange curd for a change of pace.

HANDS-ON TIME: 15 minutes
COOK TIME: 24 minutes

INGREDIENTS | SERVES 6

3 teaspoons sugar, divided
1 sheet phyllo dough, thawed to room temperature
1 tablespoon butter, melted
⅓ cup lemon curd

Homemade Lemon Curd

Although lemon curd can be purchased jarred in most grocery stores, it can be easily made and is amazingly delicious. Combine 4 large egg yolks and ½ cup granulated sugar in a small pot over low heat. Whisk in ⅔ cup fresh lemon juice and 1 teaspoon fresh lemon zest. Slowly whisk in 5 tablespoons unsalted butter, 1 tablespoon at time. Stir continuously until combined and thickened. Strain through a sieve and store covered until ready to use for up to 1 week.

1. On a flat, clean surface sprinkle 2 teaspoons of sugar over surface. Place phyllo sheet over scattered sugar. Brush butter over sheet. Sprinkle with remaining sugar. Flip dough.

2. Evenly spread lemon curd over sheet. Carefully roll one end toward the middle of sheet. Stop at the halfway point. Roll opposite side toward the middle. Refrigerate covered 30 minutes.

3. Slice double log into eighteen equal slices.

4. Preheat air fryer at 350°F for 3 minutes.

5. Place six palmiers in lightly greased air fryer basket. Cook 8 minutes. Repeat with remaining palmiers.

6. Transfer cooked palmiers to a cooling rack. Serve warm or at room temperature.

PER SERVING Calories: 120 | Fat: 4.6 g | Protein: 0.6 g | Sodium: 28 mg | Fiber: 0.1 g | Carbohydrates: 19.1 g | Sugar: 17.4 g

Butterscotch-Pear Wonton Spectaculars

The alcohol from the Scotch will cook off, leaving that rich malt flavor in these wontons. The drizzled Butterscotch Ganache is an amazing touch over the crispy wonton shells, which have been cooked on all sides in the air fryer.

HANDS-ON TIME: 10 minutes
COOK TIME: 31 minutes

INGREDIENTS | SERVES 5

Filled Wontons

2 cups peeled, cored, and small-diced Bosc pears (approximately 2 pears)

2 tablespoons Scotch whiskey

4 tablespoons unsalted butter, melted

2 tablespoons packed light brown sugar

⅛ teaspoon salt

⅛ teaspoon ground nutmeg

1 teaspoon vanilla extract

1 teaspoon lemon juice

20 wonton wrappers

Butterscotch Ganache

¼ cup heavy cream

½ cup butterscotch chips

1. In a large skillet over medium-high heat, add pears, Scotch, butter, sugar, salt, nutmeg, vanilla, and lemon juice. Stir-fry 5 minutes until pears are tender, alcohol cooks off, and juices are sticky. Set aside 5 minutes to cool.

2. Place a wonton wrapper on a cutting board. Place approximately 1½ teaspoons pear mixture in the middle of a wonton wrapper.

3. Place a small bowl of water near the working area. Dip your finger in the water and run it around the perimeter of the wonton. Form into a triangle and pinch the straight edges together. Repeat filling and forming remaining wonton wrappers.

4. Preheat air fryer at 325°F for 3 minutes.

5. Place five filled wontons in air fryer basket. Cook 6 minutes. Transfer to a plate and work the next batch. Repeat until done.

6. Transfer to a cooling rack.

7. To make ganache, in a double boiler, heat heavy cream for about 1 minute to a rolling boil. Whisk in butterscotch chips for about 1 minute until thickened. Drizzle over cooled wontons. Serve warm.

PER SERVING Calories: 411 | Fat: 19.5 g | Protein: 4.3 g | Sodium: 264 mg | Fiber: 2.3 g | Carbohydrates: 47.9 g | Sugar: 26.0 g

Chocolate-Cherry Cheesecake Crescents

Cheesecake has never been so easy to make with these prepared refrigerated crescent rolls. The creamy, sweet filling and the silky glaze creates a tasty little bakery treat without any of the hassle.

HANDS-ON TIME: 5 minutes
COOK TIME: 20 minutes

INGREDIENTS | SERVES 8

Filled Crescents

3 ounces cream cheese, at room temperature

¼ cup cherry preserves

2 tablespoons powdered sugar

Pinch salt

1 (8-ounce) container refrigerated crescent rolls

Chocolate Glaze

1 tablespoon powdered sugar

1 tablespoon unsweetened cocoa powder

2 teaspoons whole milk

1. In a small bowl, combine cream cheese, cherry preserves, powdered sugar, and salt.

2. Preheat air fryer at 350°F for 3 minutes.

3. Place 1 tablespoon cream cheese mixture on the big end of the crescent roll and spread it out leaving a ¼" perimeter uncovered. Gently roll from large end to small end. Repeat with remaining crescent rolls.

4. Lightly spray cooking oil on air fryer basket and add rolls in batches of two. Cook each batch of rolls 5 minutes. Transfer to a cooling rack.

5. Whisk together glaze ingredients in a small bowl. Drizzle over cooled rolls and serve.

PER SERVING Calories: 179 | Fat: 8.3 g | Protein: 2.9 g | Sodium: 273 mg | Fiber: 0.4 g | Carbohydrates: 22.9 g | Sugar: 11.2 g

Strawberry Cheesecake Rolls

These rolls are a play on cinnamon rolls, with strawberry cheesecake as the theme. If you are craving a taste of cheesecake but don't want an entire rich slice, these rolls help satisfy that hankering.

HANDS-ON TIME: 10 minutes
COOK TIME: 15 minutes

INGREDIENTS | SERVES 4

Rolls

1 (13.8-ounce) can refrigerated pizza dough
4 ounces cream cheese, at room temperature
¼ cup powdered sugar
2 cups sliced fresh strawberries

Glaze

2 tablespoons powdered sugar
1–2 teaspoons whole milk

1. Press out pizza dough into its rectangle shape. Combine cream cheese and sugar and spread over dough. Evenly scatter strawberries.

2. Preheat air fryer at 400°F for 3 minutes.

3. Roll small end of dough to small end tightly in a roll. Slice into eight even portions.

4. Place rolls cut side up in lightly greased round cake barrel (accessory). Cover with aluminum foil.

5. Cook 12 minutes. Uncover and cook an additional 3 minutes.

6. Transfer cake barrel to a cooling rack and let rest 10 minutes.

7. Whisk together glaze ingredients in a small bowl. Drizzle glaze over rolls, pull apart, and serve warm.

PER SERVING Calories: 404 | Fat: 11.6 g | Protein: 9.8 g | Sodium: 676 mg | Fiber: 3.2 g | Carbohydrates: 64.5 g | Sugar: 21.1 g

Orange Cheesecake

The citrus in the orange is so fresh and bright, it helps make this a nice summer dessert. Change up the flavor profile by using chocolate graham crackers or lemon cookies for the crust.

HANDS-ON TIME: 10 minutes
COOK TIME: 19 minutes

INGREDIENTS | SERVES 6

1 cup graham cracker crumbs

3 tablespoons butter, melted

12 ounces cream cheese, at room temperature

2 tablespoons sour cream

2 large eggs

½ cup sugar

1 tablespoon fresh orange zest

1 tablespoon freshly squeezed orange juice

1 teaspoon vanilla extract

Pinch salt

1. In a small bowl, combine graham cracker crumbs and butter. Press into a 7" springform pan.

2. In a medium bowl, combine cream cheese, sour cream, eggs, sugar, orange zest, orange juice, vanilla, and salt until smooth. Spoon over graham cracker crust. Cover with aluminum foil.

3. Preheat air fryer at 400°F for 3 minutes.

4. Place springform pan into air fryer basket and cook 14 minutes.

5. Reduce air fryer heat to 350°F, remove aluminum foil, and cook an additional 5 minutes.

6. The cheesecake will be a little jiggly in the center. Refrigerate covered a minimum of 2 hours to allow it to set. Release sides from pan and serve.

PER SERVING Calories: 404 | Fat: 25.5 g | Protein: 6.6 g | Sodium: 321 mg | Fiber: 0.6 g | Carbohydrates: 30.6 g | Sugar: 22.5 g

Spiced Pumpkin Cheesecake

From the gingersnap crust to the pumpkin pie spice, this pumpkin cheesecake is the perfect size for a small family gathering. It's so smooth and spiced, creamy and delicious, that there won't be any leftovers with this one!

HANDS-ON TIME: 10 minutes
COOK TIME: 19 minutes

INGREDIENTS | SERVES 6

1 cup crushed gingersnap crumbs

3 tablespoons butter, melted

1 cup pumpkin purée

8 ounces cream cheese, at room temperature

2 tablespoons sour cream

2 large eggs

½ cup sugar

¼ teaspoon pumpkin pie spice

¼ teaspoon ground cinnamon

⅛ teaspoon freshly ground nutmeg

½ teaspoon vanilla extract

Pinch salt

Nutmeg—Ground or Whole?

When you are standing in the spice aisle and looking up at the two nutmeg options—the dusty ground stuff and those whole nuts—what do you buy? This one is a no-brainer. Buy those little nuts...well, really they are seeds. Mace actually covers this seed in the wild, but that's another story. Buy the whole nutmeg and use a Microplane to shave off what you need for your recipe each time, then store the nutmeg back in its container. It will yield a more fragrant product.

1. In a small bowl, combine gingersnap crumbs and butter. Press into a 7" springform pan.

2. In medium bowl, combine pumpkin purée, cream cheese, sour cream, eggs, sugar, spices, vanilla, and salt until smooth. Spoon over gingersnap crust. Cover with aluminum foil.

3. Preheat air fryer at 400°F for 3 minutes.

4. Place springform pan into air fryer basket and cook 14 minutes.

5. Reduce air fryer heat to 350°F, remove aluminum foil, and cook an additional 5 minutes.

6. The cheesecake will be a little jiggly in the center. Refrigerate covered a minimum of 2 hours to allow it to set. Release from pan and serve.

PER SERVING Calories: 299 | Fat: 20.3 g | Protein: 5.9 g | Sodium: 277 mg | Fiber: 1.7 g | Carbohydrates: 18.7 g | Sugar: 6.3 g

Triple Chocolate Cheesecake

This dish has chocolate in the crust, in the filling, and, in the chocolate chip garnish. Most people might enjoy their slice with a tall glass of milk, but the true chocoholics will pour themselves a glass of chocolate milk!

HANDS-ON TIME: 10 minutes
COOK TIME: 19 minutes
INGREDIENTS | SERVES 6

1 cup chocolate graham cracker crumbs

3 tablespoons butter, melted

12 ounces cream cheese, at room temperature

2 tablespoons sour cream

2 large eggs

¼ cup unsweetened cocoa powder

½ cup sugar

1 teaspoon vanilla extract

Pinch salt

¼ cup mini chocolate chips

1. In a small bowl, combine chocolate graham cracker crumbs and butter. Press into a 7" springform pan.

2. In a medium bowl, combine cream cheese, sour cream, eggs, cocoa, sugar, vanilla, and salt until smooth. Spoon over chocolate graham cracker crust. Cover with aluminum foil.

3. Preheat air fryer at 400°F for 3 minutes.

4. Place springform pan into air fryer basket and cook 14 minutes.

5. Reduce air fryer heat to 350°F, remove aluminum foil, and cook an additional 5 minutes.

6. Remove cheesecake from air fryer. Garnish top with mini chocolate chips.

7. The cheesecake will be a little jiggly in the center. Refrigerate covered a minimum of 2 hours to allow it to set. Release from pan and serve.

PER SERVING Calories: 448 | Fat: 27.8 g | Protein: 7.8 g | Sodium: 327 mg | Fiber: 2.0 g | Carbohydrates: 36.4 g | Sugar: 25.9 g

Mixed Berry and Apple Crumble

This streusel-like topping has oats, almonds, and that rich brown sugar crisping up nicely in the air fryer. It's best served with vanilla ice cream or fresh whipped cream!

HANDS-ON TIME: 15 minutes
COOK TIME: 10 minutes

INGREDIENTS | SERVES 4

Filling

6 medium Granny Smith apples, peeled, cored, and diced
1 cup thawed frozen mixed berries
1 tablespoon fresh lemon juice
2 tablespoons light brown sugar
1 teaspoon ground cinnamon
Pinch ground nutmeg
Pinch salt

Topping

4 tablespoons butter, melted
1 cup quick-cooking oats
⅛ cup all-purpose flour
¼ cup chopped almonds
¼ cup packed light brown sugar
¼ teaspoon sea salt

1. In a medium bowl, combine filling ingredients and place in lightly greased cake barrel (accessory).

2. In a small bowl, combine topping ingredients until crumbly. Spoon evenly over berry mixture.

3. Preheat air fryer at 350°F for 3 minutes.

4. Place cake barrel in air fryer basket. Cook 10 minutes.

5. Transfer cake barrel to a cooling rack. Let cool 10 minutes. Serve warm.

PER SERVING Calories: 460 | Fat: 16.4 g | Protein: 6.1 g | Sodium: 142 mg | Fiber: 8.1 g | Carbohydrates: 75.7 g | Sugar: 48.5 g

Move Over Wonder Woman

There are superfoods…and then there are berries—super-superfoods! Rich in color and taste, these little babies pack a punch with flavonoids, polyphenols, probiotics, antioxidants, and vitamins. Berries can help aid cell regeneration and can protect against free radicals and premature aging. Add berries to your daily routine for pretty skin, shiny hair, and a healthy heart.

Confetti Cake

When you are celebrating something with two to four people, sometimes there is no need for an oversized sheet cake. This mini colorful cake is perfect for birthdays, anniversaries, or just for happiness.

HANDS-ON TIME: 15 minutes
COOK TIME: 25 minutes

INGREDIENTS | SERVES 6

Cake

4 tablespoons butter, melted and cooled
4 tablespoons whole milk
1 teaspoon vanilla extract
2 large eggs
1¼ cups all-purpose flour
2 teaspoons baking powder
½ teaspoon baking soda
Pinch salt
⅓ cup rainbow sprinkles, plus extra for decoration

Buttercream Frosting

1 cup powdered sugar
¼ cup butter, melted and cooled
½ teaspoon vanilla extract
1 tablespoon whole milk

Create an Aluminum-Foil Sling

You may want to fashion an aluminum-foil sling for easy pan retrieval if you don't have a pair of retriever tongs. Take a 10" × 10" square of aluminum foil and fold it back and forth until you have a 2" × 10" sling. Place sling under the pan before cooking so that you can easily lift up the heated dish when cooking is complete.

1. In a small bowl, combine butter, milk, vanilla, and eggs.

2. In a large bowl, combine flour, baking powder, baking soda, salt, and ⅓ cup sprinkles.

3. Pour wet ingredients from the small bowl into the large bowl with dry ingredients. Gently combine ingredients. Do not overmix. Spoon mixture into greased round cake barrel (accessory). Cover with aluminum foil.

4. Preheat air fryer at 350°F for 3 minutes.

5. Cook 15 minutes. Remove foil. Cook an additional 10 minutes.

6. Remove cake pan from the air fryer and transfer to a rack until cool. Flip cake onto a serving platter.

7. Once cake has cooled, prepare Buttercream Frosting by creaming together its ingredients in a small bowl. Spread frosting over cake and garnish with extra rainbow sprinkles.

PER SERVING Calories: 370 | Fat: 18.5 g | Protein: 5.3 g | Sodium: 323 mg | Fiber: 0.7 g | Carbohydrates: 48.5 g | Sugar: 27.9 g

Lemon Cake

Don't underestimate the zest on a lemon. Yes, fresh lemon juice adds a beautiful citric quality, but the vibrant oils in the zest (or skin) of a lemon takes it a step further. Every bite of this small Lemon Cake bursts with big lemon flavor.

HANDS-ON TIME: 15 minutes
COOK TIME: 25 minutes

INGREDIENTS | SERVES 6

Cake

4 tablespoons butter, melted and cooled
4 tablespoons whole milk
½ teaspoon vanilla extract
2 large eggs
1 tablespoon fresh lemon juice
1 tablespoon fresh lemon zest
1¼ cups all-purpose flour
2 teaspoons baking powder
½ teaspoon baking soda
Pinch salt

Lemon Glaze

5 tablespoons powdered sugar
4–5 teaspoons fresh lemon juice

Zesting a Lemon

There are many ways to obtain the fragrant zest of a citrus fruit. There is an actual lemon zester tool, but that will just end up in your graveyard of kitchen gadgets. A microplane or the fine side of a box grater will work the best when you rub the rind in one direction against the small blades. Although it will require a little more precision to avoid the bitter white pithy layer, a sharp paring knife can be used as well and then mince the rind.

1. In a small bowl, combine butter, milk, vanilla, eggs, lemon juice, and lemon zest.

2. In a large bowl, combine flour, baking powder, baking soda, and salt.

3. Pour wet ingredients from the small bowl into the large bowl with dry ingredients. Gently combine ingredients. Do not overmix. Spoon mixture into greased round cake barrel (accessory). Cover with aluminum foil.

4. Preheat air fryer at 350°F for 3 minutes.

5. Cook 15 minutes. Remove foil. Cook an additional 10 minutes.

6. Remove cake pan from the air fryer and transfer to a rack until cool. Flip cake onto a serving platter.

7. Once cake has completely cooled, prepare glaze by whisking together its ingredients in a small bowl. Drizzle over cake. Slice and serve.

PER SERVING Calories: 221 | Fat: 9.0 g | Protein: 5.2 g | Sodium: 216 mg | Fiber: 0.8 g | Carbohydrates: 28.2 g | Sugar: 7.4 g

Apple Pie Egg Rolls

These sweet cooked cinnamon apples are wrapped in crunchy goodness in every single bite. Enjoy these on the go or warmed and served with vanilla ice cream!

HANDS-ON TIME: 15 minutes
COOK TIME: 14 minutes

INGREDIENTS | SERVES 3

2 medium Granny Smith apples, peeled, cored, and diced small

3 tablespoons butter, divided

½ teaspoon ground cinnamon

2 tablespoons packed brown sugar

4 tablespoons pecan pieces

1 teaspoon lemon juice

Pinch salt

6 egg-roll wrappers

1. In a large skillet over medium heat, heat apples, 2 tablespoons butter, cinnamon, sugar, pecans, lemon juice, and salt. Cook 4–5 minutes until apples are tender. Remove from heat and let rest 5 minutes off the burner.

2. Drape a damp towel over stack of egg-roll wrappers. Place one egg-roll wrapper on a cutting board. Place approximately ¼ cup of apple mixture in a line in the middle of the wrapper. Fold ½" of two sides of the egg roll toward the middle. Roll to form an egg roll and place seam side down in the air fryer basket. Repeat with remaining wrappers.

3. Preheat air fryer at 325°F for 3 minutes.

4. Place egg rolls in the air fryer basket. Cook 3 minutes. Lightly brush tops of egg rolls with 1 tablespoon melted butter. Cook an additional 6 minutes.

5. Transfer to a plate. Serve warm.

PER SERVING Calories: 439 | Fat: 17.7 g | Protein: 7.6 g | Sodium: 418 mg | Fiber: 4.0 g | Carbohydrates: 62.0 g | Sugar: 20.2 g

Candied Pecans

These sweet and crunchy treats don't need to be made just at the holidays. Candied Pecans are an amazing crunchy and sweet element when added to fresh summer salads, a bowl of homemade ice cream, and even jarred as gifts.

HANDS-ON TIME: 10 minutes
COOK TIME: 16 minutes

INGREDIENTS | SERVES 6

1 large egg white
¼ teaspoon vanilla extract
¼ cup packed brown sugar
¼ cup white sugar
¼ teaspoon ground cinnamon
Pinch salt
3 cups pecan halves

1. In a large bowl, whisk egg white. Whisk in vanilla, brown sugar, white sugar, cinnamon, and salt. Add pecans and toss until well coated.

2. Preheat air fryer at 275°F for 3 minutes.

3. Place pecans in lightly greased air fryer basket. Cook 8 minutes. Stir. Cook an additional 8 minutes.

4. Let cool completely and store in an airtight container.

PER SERVING Calories: 412 | Fat: 34.0 g | Protein: 5.2 g | Sodium: 35 mg | Fiber: 4.8 g | Carbohydrates: 24.3 g | Sugar: 19.2 g

Giant Oatmeal Raisin Cookie for One

Move over cake in a mug; now you have a giant cookie for one! Pour a glass of milk and enjoy your very own moist and chewy classic cookie filled with oats, raisins, and cinnamon.

HANDS-ON TIME: 10 minutes
COOK TIME: 12 minutes

INGREDIENTS | SERVES 1

2 tablespoons butter, at room temperature
1 tablespoon white sugar
1 tablespoon packed light brown sugar
¼ teaspoon vanilla extract
1 large egg
4 teaspoons all-purpose flour
⅛ teaspoon baking soda
⅛ teaspoon baking powder
⅛ teaspoon ground cinnamon
Pinch salt
4 tablespoons quick-cooking oats
1 tablespoon raisins

1. In a medium bowl, cream together butter, white sugar, brown sugar, vanilla, and egg. Stir in flour, baking soda, baking powder, cinnamon, salt, oats, and raisins.

2. Press mixture into a greased pizza pan (accessory).

3. Preheat air fryer at 350°F for 3 minutes.

4. Place pan into basket and insert into air fryer. Cook 7 minutes. Remove pan from air fryer and let cool 10 minutes. Flip cookie onto a plate and enjoy with a glass of milk!

PER SERVING Calories: 446 | Fat: 22.6 g | Protein: 4.3 g | Sodium: 369 mg | Fiber: 2.8 g | Carbohydrates: 55.4 g | Sugar: 31.6 g

Cinnamon Raisin Nutty Tarts

These sinful, sweet, and warm pastries are filled with brown sugar, pecans, raisins, and cinnamon and topped with vanilla ice cream.

HANDS-ON TIME: 10 minutes
COOK TIME: 27 minutes

INGREDIENTS | SERVES 6

2 tablespoons all-purpose flour

¾ cup chopped pecans

¾ cup raisins

1 teaspoon ground cinnamon

¼ cup packed brown sugar

2 tablespoons white sugar

Pinch salt

3 tablespoons butter

2 sheets puff pastry, thawed to room temperature

1 large egg, whisked

6 (½-cup) scoops vanilla ice cream

1. Use 1 tablespoon of flour to sprinkle on a flat, clean surface. Set aside the other tablespoon for your hands when you start working with the dough, as well as extra for the surface if needed.

2. In a small saucepan over medium-high heat, heat pecans, raisins, cinnamon, brown sugar, white sugar, salt, and butter 2–3 minutes until sugars are melted and mixture is creamy. Set aside to cool.

3. Preheat air fryer at 375°F for 3 minutes.

4. Place sheets of puff pastry on floured surface one at a time. Cut each sheet into six equal rectangles. Place approximately 1½ tablespoons of mixture in the middle of each rectangle and spread it, leaving ½" crust around perimeter uncovered. Create twelve tarts. Brush edges with whisked egg.

5. Add two tarts to lightly greased air fryer basket. Cook 4 minutes. Transfer to a plate. Repeat until all tarts are cooked.

6. Serve warm with half a scoop of vanilla ice cream per two tarts.

PER SERVING Calories: 426 | Fat: 24.5 g | Protein: 5.5 g | Sodium: 106 mg | Fiber: 2.8 g | Carbohydrates: 46.7 g | Sugar: 31.5 g

Nutella-Banana Pockets

Better than filled doughnuts, these buttery layered puff pastry pockets are treated with care in your air fryer, heating all sides into crunchy heaven.

HANDS-ON TIME: 10 minutes
COOK TIME: 20 minutes

INGREDIENTS | SERVES 6

2 tablespoons all-purpose flour

2 sheets puff pastry, thawed to room temperature

1 cup Nutella

2 medium bananas, cut into 24 slices

1 large egg, whisked

3 teaspoons sugar

1. Use 1 tablespoon of flour to sprinkle on a flat, clean surface. Set aside the other tablespoon for your hands when you start working with the dough, as well as extra for the surface if needed.

2. Preheat air fryer at 375°F for 3 minutes.

3. Place a sheet of puff pastry on floured surface. Cut each sheet into six equal rectangles. Place 1 tablespoon of Nutella in the middle of each rectangle. Add 2 banana slices. Fold over so edges meet and lightly pinch the seams. Use the tines of a fork to pinch the borders to secure the seal. Create twelve puff pastry pockets. Brush the tops of each with whisked egg. Sprinkle each with ¼ teaspoon sugar.

4. Add three pockets to lightly greased air fryer basket. Cook 5 minutes. Transfer to a plate. Repeat until all are cooked. Serve warm.

PER SERVING Calories: 326 | Fat: 17.0 g | Protein: 4.7 g | Sodium: 66 mg | Fiber: 3.4 g | Carbohydrates: 46.7 g | Sugar: 31.9 g

Cherry Phyllo Pastries

Sweet cherry season comes in like a wave and is gone too soon. But while it's here, enjoy the ride. These buttery little pastry pillows topped with supernutritional cherries are a treat that only comes around once a year.

HANDS-ON TIME: 20 minutes
COOK TIME: 19 minutes

INGREDIENTS | SERVES 4

2 cups quartered fresh sweet cherries, pitted

½ cup instant oats

1 tablespoon packed light brown sugar

2 tablespoons white sugar

½ teaspoon fresh lime zest

Pinch salt

Pinch ground nutmeg

8 phyllo sheets

2 tablespoons butter, melted

1. In a medium saucepan over medium-high heat, cook cherries, oats, brown sugar, white sugar, lime zest, salt, and nutmeg 2–3 minutes. Remove from heat and let rest 5 minutes off the burner.

2. Lay out phyllo sheets on smooth surface. Place a damp towel over phyllo sheets so they won't dry out.

3. Retrieve one phyllo sheet from the pile. Lightly brush sheet with melted butter.

4. Place 2 tablespoons cherry mixture in the middle of the sheet, about 2" from the bottom. Fold up the bottom of the sheet over the cherry mixture. Then fold the outside thirds lengthwise toward the middle, one at a time. Gently fold the pastry like a flag, forming a triangle each time. Brush the final end with butter to seal. Lightly brush completed triangle with butter. Set aside on a plate and continue with remaining pastries.

5. Preheat air fryer at 375°F for 3 minutes.

6. Place two pastries in air fryer basket. Cook 4 minutes until lightly browned.

7. Transfer cooked pastries to a plate and continue with remaining ones. Serve warm or cooled.

PER SERVING Calories: 286 | Fat: 8.1 g | Protein: 5.0 g | Sodium: 221 mg | Fiber: 3.3 g | Carbohydrates: 48.8 g | Sugar: 19.7 g

Island Phyllo Pastries

You can't get more island-style than fresh mango and sweet pineapple with a touch of lime. Of course, if you add a touch of the creamy and crunchy nature of the macadamia nut, then life is good.

HANDS-ON TIME: 20 minutes
COOK TIME: 23 minutes

INGREDIENTS | SERVES 5

¾ cup diced fresh pineapple
¾ cup diced fresh mango
⅓ cup honey
1 tablespoon sugar
2 teaspoons cornstarch
¼ teaspoon lime juice
¼ cup crushed salted macadamia nuts
10 phyllo sheets
⅓ cup butter, melted

1. In a medium saucepan over medium-high heat, add pineapple, mango, honey, sugar, cornstarch, lime juice, and crushed nuts. Bring to a boil and then reduce to a simmer 3 minutes. Remove from heat and let rest 5 minutes off the burner.

2. Lay out phyllo sheets on smooth surface. Place a damp towel over phyllo sheets so they won't dry out.

3. Retrieve one phyllo sheet from the pile. Lightly brush sheet with melted butter.

4. Place 2 tablespoons fruit mixture in the middle of the sheet, about 2" from the bottom. Fold up the bottom of the sheet over the fruit mixture. Then fold the outside thirds lengthwise toward the middle, one at a time. Gently fold the pastry like a flag, forming a triangle each time. Brush the final end with butter to seal. Lightly brush completed triangle with butter. Set aside on a plate and continue with remaining pastries.

5. Preheat air fryer at 375°F for 3 minutes.

6. Place two pastries in air fryer basket. Cook 4 minutes until lightly browned.

7. Transfer cooked pastries to a plate and repeat with remaining ones. Serve warm or cooled.

PER SERVING Calories: 378 | Fat: 18.4 g | Protein: 3.8 g | Sodium: 209 mg | Fiber: 2.1 g | Carbohydrates: 49.9 g | Sugar: 27.2 g

S'more Brownies

If it's too rainy or windy outside for setting up a campfire, take cover in a warm home and serving up a tray of these "s'more-licious" brownies!

HANDS-ON TIME: 10 minutes
COOK TIME: 12 minutes

INGREDIENTS | SERVES 4

2 full graham cracker sheets

½ cup all-purpose flour

2 tablespoons unsweetened cocoa powder

⅓ cup sugar

¼ teaspoon baking soda

3 tablespoons unsalted butter, melted

1 large egg

Pinch salt

⅓ cup semisweet chocolate chips

⅓ cup mini marshmallows

1. Place graham crackers in a sandwich bag. Crush them into chunky pieces, not into crumbs.

2. In a medium bowl, combine flour, cocoa, sugar, baking soda, and butter. Stir in egg and salt. Add chocolate chips, marshmallows, and graham crackers. Mixture will be thick and sticky.

3. Preheat air fryer at 350°F for 3 minutes.

4. Press mixture into a greased square cake barrel (accessory).

5. Place pan into basket and insert into air fryer. Cook 12 minutes. Remove pan from air fryer and let cool 10 minutes.

6. Slice into eight sections and serve warm or at room temperature.

PER SERVING Calories: 337 | Fat: 14.6 g | Protein: 5.0 g | Sodium: 167 mg | Fiber: 2.6 g | Carbohydrates: 48.8 g | Sugar: 29.2 g

Peanut Butter and Chocolate Brownies

If your sweet tooth is acting up but you don't want a huge tray of brownies, this small dish of treats will curb that craving without all the leftovers.

HANDS-ON TIME: 10 minutes
COOK TIME: 12 minutes

INGREDIENTS | YIELDS 9 BROWNIES

½ cup all-purpose flour

2 tablespoons unsweetened cocoa powder

⅓ cup sugar

¼ teaspoon baking soda

3 tablespoons unsalted butter, melted

1 large egg

Pinch salt

¼ cup semisweet chocolate chips

⅓ cup peanut butter chips

1. In a medium bowl, combine flour, cocoa, sugar, baking soda, and butter. Stir in egg and salt. Add chocolate chips and peanut butter chips. Mixture will be thick and sticky.

2. Preheat air fryer at 350°F for 3 minutes.

3. Press mixture into a greased square cake barrel (accessory).

4. Place pan into basket and insert into air fryer. Cook 12 minutes. Remove pan from air fryer and let cool 10 minutes.

5. Slice into nine sections and serve warm or at room temperature.

PER SERVING Calories: 169 | Fat: 8.4 g | Protein: 3.7 g | Sodium: 78 mg | Fiber: 1.2 g | Carbohydrates: 21.4 g | Sugar: 13.8 g

CHAPTER 15

Sauces and Dips

Cocktail Sauce

With this desired dipping sauce for seafood, home chefs sometimes make the mistake of only mixing together ketchup and horseradish. Take the time to add the rest of the ingredients, as they lend depth of flavor and give balance to your homemade sauce.

HANDS-ON TIME: 5 minutes
COOK TIME: 0 minutes

INGREDIENTS | YIELDS APPROXIMATELY 1¼ CUPS

1 cup ketchup
2 tablespoons prepared horseradish
1 tablespoon lemon juice
½ teaspoon Worcestershire sauce
⅛ teaspoon Tabasco sauce
⅛ teaspoon chili powder
¼ teaspoon salt
Pinch freshly ground black pepper

Combine ingredients in a small bowl and refrigerate covered until ready to use, up to 1 week.

PER SERVING (2 tablespoons) Calories: 26 | Fat: 0.0 g | Protein: 0.3 g | Sodium: 292 mg | Fiber: 0.2 g | Carbohydrates: 7.1 g | Sugar: 5.4 g

Blue Cheese Dipping Sauce

Tangy and sharp in taste, the fresh blue cheese crumbles in this homemade version make it heads and tails above the products found on shelves. This sauce is also terrific drizzled over a fresh steak salad!

HANDS-ON TIME: 10 minutes
COOK TIME: 0 minutes

INGREDIENTS | YIELDS APPROXIMATELY 1½ CUPS

1 cup crumbled blue cheese
½ cup mayonnaise
½ cup plain Greek yogurt
1 tablespoon whole milk
¼ cup chopped fresh parsley
½ teaspoon salt
¼ teaspoon freshly ground black pepper

Combine all the ingredients in a small bowl and refrigerate covered until ready to use, up to 1 week.

PER SERVING (2 tablespoons) Calories: 112 | Fat: 10.3 g | Protein: 3.4 g | Sodium: 288 mg | Fiber: 0.1 g | Carbohydrates: 0.9 g | Sugar: 0.6 g

Cilantro-Jalapeño Ranch Dip

*Whether you are frying vegetables and need a flavorful dip or have prepared
tacos or a beautiful salad and need a dressing, this is your dip. Add a teaspoon
or two of milk if you need to thin this dip out for a dressing.*

HANDS-ON TIME: 5 minutes
COOK TIME: 0 minutes

**INGREDIENTS | YIELDS APPROXIMATELY
2 CUPS**

½ cup chopped fresh cilantro

2 medium jalapeños, stems discarded
(remove seeds for less heat)

Juice of 1 medium lime

Pinch salt

1 cup mayonnaise

1 cup plain Greek yogurt

1 (1-ounce) packet dry ranch dip mix

1. Pulse cilantro, jalapeños, and lime juice in a food processor until a paste is formed. Transfer mixture to a medium bowl.

2. Add remaining ingredients and stir to combine.

3. Refrigerate covered until ready to use, up to 5 days.

PER SERVING (2 tablespoons) Calories: 452 | Fat: 43.1 g | Protein: 5.7 g | Sodium: 937 mg | Fiber: 0.3 g | Carbohydrates: 7.7 g | Sugar: 3.0 g

Basic Honey Mustard Sauce

*This sauce is terrific with air-fried vegetables, with chicken bites, as a salad dressing,
and even on tacos. Whisk in a little barbecue sauce to make Honey BBQ Sauce!*

HANDS-ON TIME: 5 minutes
COOK TIME: 0 minutes

**INGREDIENTS | YIELDS APPROXIMATELY
¾ CUP**

¼ cup honey

¼ cup yellow mustard

⅛ cup mayonnaise

1 tablespoon apple cider vinegar

1 teaspoon freshly ground black pepper

Combine all the ingredients in a small bowl and refrigerate covered until ready to use, up to 1 week.

PER SERVING (2 tablespoons) Calories: 81 | Fat: 3.7 g | Protein: 0.5 g | Sodium: 144 mg | Fiber: 0.5 g | Carbohydrates: 12.5 g | Sugar: 11.7 g

Fancy-Pants Honey Mustard Sauce

If you are enjoying your air-fried chicken tenders with your pinky finger extended and don't want to feel like you're eating a kids' meal, try "upping the snooty" on your ingredients!

HANDS-ON TIME: 5 minutes
COOK TIME: 0 minutes

INGREDIENTS | YIELDS APPROXIMATELY ¾ CUP

¼ cup honey

¼ cup Dijon mustard

⅛ cup mayonnaise

1 tablespoon white wine vinegar

1 teaspoon freshly ground black pepper

Pinch cayenne pepper

Combine all the ingredients in a small bowl and refrigerate covered until ready to use, up to 1 week.

PER SERVING (2 tablespoons) Calories: 95 | Fat: 4.4 g | Protein: 0.9 g | Sodium: 279 mg | Fiber: 0.1 g | Carbohydrates: 12.7 g | Sugar: 11.6 g

Varieties of Mustard

There are so many varieties of mustard sold today, so take advantage of these flavors when making your sauces. Beer mustard mixed in would work well with grilled brats. Spicy brown is excellent spread on a pastrami-on-rye. Honey would temper the heat of a Chinese mustard; use it as a dip for your homemade air-fried egg rolls!

Marinara Sauce

One of the tastiest and most versatile tomato-based sauces out there, Marinara Sauce is perfect for pasta, fried eggplant, mozzarella, and even St. Louis toasted ravioli.

HANDS-ON TIME: 10 minutes
COOK TIME: 30 minutes

INGREDIENTS | YIELDS 4 CUPS

1 (28-ounce) can crushed tomatoes, including juice
1 medium stalk celery, finely diced
1 medium carrot, peeled and finely diced
½ medium red onion, peeled and finely diced
4 cloves garlic, quartered
2 tablespoons chopped fresh basil
2 tablespoons chopped fresh Italian flat-leaf parsley
1 tablespoon fresh thyme leaves
1 teaspoon sea salt
½ teaspoon freshly ground black pepper
½ cup beef broth

1. Combine all ingredients in a large heavy-bottomed pot over high heat. Bring to a boil. Reduce heat and simmer covered 30 minutes.

2. Use an immersion blender to blend the sauce in the pot until smooth. Let cool.

3. Pour the sauce into a lidded container or jar and refrigerate until ready to use. Use within 5 days.

PER SERVING (½ cup) Calories: 42 | Fat: 0.3 g | Protein: 2.2 g | Sodium: 445 mg | Fiber: 2.5 g | Carbohydrates: 9.5 g | Sugar: 5.1 g

Spicy Marinara Sauce

*If you like a little heat with your marinara, add some red chili flakes to this sauce
to kick it up a notch. Taste as you go to hit the level that you can handle.*

HANDS-ON TIME: 10 minutes
COOK TIME: 30 minutes

INGREDIENTS | YIELDS 4 CUPS

1 (28-ounce) can crushed tomatoes, including juice

1 medium carrot, peeled and finely diced

½ medium red onion, peeled and finely diced

4 cloves garlic, quartered

½ teaspoon red chili flakes

1 tablespoon balsamic vinegar

2 tablespoons chopped fresh basil

2 tablespoons chopped fresh Italian flat-leaf parsley

1 teaspoon sea salt

½ teaspoon freshly ground black pepper

½ cup beef broth

1. Combine all ingredients in a large heavy-bottomed pot over high heat. Bring to a boil. Reduce heat and simmer covered 30 minutes.

2. Use an immersion blender to blend the sauce in the pot until smooth. Let cool.

3. Pour the sauce into a lidded container or jar and refrigerate until ready to use. Use within 5 days.

PER SERVING (½ cup) Calories: 43 | Fat: 0.3 g | Protein: 2.1 g | Sodium: 441 mg | Fiber: 2.3 g | Carbohydrates: 9.6 g | Sugar: 5.3 g

Rosemary Mayonnaise

*Rosemary is an herb that makes this an ideal mayonnaise to slather on a leftover
turkey sandwich after Thanksgiving. It's also good with grilled shrimp, sweet-
potato fries, and even slathered on a beef or turkey burger!*

HANDS-ON TIME: 5 minutes
COOK TIME: 0 minutes

INGREDIENTS | YIELDS ½ CUP

½ cup mayonnaise

1 tablespoon finely chopped fresh rosemary

½ teaspoon fresh lemon juice

½ teaspoon fresh lemon zest

¼ teaspoon sea salt

⅛ teaspoon cayenne pepper

Combine all the ingredients in a small bowl and refrigerate covered until ready to use, up to 1 week.

PER SERVING (2 tablespoons) Calories: 187 | Fat: 20.2 g | Protein: 0.3 g | Sodium: 272 mg | Fiber: 0.1 g | Carbohydrates: 0.4 g | Sugar: 0.2 g

Tomato Curry Sauce

This creamy nondairy sauce is excellent served over cauliflower "rice," seafood, chicken, and even your breakfast eggs! Full of flavor and Indian spices, this recipe is heavenly.

HANDS-ON TIME: 10 minutes
COOK TIME: 15 minutes

INGREDIENTS | YIELDS 2 CUPS

1 (14.5-ounce) can crushed tomatoes, including juice

2 tablespoons minced onion

2 cloves garlic, quartered

1 teaspoon ground ginger

¼ teaspoon garam masala

¼ teaspoon ground turmeric

⅛ teaspoon red pepper flakes

⅛ teaspoon ground cinnamon

2 teaspoons fresh thyme leaves

½ teaspoon sea salt

¼ teaspoon freshly ground black pepper

¼ cup canned coconut milk

1. Combine all ingredients in a large heavy-bottomed pot or Dutch oven. Bring to a boil over high heat. Reduce heat and simmer covered for 20 minutes.

2. Use an immersion blender to blend the sauce in the pot until smooth.

3. Pour sauce into a lidded container or jar and refrigerate until ready to use. Use within 5 days.

PER SERVING (½ cup) Calories: 67 | Fat: 3.1 g | Protein: 2.2 g | Sodium: 483 mg | Fiber: 2.3 g | Carbohydrates: 9.6 g | Sugar: 4.8 g

What Is Coconut Milk?

Coconut milk is simply coconut meat and coconut water. Period. Be mindful of labels when purchasing coconut milk, as some brands add emulsifiers and fillers. You should be able to easily buy canned versions from reputable companies. Stay away from the "light" varieties, as this takes away from the natural healthy fats found in coconut and is counter to the whole-food mentality.

Super Easy Romesco Sauce

*This roasted red pepper and almond–based sauce can be stirred into pasta,
spread on sandwiches, and also used as a dip for a crudités tray.*

HANDS-ON TIME: 5 minutes
COOK TIME: 5 minutes

**INGREDIENTS | YIELDS APPROXIMATELY
2 CUPS**

1 (12-ounce) jar roasted red peppers, drained

1 (1-ounce) slice ciabatta bread, cubed

¼ cup diced tomatoes, drained

⅓ cup chopped fresh parsley

2 cloves garlic, halved

½ cup chopped almonds

¼ cup olive oil

1 tablespoon cooking sherry

½ teaspoon smoked paprika

2 teaspoons sriracha

½ teaspoon salt

¼ teaspoon freshly ground black pepper

1. In a medium saucepan, add all ingredients and heat over medium heat 5 minutes, stirring occasionally.

2. Use an immersion blender to blend the sauce in the saucepan until smooth.

3. Pour sauce into a lidded container or jar and refrigerate until ready to use. Use within 5 days.

PER SERVING (2 tablespoons) Calories: 57 | Fat: 4.8 g | Protein: 1.1 g | Sodium: 390 mg | Fiber: 0.8 g | Carbohydrates: 2.9 g | Sugar: 0.4 g

Remoulade Special Sauce

Invented in France and adopted by Louisiana, this mayonnaise-based sauce is excellent on po'boy sandwiches, on air-fried oysters, and even as a base in a cold shrimp or crab salad. If you want to create umami (taste sensation), finely chop a few anchovies and throw them in.

HANDS-ON TIME: 5 minutes
COOK TIME: 0 minutes

INGREDIENTS | YIELDS APPROXIMATELY 1½ CUPS

1 cup mayonnaise

¼ cup Dijon mustard

1 tablespoon sweet paprika

2 teaspoons Cajun seasoning

1 teaspoon lemon juice

1 tablespoon sweet pickle relish

2 cloves garlic, minced

1 tablespoon finely chopped fresh parsley

¼ teaspoon hot sauce

Combine all the ingredients in a small bowl and refrigerate covered until ready to use, up to 1 week.

PER SERVING (2 tablespoons) Calories: 138 | Fat: 14.0 g | Protein: 0.2 g | Sodium: 296 mg | Fiber: 0.2 g | Carbohydrates: 1.3 g | Sugar: 0.2 g

Tartar Sauce

Tartar Sauce is a mayonnaise-based sauce traditionally served with fried seafood. It's also good on seafood tacos. There are many who also swear by dipping the ever-humble French fry in it, so give it a try!

HANDS-ON TIME: 5 minutes
COOK TIME: 0 minutes

INGREDIENTS | YIELDS APPROXIMATELY 1 CUP

½ cup mayonnaise

1 tablespoon Dijon mustard

½ cup small-diced dill pickles

Pinch salt

¼ teaspoon freshly ground black pepper

Combine ingredients in a small bowl and refrigerate covered until ready to use, up to 1 week.

PER SERVING (2 tablespoons) Calories: 98 | Fat: 10.3 g | Protein: 0.3 g | Sodium: 224 mg | Fiber: 0.1 g | Carbohydrates: 0.4 g | Sugar: 0.2 g

Comeback Sauce

Comeback Sauce will have you coming back again and again. Well, that's what Southerners think. This traditional sauce pretty much goes with everything. A little sweet, a little spicy—this sauce is excellent with fries, burgers, and even fried oysters!

HANDS-ON TIME: 5 minutes
COOK TIME: 0 minutes

INGREDIENTS | YIELDS 1 CUP

½ cup mayonnaise

2 tablespoons honey

2 tablespoons ketchup

½ teaspoon Worcestershire sauce

½ teaspoon Dijon mustard

½ teaspoon sriracha

1 clove garlic, minced

¼ teaspoon smoked paprika

¼ teaspoon salt

¼ teaspoon freshly ground black pepper

Combine all the ingredients in a small bowl and refrigerate covered until ready to use, up to 1 week.

PER SERVING (2 tablespoons) Calories: 115 | Fat: 10.1 g | Protein: 0.3 g | Sodium: 216 mg | Fiber: 0.1 g | Carbohydrates: 5.9 g | Sugar: 5.4 g

Horseradish-Lemon Aioli

In modern terms, aioli has come to mean a flavored mayonnaise. This Horseradish-Lemon Aioli is delicious paired with crab cakes or fried shrimp, or spread on the buns of seafood sliders!

HANDS-ON TIME: 5 minutes
COOK TIME: 0 minutes

INGREDIENTS | YIELDS APPROXIMATELY ¾ CUP

½ cup mayonnaise

4 teaspoons prepared horseradish

2 teaspoons fresh lemon zest

¼ teaspoon fresh lemon juice

Combine all the ingredients in a small bowl and refrigerate covered until ready to use, up to 1 week.

PER SERVING (2 tablespoons) Calories: 126 | Fat: 13.4 g | Protein: 0.2 g | Sodium: 130 mg | Fiber: 0.2 g | Carbohydrates: 0.6 g | Sugar: 0.4 g

Sriracha Mayonnaise

If spicy is your thing, just add a squirt or two more of the sriracha. Also, if you are using this for tacos, add the mayonnaise to a squirt bottle for a pretty drizzle on your food. Alternatively, spoon the mayonnaise mixture into a plastic sandwich bag and snip off just the tip of the corner.

HANDS-ON TIME: 5 minutes
COOK TIME: 0 minutes

INGREDIENTS | YIELDS APPROXIMATELY ½ CUP

½ cup mayonnaise
2 teaspoons sriracha
1 teaspoon lime juice
Pinch salt

Combine all the ingredients in a small bowl and refrigerate covered until ready to use, up to 1 week.

PER SERVING (2 tablespoons) Calories: 189 | Fat: 20.1 g | Protein: 0.3 g | Sodium: 260 mg | Fiber: 0.0 g | Carbohydrates: 0.8 g | Sugar: 0.7 g

Curry Dip

Curry Dip harkens back to a time when disco was cool and jeans were belled. But guess what? It holds up! Fix this dip the night before, as the curry tends to blossom overnight and become a little spicier.

HANDS-ON TIME: 10 minutes
COOK TIME: 0 minutes

INGREDIENTS | YIELDS APPROXIMATELY 1 CUP

½ cup mayonnaise
½ cup sour cream
2 tablespoons ketchup
1 tablespoon curry powder
1 tablespoon grated yellow onion
1 teaspoon Worcestershire sauce
¼ teaspoon prepared horseradish
½ teaspoon salt

Combine all the ingredients in a small bowl and refrigerate covered until ready to use, up to 1 week.

PER SERVING (2 tablespoons) Calories: 128 | Fat: 12.7 g | Protein: 0.6 g | Sodium: 285 mg | Fiber: 0.5 g | Carbohydrates: 2.4 g | Sugar: 1.6 g

Sweet Chili Sauce

The spices and heat from the sambal oelek is tempered and sweetened by the added sugar, creating an addictive balance in this sauce, which also makes an amazing dip for egg rolls.

HANDS-ON TIME: 10 minutes
COOK TIME: 3 minutes

INGREDIENTS | YIELDS APPROXIMATELY ½ CUP

2 tablespoons sambal oelek
4 cloves garlic, halved
1 cup sugar
1 cup rice vinegar
½ teaspoon salt
¾ cup plus 1 tablespoon water, divided
1 tablespoon cornstarch

1. In a medium saucepan, add sambel oelek, garlic, sugar, vinegar, salt, and ¾ cup water. Bring to a rolling boil, 2 minutes.

2. In a small bowl, create a slurry by adding 1 tablespoon water to the cornstarch.

3. Slowly whisk slurry into boiling sauce mixture. Reduce heat and allow to simmer 1 additional minute to thicken. Discard garlic. Allow mixture to cool. Refrigerate covered until ready to use, within 7 days.

PER SERVING (1 tablespoon) Calories: 107 | Fat: 0.0 g | Protein: 0.1 g | Sodium: 83 mg | Fiber: 0.0 g | Carbohydrates: 26.4 g | Sugar: 25.2 g

What Is Sambal Oelek?

Sambal oelek is an Indonesian chili paste usually containing salt, vinegar, and other spices. It can be found at most grocers in the ethnic aisle. It actually has the same ingredients and heat level as sriracha but it has zero sugars, so if you are adhering to a carb-free diet, this is your hot sauce!

Pico Guacamole

Pico Guacamole is the baby from the marriage of salsa and guacamole. When dicing the avocado, be sure to immediately toss the cubes in the lime juice to avoid browning. Serve over scrambled eggs, with tacos, or as a dip with air-fried tortilla chips.

HANDS-ON TIME: 10 minutes
COOK TIME: 0 minutes

INGREDIENTS | YIELDS APPROXIMATELY 1 CUP

Juice of 1 small lime

2 medium avocados, peeled, pitted, and diced

4 cloves garlic, minced

1 teaspoon sriracha

1 teaspoon sea salt

¼ cup chopped fresh cilantro

2 medium Roma tomatoes, seeded and diced

1. Combine lime juice and diced avocado in a small bowl. Using the back of a fork, press avocado so it is half smooshed. Stir in remaining ingredients.

2. Serve immediately. Cover and refrigerate any leftovers (to avoid browning) up to 3 days.

PER SERVING (2 tablespoons) Calories: 63 | Fat: 4.7 g | Protein: 0.9 g | Sodium: 211 mg | Fiber: 2.6 g | Carbohydrates: 4.5 g | Sugar: 0.7 g

Hollandaise Sauce

Primarily found served over eggs Benedict, this creamy, dreamy emulsion can also be served over fish cakes, salmon, asparagus, and crab dishes.

HANDS-ON TIME: 10 minutes
COOK TIME: 5 minutes

INGREDIENTS | YIELDS APPROXIMATELY 1½ CUPS

4 large egg yolks

1 tablespoon lemon juice

½ cup unsalted butter, cut into 8 pats

Pinch salt

Pinch cayenne pepper

Pinch ground white pepper

1. Whisk egg yolks and lemon juice together over a double boiler.

2. Quickly whisk in one pat of butter at a time until all of the butter is used and sauce has thickened. Sprinkle in seasonings. If sauce starts to curdle, add in a little of the hot double-boiler water and whisk. Serve immediately.

PER SERVING (2 tablespoons) Calories: 86 | Fat: 8.6 g | Protein: 1.0 g | Sodium: 15 mg | Fiber: 0.0 g | Carbohydrates: 0.3 g | Sugar: 0.1 g

Horseradish Sauce

Traditionally served with prime rib, this Horseradish Sauce also confers its benefits on roast beef sandwiches. Or stir some into room-temperature cream cheese for a raw vegetable dip!

HANDS-ON TIME: 10 minutes
COOK TIME: 0 minutes

INGREDIENTS | YIELDS APPROXIMATELY 1 CUP

¼ cup mayonnaise

¼ cup sour cream

¼ cup prepared horseradish, plus more if needed

2 teaspoons Dijon mustard

1 tablespoon lemon juice

¼ teaspoon hot sauce

½ teaspoon Worcestershire sauce

½ teaspoon freshly ground black pepper

Combine all the ingredients in a small bowl. Taste and add more horseradish for more kick if desired. Refrigerate covered until ready to use, up to 1 week.

PER SERVING (2 tablespoons) Calories: 114 | Fat: 11.5 g | Protein: 0.5 g | Sodium: 157 mg | Fiber: 0.3 g | Carbohydrates: 1.5 g | Sugar: 1.0 g

Traditional Pesto

Pesto is a great sauce to make when your garden is overflowing with herbs. Traditionally made with basil and/or parsley, try swapping out herbs for different main dishes. For example, mint pesto is amazing served with lamb kebabs.

HANDS-ON TIME: 5 minutes
COOK TIME: 0 minutes

INGREDIENTS | YIELDS APPROXIMATELY ½ CUP

3 cups fresh basil leaves

⅓ cup pine nuts

4 cloves garlic, halved

¾ cup freshly grated Parmesan cheese

3–4 tablespoons olive oil

Pinch salt

Pulse basil and pine nuts in a food processor. Add garlic, cheese, and 1 tablespoon olive oil. Pulse. Slowly add remaining oil until desired consistency is reached. Add a pinch of salt. Transfer to a jar and refrigerate. Use within 5 days.

PER SERVING (2 tablespoons) Calories: 180 | Fat: 13.0 g | Protein: 7.6 g | Sodium: 375 mg | Fiber: 0.8 g | Carbohydrates: 5.6 g | Sugar: 0.5 g

Vegan Walnut-Mint Pesto

Nutritional yeast replaces the traditional Parmesan cheese in this super yummy and fresh pesto. Also, if you have nut allergies, try using sunflower seeds instead of the walnuts.

HANDS-ON TIME: 5 minutes
COOK TIME: 0 minutes

INGREDIENTS | YIELDS APPROXIMATELY ½ CUP

2 cups fresh mint leaves
1 cup chopped fresh parsley
⅓ cup walnut pieces
4 cloves garlic, halved
¼ cup nutritional yeast
3–4 tablespoons olive oil
Pinch salt

Pulse mint, parsley, and walnuts in a food processor. Add garlic, yeast, and 1 tablespoon olive oil. Pulse. Slowly add remaining oil until desired consistency. Add a pinch of salt. Transfer to a jar and refrigerate. Use within 5 days.

PER SERVING (2 tablespoons) Calories: 202 | Fat: 18.0 g | Protein: 4.6 g | Sodium: 55 mg | Fiber: 3.0 g | Carbohydrates: 6.5 g | Sugar: 0.4 g

Tzatziki Sauce

This yogurt-based sauce has a mix of very fresh flavors, such as cucumber, dill, mint, and lemon. This sauce is served mostly with Greek dishes, such as gyros, salads, and Greek meatballs, also known as keftedes. But it is also a great choice for chicken or fish.

HANDS-ON TIME: 10 minutes
COOK TIME: 0 minutes

INGREDIENTS | YIELDS APPROXIMATELY 2½ CUPS

2 cups plain Greek yogurt
1 medium English cucumber, peeled and diced small
2 teaspoons chopped fresh dill
2 teaspoons chopped fresh mint
1 teaspoon salt
2 teaspoons lemon juice
3 cloves garlic, minced

Combine all the ingredients in a medium bowl and refrigerate covered until ready to use, up to 1 week.

PER SERVING (2 tablespoons) Calories: 23 | Fat: 1.1 g | Protein: 2.1 g | Sodium: 124 mg | Fiber: 0.1 g | Carbohydrates: 1.3 g | Sugar: 1.1 g

Standard US/Metric Measurement Conversions

VOLUME CONVERSIONS

US Volume Measure	Metric Equivalent
⅛ teaspoon	0.5 milliliter
¼ teaspoon	1 milliliter
½ teaspoon	2 milliliters
1 teaspoon	5 milliliters
½ tablespoon	7 milliliters
1 tablespoon (3 teaspoons)	15 milliliters
2 tablespoons (1 fluid ounce)	30 milliliters
¼ cup (4 tablespoons)	60 milliliters
⅓ cup	80 milliliters
½ cup (4 fluid ounces)	125 milliliters
⅔ cup	160 milliliters
¾ cup (6 fluid ounces)	180 milliliters
1 cup (16 tablespoons)	250 milliliters
1 pint (2 cups)	500 milliliters
1 quart (4 cups)	1 liter (about)

WEIGHT CONVERSIONS

US Weight Measure	Metric Equivalent
½ ounce	15 grams
1 ounce	30 grams
2 ounces	60 grams
3 ounces	85 grams
¼ pound (4 ounces)	115 grams
½ pound (8 ounces)	225 grams
¾ pound (12 ounces)	340 grams
1 pound (16 ounces)	454 grams

OVEN TEMPERATURE CONVERSIONS

Degrees Fahrenheit	Degrees Celsius
200 degrees F	95 degrees C
250 degrees F	120 degrees C
275 degrees F	135 degrees C
300 degrees F	150 degrees C
325 degrees F	160 degrees C
350 degrees F	180 degrees C
375 degrees F	190 degrees C
400 degrees F	205 degrees C
425 degrees F	220 degrees C
450 degrees F	230 degrees C

BAKING PAN SIZES

American	Metric
8 × 1½ inch round baking pan	20 × 4 cm cake tin
9 × 1½ inch round baking pan	23 × 3.5 cm cake tin
11 × 7 × 1½ inch baking pan	28 × 18 × 4 cm baking tin
13 × 9 × 2 inch baking pan	30 × 20 × 5 cm baking tin
2 quart rectangular baking dish	30 × 20 × 3 cm baking tin
15 × 10 × 2 inch baking pan	38 × 25 × 5 cm baking tin (Swiss roll tin)
9 inch pie plate	22 × 4 or 23 × 4 cm pie plate
7 or 8 inch springform pan	18 or 20 cm springform or loose bottom cake tin
9 × 5 × 3 inch loaf pan	23 × 13 × 7 cm or 2 lb narrow loaf or pâté tin
1½ quart casserole	1.5 liter casserole
2 quart casserole	2 liter casserole

Index

THE COOKBOOK THAT MAKES USING YOUR INSTANT POT®
EASIER THAN EVER!

With 300 delicious and simple recipes perfect for Instant Pot®
beginners, you'll be making hundreds of great meals sure to
impress your friends and family in no time!

Whether you're looking for an easy breakfast dish,
a savory snack, or a scrumptious supper for the family,
let the Instant Pot® change your life!

The Everything® Easy Instant Pot® Cookbook
978-1-5072-0940-0
978-1-5072-0941-7

adamsmedia
An Imprint of Simon & Schuster
A CBS COMPANY